DESIGN
PORTFOLIOS

DESIGN PORTFOLIOS

A Recruiter's View

MARK W. SMITH, ASLA

WILEY

Published by John Wiley & Sons, Inc., Hoboken, New Jersey.
Published simultaneously in Canada.

For general information on our other products and services or for technical support, please contact our Customer Care Department within the United States at (800) 762-2974, outside the United States at (317) 572-3993 or fax (317) 572-4002.

Wiley also publishes its books in a variety of electronic formats. Some content that appears in print may not be available in electronic formats. For more information about Wiley products, visit our web site at www.wiley.com.

Library of Congress Cataloging-in-Publication Data Applied for

ISBN: 9781394150465 (Paperback)
ISBN: 9781394150472 (epdf)
ISBN: 9781394150472 (epub)

Cover Design: Wiley
Cover Image: © Alexander/Adobe Stock Photos

SKY10042286_020223

Contents

Foreword

Most people have been told that the 3-Rs of education are "reading, writing, and 'rith-matic," but Bruce Archer, the influential British design educator, quoted a family matriarch who said that the 3-Rs were, "reading and writing, reckoning and figuring, and wroughting and wrighting."[1] The first two pairs of words in this alternative view cover literacy and numeracy, both of which are emphasized in most primary and secondary schooling. The last pair, though, uses terms that can be unfamiliar. *Wroughting* concerns knowing how the things in our world are brought about or technology; *wrighting* concerns crafts of making and practices of designing. The notion that know-ing how to make and design things is its own fundamental kind of understanding will be obvious to those who are completing any sort of design degree but may seem novel to others. After all, for whatever reasons, experiences in sustained formal coursework in design—or even a single semester-long class—often occur only when a person enters college or even later when they enroll in a graduate program. More needs to be said on this important point, but before that, what does it mean to learn about and to learn how to design?

An inherent aspect of design practice is taking on what are called *ill-structured problems*.[2] By contrast, an example of a very well-structured problem is a jigsaw puz-zle: At the start, a person has all the pieces, the intended configuration is provided on a box cover, and the pieces can fit together in only one way. A game of chess is less well-structured: At the start, all the pieces are seen in pre-established positions on a standard board, there is a decisive endpoint condition (checkmate), and the rules about how each piece can move and capture another are known to both players. An ill-structured design problem is not so simple: At the start, all the information about the existing conditions is rarely available (and might never be fully knowable), the criteria for a successful end state are vague, and the ways to bring about a satisfac-tory outcome are not clear. Some design problems are even called *wicked* because the criteria for preferred outcomes are politically contentious.[3] In this light, the common feature of all design education—including product design, industrial design, interior design, architecture, landscape architecture, urban design, and all the other design professions—is that the student learns to structure ambiguities and uncertainties of ill-structured problems so that resolutions can be found.

---

[1] B. Archer, "Whatever Became of Design Methodology?," *Design Studies* 1:1 (1979), pp. 17–20.

[2] A. Newell, J.C. Shaw, and H. Simon, "The Process of Creative Thinking," In: *Contemporary Approaches to Creative Thinking*, H.E. Gruber, G. Terrell, and M. Wertheimer (Eds.) (New York: Atherton Press, 1962), pp. 63–199.

[3] H.W.J. Rittel and M.M. Webber, "Dilemmas in a General Theory of Planning," *Policy Sciences*, 4 (1973), 159–169.

Getting to a resolution begins with the designer asking a "What if...?" question. The topic might be about locations, dimensions, or materials; about parameters or interactions within a system; about a social ideal or utopian impulse; or, about an aspect that is of special interest to a profession—such as qualities of light for interior design or ephemerality of plants for landscape architecture. Regardless of whatever self-directed prompt is employed, the question and the provisional answer are not idle speculations. Instead, they provide a generative conjecture that begins to establish intellectual order to the ill-structured problem. The conjecture is then tested and expanded against facts and assumptions through diagrams, plans, sections, elevations, renderings, and models (and increasingly through animations and Virtual Reality simulations). The asking and answering process is never straightforward. Many lines of inquiry lead to disappointing or unacceptable results, but as promising conjectures are re-tested and re-expanded again and again and again, the problem becomes increasingly structured. In the end, the designer has developed a consistent argument for purposeful, meaningful, and beneficial change.

So how after three, four, or five years of learning to structure ill-structured problems—that is, of learning design thinking—how does someone demonstrate this kind of knowing to possible employers and others? Mark Smith wants designers to tell their *stories*. In this book, he generously shares how to tell effective stories through the making of portfolios, résumés, and cover letters.

Sharing stories about one's work and oneself enables connections with an audience through what is perhaps the most widely sharable form of representation: narrative. The French philosopher and literary critic Roland Barthes wrote, "narrative is present in every age, every place, every society ... narrative is international, transhistorical, transcultural: it is simply there like life itself."[4] In addition to being pervasive across cultures, psychologists and neuroscientists have aided our understanding of the ways storytelling is a shared cognitive tool that can be used to explain and to influence. It has even been argued that the human mind evolved to process stories.[5]

In part, a story appeals to an audience by interrelating specific aspects of life, rather than by declaring abstract principles.[6] Story logic not only presents actions and events over time, it calls attention to why things occur and why actions matter. According to novelist E.M. Forster, the more attention given to causation, the better the plot: "The king died and then the queen died," is a basic story, but "The king died, and then the queen died of grief," is an engaging plot.[7] But perhaps the most important aspect of storytelling is that a story also allows a temporary willing suspension of disbelief that may not occur in more typical forms of professional communication, such as the

---

[4] R. Barthes, "Introduction to the Structural Analysis of Narratives," *Image, Music, Text*, Stephen Heath (trans.), (New York: Hill and Wang, 1977), pp. 79–124, this note, p. 79.

[5] B. Boyd, *On the Origin of Stories: Evolution, Cognition, and Fiction* (Cambridge, MA: Belknap Press of Harvard University Press, 2009).

[6] J. Bruner, *Actual Minds, Possible Worlds* (Cambridge, MA: Harvard University Press, 1986).

[7] E.M. Forster, *Aspects of the Novel* (San Diego: Harcourt, 1927), p. 86.

tables, charts, graphs, and maps used to present various analyses.[8] As a result, audiences want to get to the end of the tale to learn the outcome. (Forster also noted that the intelligent audience member knows that making complete sense of each new piece of information encountered in a story might not be possible until the very end.[9]) To avoid any misunderstanding on this point, *yes*, in all kinds of professional practice, the technical forms of representation used for inventories, analyses, and evaluations are vitally important for making sound decisions; but they will not matter if decision makers do not know why they should care about the details. Telling effective stories about relatable experiences and meaningful relationships can help ensure everyone gives full attention until the end and grasps the significance of everything said.

A design project story guides the audience through key points of the process to structure the ill-structured problem. Part of this story will involve showing specialized methods and techniques to envision possible change. Many compelling examples of such graphics can be seen throughout this book. But, as accomplished and as evocative as these illustrations are (and they are!), they do not convey the whole stories about what went into making them or why they contribute to problem solving. To underscore a theme across the chapters of this book, establishing the context of a design problem allows the content of the design resolution to be understood. Each profession is situated within a discipline that includes not only the professionals, but also those whose interests and ideas influence design activities. And each discipline is situated within a discourse about how communities establish priorities. That is, design practices are embedded within the larger world. The successful resolution to a design problem not only satisfies the opinions of the designer and the aspirations of the client, it also informs the larger discipline and contributes to still larger societal discourse. Design stories use graphics and words to reveal links across the motives for change, the means for change, and the ends of change.

In addition to helping share ideas about designs with others, composing stories about past work supports *reflective practice*, which centers on learning general principles from one's own specific profession-related experiences. No two design problems are identical, but some share features. Grasping lessons about what produced good results and what did not within one project can help a designer make quicker and even better decisions as related problems are encountered. As the number of lessons grows and as the lessons become interconnected, design knowledge becomes design wisdom.

Developing stories about the past as part of a reflective practice also helps develop skills to project stories into the future. This extension might be thought of as going from reflective practice to *projective practice*. Projective practice can help a designer answer a very common interview question: "How would you approach ... [insert some kind of project that you have never done, but that some client needs doing

---

[8] P. Schwartz, *The Art of the Long View: Paths to Strategic Insight for Yourself and Your Company* (New York: Currency Doubleday, 1996).

[9] Forster, op. cit., p. 87.

tomorrow]?" As an educator, I have often thought that a revealing comprehensive examination would similarly ask soon-to-graduate students how they would engage in a project not done in one of their studios but is in a growing area of contemporary professional practice. (For the record, the program in which I teach does not require such a test.) The grade would be based on a demonstration of being able to connect past, present, and projected futures and to identify cause-and-effect inflection points in the plot at which a designer could have influence through their professional skills. Specific details about how design practices would operate within the scenario would count most. That is, following E.M. Forster, the goal would be to provide a good plot with the designer having a meaningful role.

The more advanced version of this comprehensive exam question would have the same rules for grading, but require considerations of greater ambiguity and acceptance of broader suspensions of disbelief: "How would you approach … [insert a topic (not just a project) that the faculty and leading professionals do not know how to fully address or perhaps that they cannot even imagine]?" One might feel such a question is unfair, but history—including recent history—has shown that each generation encounters challenges that previous generations did not foresee. The continual advance of technologies results in the evolution of political, social, and economic relationships that create conditions for new ways to solve old problems. It must also be recognized that past actions made with the best intentions sometimes result in harmful consequences. We train our students for their first job, but we educate them to replace those who initially hired them. I will offer the position that an indicator of successful professional education is that students are able to tell stories about uncertain futures in which they used what they have learned to contribute to a positive outcome. Developing the ability to envision and share these kinds of stories—stories told from a person's own perspective, with a person's own style, and filled with details of substance gained from education—begins with learning how to tell stories about experiences with completed projects.

In addition to helping the audience understand past or future projects, design stories enable the author (the designer) to demonstrate imagination, agency, and sense of responsibility. An aspect of storytelling that must never to be forgotten—and one that is emphasized by Smith throughout this book—is that stories are told from the author's perspective and any such perspective is based on a lifetime of experiences. When a student's perspective on resolving ill-defined problems is clearly expressed through the style and substance of the portfolio, résumé, and cover letter, potential employers have a better understanding of the job candidate's career goals and potential contributions as a professional. The point that perspectives are multifaceted connects to the earlier observation that formal design instruction does not often occur before the collegiate or graduate-levels of schooling. Design is about inserting oneself into the world and helping make it tangibly better. It would be difficult to argue that such thinking cannot start soon enough. It must also be recognized, though, that resolving complex relationships among facts and assumptions that stem from goals and constraints is difficult work—it is incredibly rewarding, but very challenging. Perspectives and insights gained from "reading and writing" and "reckoning and figuring" are needed for responsible design—that is, not change that *could* occur, but change that *should* occur. Part of one's story as a designer is how knowledge from these other ways of understanding helps "wroughting and wrighting" to meet the needs of the present and aspirations for the future.

Allan W. Shearer, Ph.D., FASLA, FCELA
Associate Dean for Research and Technology
The University of Texas at Austin School of Architecture

Acknowledgments

It's one thing to casually tell someone your story in an interview; it's an entirely different challenge to convey that story using only your portfolio and to do so convincingly enough to get that person to hire you. Telling your story through your work is what this book is all about. Most design students seem to be experts at sharing their *project experience,* but they are not so good at telling their *story.*

A big part of understanding how to tell one's story effectively comes from good mentorship. From my earliest days as a student at Louisiana State University, throughout my years of professional practice, and finally the writing of this book, I was fortunate enough to have extraordinary teachers, mentors, and friends help me to understand the importance of *story.* Collectively, these individuals taught me the fundamentals of portfolio design, helped mold me into a designer, and ultimately led me through the myriad of challenges inherent to writing and publishing a book. Without them, this book would not have been possible. I am deeply indebted to the following people:

I owe an enormous debt of gratitude to Dr. Robert S. Reich (1913–2010). "Doc," as he was affectionately known, was the Director of the LSU Department of Landscape Architecture from 1946–1983. Without Doc, it's very unlikely that I would have ever become a designer at all. In the briefest of interviews during my first week of college, Doc somehow recognized that design would be my life's work (long before I did). It's hard for me to imagine what I might be doing today had it not been for his less-than-subtle insistence that I attend his *Introduction to Landscape Architecture* class on that crisp fall day in 1974. I also benefited from the teachings of a tireless and dedicated faculty during my years in the LSU Department of Landscape Architecture. Among them, Dennis Gail ("Buck") Abbey, Max Conrad, Van Cox, Dr. Neil Odenwald (1935–2021), James Turner, and Wayne Womack (1932–2019) were very influential in the development of my creative skills and, ultimately, my desire to create the best portfolio possible. I wish to extend a special thanks to Assistant Professor Seishiro Tomioka for his willingness to work with me week after week during my final semester at LSU and to critique my evolving portfolio. His experience in the "real world" and his honest feedback helped me to understand the core function of a design portfolio: to tell one's story.

I am immensely grateful to Carlos Cashio (1942–2011) and L. Azeo Torre ("Ace") of Cashio Cochran Torre/Design Consortium (CCT/DC) for giving me a start as a designer. In the course of a short 10-minute interview, Carlos saw *something* in my design portfolio that compelled him to offer me my first professional design job. Surely, it wasn't my interview abilities (it was my first interview...ever). Throughout my tenure at CCT/DC, Ace worked patiently with me to develop confidence in design and conceptualization skills that would serve me well throughout my career as a designer. That position provided me with the kind of project experience that I was proud of and would serve as the foundational content of my professional portfolio.

I am deeply indebted to Dr. Allan Shearer (Associate Professor and Associate Dean for Research and Technology: University of Texas School of Architecture), without whom my experience leading student portfolio reviews might never have been realized. In early spring 2011, Allan called me and proposed that we work together to host the first *Annual UT/ASLA Student Portfolio Review* (aka "Portfolio Palooza"). The aim was simply to provide a meaningful portfolio review experience for students. What we've ended up with is a student/professional portfolio review program that has now been integrated into the School of Architecture's curriculum and has been held annually ever since. The program we developed has since expanded to other universities. I also want to thank the students and faculty at all the universities who have taken part in the many portfolio review sessions that have inspired and provided the basis for this book.

My deepest appreciation goes to Peter Dufrene (Associate Principal at RVi Planning + Landscape Architecture). Without his encouragement, I might never have even thought of writing this book. On the long drive home from leading a student portfolio review at Texas Tech University back in 2018, Peter casually suggested that I should write a book on portfolio design. Wow, why hadn't I thought of that! I took his suggestion to heart and initiated this project a week later.

I wish to thank all of the students (each is credited on their respective exhibits) who had enough faith early in this project to allow me to use their portfolio content to illustrate the concepts presented. Coming from many different areas of design study, these students immediately recognized the need for a new book on portfolio design for students and generously agreed to the use of their entire portfolio. Without them, it would not have been possible for me to show you how to tell your story!

My sincerest thanks go to Professor Lake Douglas (MLA Coordinator for LSU Landscape Architecture and friend) for his on-going encouragement and support of this project. As the author of numerous books, his deep knowledge of publishing, his thorough editorial eye, and his candid feedback gave me the confidence (and the occasional kick in the pants) to complete the manuscript and find a willing publisher.

I would also like to thank Tim Augustine, Senior Vice President of Atwell, and author of the book series *How Hard Are You Knocking?*, for his continued support. Tim's own success in writing about the job search motivated me and his mentorship and encouragement inspired me to stay the course as I worked on this manuscript.

I wish to thank my wife Donna and my son Austin for their unwavering support of my career and this literary endeavor. Writing this book was an arduous undertaking that took time away from family activities on many occasions. Their understanding (and occasional cheerleading) of my ambitions made it possible to see this work through to completion.

And, finally, a big thanks goes to the numerous individuals at Wiley Publishing who helped to mold this raw manuscript into a publishable book. A very special thanks goes to Wiley Executive Editor Todd Green for his willingness to give my first book a shot, and to copy-editor Susan Dunsmore, whose skillful editing helped to make sure that my inaugural literary effort was polished and professional.

Introduction

Qualified candidates should submit a cover letter, résumé, and portfolio for consideration.

How many times have you seen this worn-out submittal requirement in a job advertisement? Just about every ad ever posted for a designer, regardless of the position or level of experience sought, has included a request for these three documents. *Don't things ever change?*

Actually...they *don't*. Like it or not, the need for both students *and* professional designers to produce and maintain a portfolio of their creative work and the inevitability that a recruiter will ask to review it are the facts of life for designers engaged in a job search. Despite the near complete overhaul of the design industry brought about by digital technologies over the last quarter century, the good old-fashioned portfolio is *still* very much at the heart of the recruiting process. Though the methods by which we create and share our portfolios have changed dramatically, the song remains the same—we must still present a compendium of our best work to qualify for and get the job.

In my position as recruiting manager for a large multi-discipline design firm, I spend a lot of time interviewing students, reviewing portfolios, and lecturing in university-level design programs. Hands down, the subject I am most frequently asked to address in these lectures is "making the transition from full-time student to working design professional." As you might imagine, portfolio design is central to this topic. It seems that, regardless of which design school you attend or the length of your degree program, most curricula struggle with fully preparing students for the challenge of finding their first professional job. It's not that your teachers aren't trying—it's just that there is only so much they can teach in the short amount of time they have with you before you graduate. To make matters worse, with increased competition to attract students and mounting pressure to control student debt, some schools are reducing the length of their degree programs. With shorter programs, they will have even less time to address this concern than before! Unfortunately, teaching job hunting skills doesn't rank up there with teaching fundamental design skills and technical knowledge.

As an adjunct to my academic speaking engagements, I routinely work with university faculty to host portfolio reviews for juniors and seniors. A typical review brings together a group of design professionals from the community to review the work of anywhere from 10 to 30 students and help them prepare their portfolios for their first job interview. What I have come to realize after hosting dozens of these reviews is that virtually every student who participates is hungry for answers to basic questions about what constitutes a winning portfolio. During reviews, students often ask questions like, *"What should I put on my cover?" "How many pages should my portfolio have?"* or *"Should I put my intern work in the front or the back?"* And we do our best to provide them with straightforward answers. At the end of *every* review, the students tell us that that they've never received better feedback and guidance on portfolio design.

The regularity with which we hear such basic questions began to make me wonder; *Why are these reviews so valuable to students? Aren't they getting good portfolio advice in school?* The teachers in every design program I visit tell me that they provide portfolio guidance for their students. But they also tell me that the instruction they provide sometimes goes in one ear and out the other. They often say that what students *really* want to hear is what practicing professionals think about their work. One professor told me during a recent portfolio review, "The students seem to feel that, since professionals are out there in the trenches working every day, they *must* know more about portfolio design than we do."

Whether you agree with this viewpoint or not, I can relate to the concern; I too felt that way as a student. Now, if you don't feel that your teachers are providing all the answers, where can you go? As it turns out, your choices are limited. After researching the availability of published material on design portfolio design, I uncovered a relative scarcity of resources; a class here and there, a handful of books (mostly expensive glossy texts targeting working design professionals), and a few podcasts, online articles, and blogs. And, most notably, I found virtually nothing to help students understand what *recruiters* are actually looking for when they review a student portfolio.

Understanding what recruiters look for in a portfolio is an important part of successful job hunting. Recruiters have a unique perspective on portfolio design and content that comes from years of reviewing portfolios, interviewing candidates, and giving their all to hiring the best employees they can find. They experience, in real time, which portfolios represent a good potential hire, and which don't. Through trial and error, recruiters develop an intuitive sense that makes it possible for them to quickly review and set aside weak submittals, then focus their full attention on those that represent real promise. Your goal as you design your portfolio, however, is not to try and anticipate what recruiters expect; it is to guide them to what they need to know about you and help them conclude during that brief review of your submittal that *you* are a candidate with real promise.

So, what are they looking for? This may sound idealistic, but most recruiters are looking for a highly skilled candidate to fill an extremely specific role in their organization; just "anyone" won't do. While it was quite common fifty years ago to hire entry-level employees solely for their drafting abilities, hiring for such a narrow bandwidth of skills is no longer the norm. Today's recruiters are looking for designers who, in addition to drafting abilities, can think, conceptualize, draw, research, present, collaborate ... you get the idea. And to make that determination, recruiters are looking to your submittal to answer three fundamental questions:

1. Do you possess the skill set required to fill the position?
2. Would you be a good fit in their office culture?
3. What is your future potential to learn and grow?

As you might imagine, they flip through submittal after submittal in search of that elusive "perfect" candidate. Finding such a candidate can take weeks, even months. Allowing an over-embellished résumé and flashy graphics to influence such an important hiring decision only wastes time and money on unqualified candidates. Sure, the appearance and the content of your portfolio are important. More importantly, however, recruiters are also looking for clues about your potential, such as your attention to detail, your ability to communicate ideas effectively, and the thoroughness and organization of your submittal. Like it or not, this review occurs as a recruiter thumbs through your entire body of work in a few short minutes. You don't have much time to make an impression. If you want to make the next cut and be invited to an interview, your portfolio must answer these core questions and make an impactful impression on the recruiter almost immediately.

What can I do to help my portfolio outshine those submitted by other candidates going after the same position? You can start by understanding what recruiters look for as they evaluate your work and using that knowledge to design a portfolio that will have the greatest impact during that brief review. My objective in authoring this book is to provide a student-friendly resource, written from the perspective of a design industry recruiter *and* a designer, that will help you understand what recruiters look for as they review your portfolio. This book will provide valuable guidance on creating a professional-quality design portfolio that will get you to that all-important next step in the recruiting process—the interview.

Let's get started!

Chapter 1
Why Do I Need a Portfolio?

Why all the fuss about design portfolios? I already have great-looking project cutsheets!

If you are a student of design, just getting started in your chosen creative industry, this is a reasonable question. Without any guidance on the matter, it would be easy to believe that all a recruiter really needs to know is that you do decent work. Unfortunately, the portfolio is a convention of the design industry and, to get a job, you must have one; it's the universal measure of your progress and abilities. Design firms just don't hire designers fresh out of school without first reviewing their student portfolios. Unlike many other occupations (think, for example, auto sales, accounting, or nursing) where a résumé may be the only document ever submitted in a job application, every designer must present a résumé *and* a portfolio for review if they are to be considered a credible candidate.

Despite this vital role in the search for professional employment, the design portfolio just doesn't get much exposure in the classroom. As a student of landscape architecture, I don't recall ever even seeing a portfolio until my junior year. At that point in my emerging career, my portfolio (I'm being generous with the term here; I was not a highly organized student) was little more than a roll of drawings and a few beat-up presentation boards in the back of my dorm closet. As graduation loomed, I began to realize (with some anxiety, I might add) the importance of assembling something that would be suitable for sharing with prospective employers and for presentation during interviews. While most programs now do a better job of stressing the importance of the portfolio and providing useful resources for students, I still feel that many programs could improve on this.

But what should my portfolio contain? What should it look like? As I was nearing graduation from college, we had just two options: a presentation binder containing expensive reproductions and photos or full-size original drawings. Color copiers, digital plotters, computers, email, and overnight delivery had not yet been invented. Primitive times, indeed! When asked to share a portfolio, we had little choice but to either visit the office and present it in person or send expensive photographic reproductions by snail mail (with a hopeful request that they would be returned). "It'll *probably* get there by the end of the week" was as reassuring as a postal worker would get about delivery in those days. Understandably, most of us were hesitant to send something we had so much time and money invested in through such an unreliable service. In a pinch, we sometimes used our original drawings for an interview, though unrolling those large rolled-up drawings in an interview was always a little awkward. The classic design portfolio was (and still is) the better option. If assembled professionally and presented well, it communicates your skill set at the same time it reveals that you have a good sense of organization and an aptitude for presentation.

Today, digital technology has utterly transformed how we create, store, and transmit our creative work. We now handle portfolios in ways that we could not have imagined when I entered the profession. Everything you need to produce and share your portfolio is right there on your computer desktop. Unlike the dark ages of the twentieth century, when a portfolio was essentially a glorified scrapbook, we no longer need all those old analog tools—double-stick tape, photographic darkrooms, press-on letters—to put together a portfolio. Better yet, it costs absolutely nothing to create an unlimited number of copies for distribution. And, by simply pushing the "Send" button, you can forward your portfolio anywhere on the planet instantly. How could this get any easier?

This ease of production and sharing has, unfortunately, also created a bit of a "production line" mindset. Because portfolios are so easy to package and share, many candidates (students and professionals alike) believe that simply attaching an assortment of PDFs of their work to an email and blasting it off to as many firms as possible is all one has to do to secure a job. You *might* get lucky with that approach, but chances are, most recruiters who review such a submittal will see it for what it is—an untargeted portfolio assembled with little regard for what it says about you or your suitability for the position they are trying to fill.

Your portfolio must be more than a bunch of school projects hastily clamped together! Your portfolio is THE document by which you communicate everything about your academic and professional self to a prospective employer—your personality, your skill set, how you think, your ability to present yourself, why you are the best candidate; all of this and more are determined by a recruiter without you even being in the room. You need to control this narrative!

After years of leading university-level portfolio reviews, I've observed that many of the students who participate in these sessions are nervous about the design of their first portfolio and they understandably ask a lot of questions. When I first started hosting these reviews, I presented examples of nicely designed portfolios and pointed out why they were "good." That, however, didn't always fully address the students' questions. In fact, highlighting beautiful portfolios likely made the whole thing even more challenging for some students. In the hope of making the topic more approachable, I dissected the portfolio and began to talk in detail about its individual components: cover, table of contents, project cutsheets, etc. But that too had its limitations.

I came to realize that I had been presenting the portfolio as though it was still a professional scrapbook. It wasn't until I reflected on what I, as a recruiter, look for in a portfolio that I realized I was approaching it all wrong. Of course, you need an attractive cover and informative project cutsheets to show off your talents, but those things don't tell the whole story. To get onto my interview shortlist, your portfolio also needs to reveal your potential to be a member of our team. *Do you communicate and work well with others? Are you creative? Do you have strengths that will make our firm better?* Beyond understanding your skill set, I need to know *who* you are.

While it is clear that the students who attend our portfolio reviews are looking for technical advice on portfolio design, I've found that many students also need a little emotional support. *How do you feel about my portfolio? Do you think I can get a job with it?* Thinking back to my senior year in school, I recall the technical challenges of designing my first portfolio, but I also remember the huge emotional impact it had on me during that period. Through the course of a single year, I went from a state of **confusion** (*Where do I start?*) to being **overwhelmed** (*How am I ever going to finish?*) to **confidence** (*Boy, this looks great!*) to **uncertainty** (*What if they don't like it?*) to being completely **discouraged** (*I didn't get the #!&# job!*) to **exhilaration** (*I got my first job offer!*). These emotions are part of the challenge inherent to making the transition from student to working professional and they need to be addressed.

What has evolved from years of reviewing student portfolios, hosting university portfolio reviews, and engaging in one-on-one interviews with students is a "plan of action" for portfolio design that I now call *The Four S's*. Rather than dwelling entirely on portfolio content and production, *The Four S's* is an organizational mindset focused on the added value of telling your story, revealing your style, demonstrating your strengths, and sharing all of it effectively. You are so much more than a grade point average and an infographic full of software skills!

The Four S's are:

1. **Story**: Telling Your Story.

2. **Style**: Defining Your Style.

3. **Substance**: Giving It Substance.

4. **Sharing**: Sharing Your Work.

To ensure that each "S" is thoroughly addressed, a full chapter of this book has been dedicated to each topic. Each chapter is further subdivided into the three key deliverables of the typical professional job application: (1) the **Cover Letter**; (2) the **Résumé**; and (3) the **Portfolio**. To illustrate how these concepts can be applied to your design portfolio, I've assembled examples from a variety of student portfolios I've received in recent years that I feel have expertly integrated The Four S's into their portfolios. Let me introduce you to The Four S's.

STORY

First, the obvious. The good old days of submitting that wadded-up old résumé for a summer job at the corner grocery are now behind you. As a graduate of a university design program with a certificate or professional degree, you now need a much more sophisticated and visual way to communicate your new skill set to potential employers. Your résumé is still important, of course, but it must now be supplemented with a design portfolio containing examples of your best student work. As you set out to assemble your portfolio, one question should loom large: *"How can I differentiate myself from my classmates?"* The answer, in part, lies in how well you tell your *Story*. What is your unique *Story*?

At a time when most graduates of design school have mastered AutoCAD, InDesign, and Photoshop, software skills alone rarely set candidates apart. Most young designers are so proficient with design and drafting software that these abilities are now considered a baseline competency, just as drafting (by hand, of course) was in the days before computers. You don't have to look at many job ads to see that, "Proficiency with AutoCAD," is the lowest common denominator of every entry-level position advertised; nothing unique there.

During interviews, to better understand a candidate's story, I ask them to describe their strengths (note that I didn't use the word *digital*; I'm hoping you will tell me something unique about yourself like "I'm an organized designer" or "I'm a great conceptualizer"—it's not a software kind of question). To my dismay, the answer is usually "I'm great with AutoCAD" or Lumion or Rhino or whatever the software *du jour* is. Unless you're seeking a CAD Tech position, software skills will not be the primary focus of most interviews. You'll need something more valuable than that to make yourself stand out.

Yes, recruiters *are* looking for candidates with well-developed software skills, but they expect that of *everyone* who applies. What they want are well-rounded employees who have software skills *and* who can think and can write and can work well with others and can make presentations—the list of good answers to this question of "strengths" is surprisingly long. We can train you to improve your technical and software skills; it's much harder to teach you to be collaborative or to be organized if you don't already possess such traits. Identifying and then building your portfolio around your strengths are central to telling your story.

In a recent article on *The Motley Fool* website, "10 Soft Skills Hiring Managers Are Looking For,"[1] author Maurie Backman reinforces this notion that the best candidates aren't necessarily the most technically proficient. The best candidates are those who are technically proficient *and* possess a range of well-developed soft skills. Unlike job-specific technical skills (hard skills), soft skills are skills that are not unique to a

---

[1] Backman, Maurie. "10 Soft Skills Hiring Managers Are Looking For." *The Motley Fool.* 7 January 2018. Web. 11 April 2018.

particular job; they can be applied universally in the workplace. Backman's article identified ten interpersonal soft skills that are highly valued by recruiters:

1. Oral and written communication

2. Attention to detail

3. Customer service

4. Personal drive

5. Integrity

6. Problem-solving capacity

7. Independence

8. Organization

9. Teamwork

10. Troubleshooting ability

Do you possess any of these sought-after soft skills? Backman stresses that soft skills are as important in the workplace as technical skills and that recruiters look for them in *every* candidate. While few of us possess *all* these skills, most of us are naturally good at *some* of them. As you prepare to graduate, recognize that you now command a unique blend of education, technical skills, project experience, *and* soft skills that will make you a valuable addition to the right office. To maximize your chances of getting to an interview, inventory your soft skills, integrate them into your portfolio, and be prepared to confidently demonstrate them during interviews.

In Chapter 2, "Tell Your Story," we'll look at specific techniques you can utilize to create a portfolio that stands out from the crowd. As you read on, give some thought to what makes you a unique candidate. Those qualities are there—you just need to be aware of them. There may be a few recruiters out there who don't care about what makes you unique—they only need your technical abilities. I can assure you, however, that not all recruiters are that shallow; the good ones really do want to get to know you. It's your job to help make that happen. Hiring a new employee is time-consuming and every recruiter wants to be sure that you'll be a good fit in their workplace "family." The more effectively you communicate your *Story* and illustrate that you are both a capable *and* unique candidate, the quicker you'll find yourself in an interview.

STYLE

Once you've settled on the elements of your *Story*, you will need to determine how to best communicate it to others—both digitally and in person—in your own unique *Style*. One of the chief complaints I hear from fellow recruiters about digital portfolios is, "They all look alike these days." I don't totally agree with this view, but I do understand why a recruiter would say this. With most students using the same software to create portfolios and recruiters using the same office equipment to review and print them, it just makes sense that we would see many similarities among the portfolios we review.

With high-resolution graphics and the universal availability of desktop publishing software creating a level playing field for candidates, the challenge now is to find a way to introduce your *Style* in a way that will stand out and be noticed. In large part, this is a function of good organization, competent graphic design, and an understanding of what looks professional, both on a monitor and in a printed document. Much of your appeal as a candidate depends upon this.

Starting with the opening page and concluding with the back cover, your portfolio must present your unique style in a smooth and compelling viewing experience for the recruiter. Ease of navigation, clear organization, high legibility—these are just a few of the elements that contribute to a positive digital viewing experience. Consider the experience of reading a good online book: you download the book with one click, double-click on it and immediately open to a well-designed and relevant cover, scan the table of contents, read the introduction, and then dig into the story. This is Publishing 101—an orderly well-designed presentation orients readers and guides them effortlessly through the story. Your goal should be to create a similar user experience for your portfolio.

And it's not all digital. You also need a professional-quality hardcopy presentation portfolio for those pesky in-person meetings—interviews. Over the last two years, the Covid-19 global pandemic has prevented us from hosting in-person interviews, and we have been doing interviews by video. That, however, is not expected to be the case for much longer. With the nationwide vaccine program already in place, we can already see the workplace beginning to return to normal. When that happens, upon being shortlisted, you may be asked to visit the office and present your work in person. The degree to which you leave a good impression on your interviewer will depend not only on your portfolio content, but also its tactile and visual quality and how well you present it.

In Chapter 3, "Define Your Style," we'll review the elements of *Style* using a range of samples from well-designed student portfolios, discuss current trends, and look at ways you can add your individualized touch to your presentation.

SUBSTANCE

Regardless of how wonderful your portfolio may look, it's only as good as the content—the *Substance*—that backs up your claim that you are a competent designer and that you can make a valuable contribution to the recruiter's firm. Yes, you do need good imagery, but polished graphics are only window dressing here—you still need something to lure your customer into the store and buy your product.

Most recruiters, unfortunately, don't take the time to review every drawing and read every project description in your portfolio. Sure, they'll scan your project cut-sheets (e.g., project summaries), but they probably won't notice that your design solution reduces local hydrocarbon emissions by 35% or that you used chamfered tropical hardwood on that rooftop deck. They want to know what your strengths and skills are, understand your role in the project and, most importantly, determine your potential to be a designer and future employee in their firm. As they review your portfolio, they're asking themselves questions like, "Were you the team coordinator?" or "Did you create these awesome renderings?" or "Did you develop that cool design concept?" *Does your portfolio answer "substance" questions like these?*

You could come right out and say, "I understand design conceptualization" or "I'm very creative" in your cover letter or résumé but seeing is believing. Recruiters want visual evidence to confirm that you have the technical skills you claim to have. That said, a portfolio containing work that illustrates, rather than describes, your technical prowess is a more effective portfolio. How do you go about *showing* rather than *telling*? Well-designed and consistent project cutsheet templates might illustrate your graphic design skills. The inclusion of your concept development doodles might reveal how you work through a design challenge. Placing well-written descriptive captions below every graphic might show off your writing skills and identify the software skills you used to create them. These are just a few techniques you could use to illustrate your unique abilities and help a recruiter clearly "see" your *Substance*.

In Chapter 4, "Give It Substance," we'll look at samples from well-designed student portfolios and discuss how they address the *Substance* that recruiters look for. Remember, recruiters typically have only a few minutes to review your work and make an informed decision regarding your suitability for a position. Helping them quickly find what's important and determine that you are, in fact, a qualified candidate will increase your odds of being shortlisted.

SHARING

Now that you've put in all this demanding work and created a portfolio that you are proud of, it's time to put it to the test and submit it for a job. The design portfolio is *the* industry standard for the presentation and evaluation of an artist's or designer's capabilities—it's the price of admission for *every* interview. Virtually every employer you communicate with from this day forward will ask to review your portfolio before they consider inviting you to interview. Unbelievably, the way you share your portfolio with a recruiter can have as much impact on how you are perceived as a candidate as the actual content of your portfolio itself.

In Chapter 5, "Share Your Work," we will look at different techniques you can use to share your portfolio. You should, by the time you start networking and applying for jobs, have your digital portfolio and its companion hardcopy presentation portfolio in "ready" mode and have a clear plan for sharing them quickly and effectively with recruiters. This is not the time to be experimenting with file formats or fumbling around with cutsheet layout—you should have these details worked out and be ready to confidently press "Send" the moment you get a request. When you do get that call for an interview, being ready to meet immediately communicates that you are a candidate who takes your job search seriously. You may never "finish" your portfolio, but you'd better have it "ready" to share when a recruiter calls!

Assembling your first design portfolio may feel like a monumental undertaking as you get started—it did to me as I set out to create mine. Truth be told...it does take a *lot* of arduous work to do it right. But don't let that overwhelm you. You've had plenty of practice in school tackling complex semester-long design projects, right? You've used the design process in school to break those projects down into more manageable chunks. One step at a time. The only difference between those projects and this one is that this project is focused entirely on YOU and you'll be working on it for the rest of your career. This challenge may seem daunting, but you can do this. *No one understands this subject matter better than you!*

Chapter 2
Tell Your Story

So...tell me a little bit about yourself.

You've made it to the interview. Congratulations! Once introductions have been made and we've settled in around the conference table, this innocuous sounding request is usually the first thing to come out of my mouth in an interview. While it sounds simple enough, this common interview opener is one that sometimes makes a candidate fidget. *Is this a trick question...how should I respond?* Knowing how to respond is easier if you understand why I would make such a request in the first place. It's not really a trick question; it's part curiosity and part test. Just as it might be in any other conversation, the question is simply an icebreaker intended to help me better understand who you are and how you present yourself, as well as to enable a more meaningful conversation with you. What I'm asking for here is your elevator pitch; your *Story*.

If you stop and consider why recruiters require that you submit a cover letter, résumé, and portfolio with a job application, you'll realize that the purpose of that package is much like that of the interview question I just described. You are being asked to introduce yourself to a potential employer and make a pitch for why you might be the right candidate for the position. Consider it your "digital" elevator pitch. The difference, of course, is that you aren't there to make the presentation; your submittal must do *all* the talking.

As you might imagine, the way I review a digital submittal is different from the way I handle an interview. In the hypothetical interview above, you may have 30 minutes to introduce yourself, present your work, and make a case for being hired. As I open your digital submittal, you may have just two or three minutes to achieve that same goal. As in the interview, however, a similar thought goes through my mind as I open your email; *Tell me about yourself.*

As I review your package, odds are I won't know you. I receive hundreds of submittals every year and, unless we've met in a class or an informational interview, you are just one of many students looking for work. At this stage in the process, every submittal is equal; a digital calling card in my email inbox waiting to be opened. When I do get around to opening your package, my hope is that it will reveal that you are *the* candidate that we are looking to hire.

What's the secret to creating that kind of submittal? There is no secret. Creating a submittal that will capture and hold a recruiter's attention requires assembling a package that satisfies three basic objectives:

1. It provides all the materials requested.

2. It clearly demonstrates that you have the qualifications required for the position.

3. It illustrates that you possess unique skills, talents, and experience that would bring added value to the employer.

To get this right isn't really that challenging, but you'd be surprised at how many candidates just don't get there. There's always a handful of candidates who simply fail to provide the required documents and are immediately disqualified.

Then, there's the group of candidates who provide only what's required; they send a cover letter, résumé, and portfolio. Some of these candidates may not actually be qualified, but, by gosh, they have submitted the required documents.

A much smaller group of candidates provide the required materials *and* successfully demonstrate that they possess all the qualifications required for the position.

And, finally, a select few submit all the materials required, confirm that they are qualified for the position, *and* put in the extra effort required to show that they bring something unique to the table. Of course, your degree or certificate and your software skills are important, but those are the baseline qualifications and skills *every* candidate must have. As I review your package, I'm looking to confirm that you're qualified *and* that you have that extra something that sets you apart from other applicants.

Does your portfolio have that "special sauce" needed to stand out from the crowd? For a designer who is talented with their hands, this might be represented by examples of exceptional graphic design or by study models they have built. Though the creative world has gone digital, recruiters still like to see candidates with well-developed handcraft abilities. **Brynn Macinnis** (Colorado State University: Bachelor of Science in Interior Architecture and Design, 2016) created a project cutsheet that presents a hardwood and string model she constructed to study site layout and travel distances for her capstone project; a proposed therapy center in Sea Island, GA (Figure 2.1). I found this model fascinating! Brynn's use of string to depict travel times and distance is unique and imaginative. In addition to being engaging and informative, the cutsheet provides tangible evidence of Brynn's graphic design and model building talents, while her project description provides a sample of her writing skills and describes how she approaches her creative work. This is *much* more interesting than any AutoCAD plan would ever be.

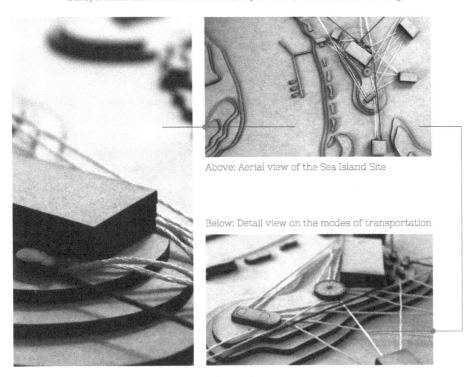

SITEMODEL : **THE CLOISTER HOTEL**

The Model:
For this model, I chose to use a hardwood for the material and a laser cutter for the stylizing. Topographical information as well as relevant building locations came into play when deciding what to include into this site model. The strings included contain information about timing and distances to relevant areas on Sea Island. The green string stands for the shortest time distance. The grey string stands for the middle amount of time. The black string stands for the longest amount of travel time on the island to relevant business locations. Each of the strings are connected to a form of transportation that stand for foot travel, bicycle travel, and automobile traveling.

Above: Aerial view of the Sea Island Site

Below: Detail view on the modes of transportation

4

Figure 2.1 Brynn Macinnis modeling.
Source: Brynn Macinnis.

Designers are often good photographers, but few take the time to effectively share that skill in their portfolios. When they do, it sometimes feels like an afterthought; "I'll just throw a few of my travel photos onto the last page here." Sure, you can add a *Photography* section to your portfolio but, if you're good at it, why not show it off in project cutsheets throughout your portfolio? If you are good with photography, use your skill to take and provide images for cutsheets of your internship projects, models, volunteer projects—there are so many opportunities to reveal your talent. Design firms are always in need of good project photography and there's nothing better than having a talented photographer on staff!

Someone with advanced artistic talent might consider adding a *Personal Skills* section that provides examples of work done outside of the classroom. Recruiters look for designers with personal interests and unique skills that might translate well to the creative workplace. **Elliot Williams** (Texas A&M University: Bachelor of Landscape Architecture, 2016) created a *Digital Painting* cutsheet to show off his advanced digital media skills (Figure 2.2). The cutsheet highlights Elliott's artistry and tells us that he also creates illustrations for a science fiction writer. At a glance, I can see that he is talented *and* ambitious. I also like that he provided a link to a website where I could see more examples of his work. As a recruiter, I am always thrilled when I come across a portfolio that reveals a candidate's personal initiative and diversity.

A candidate with student internship experience might consider downplaying some of their academic work to better emphasize their internships. Why? Because recruiters recognize that a former intern already understands how to work in an office and will be more productive on their first day at work than a non-intern candidate. **Wes Gentry** (Louisiana State University: Bachelor of Landscape Architecture, 2015) prepared a series of informative project cutsheets to illustrate the professional experience he obtained during his student internships (Figure 2.3). Wes's cutsheets show that he worked on a variety of interesting signage, site graphics, and master planned community projects during his internship. Wes wisely inserted descriptive captions below each image identifying the project and the software he used to produce it. The clean layout, the diversity of the work, and the high quality of his renderings communicate that Wes is exceptionally talented and capable of producing professional-quality work.

What sets you apart from your classmates? Whether you realize it or not, you possess a distinctive blend of personal attributes, talents, skills, and credentials that, when brought together, create a unique *Story*; it's what sets you apart from every other student looking for work. Your challenge is to know your story and tell it in a way that quickly captures a recruiter's attention. When our firm advertises a new entry-level position, we sometimes receive dozens of portfolios the day the job is posted. That's a lot of information to take in! You've need to find a way to stand out!

I like to think of reviewing a large batch of job applications as being like going to a party where I don't know anyone. I love the challenge of meeting new people but if I'm going to meet someone interesting, I'll have to work the crowd. So, I walk around, meet new people, and strike up a conversation or two—you know, idle chit-chat; "How's the weather?" or "That *was* a great football game." Nothing too exciting. The party gets much more interesting, however, when I bump into someone who is different from the other guests … someone with a unique story to tell; "*…and just as the helicopter banked so I could get a clear overhead photo of the project, my seat came*

DIGITAL PAINTING

expanding to new media

In addition to personal practice, I have fulfilled multiple commissions and illustrated concepts for an amateur science fiction writer.

For more artwork visit

ejw333.wix.com/elliot

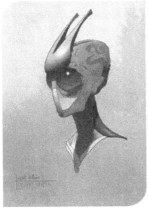

DESERT QUEEN

FATIMA

Loch Ness on a calm day.

14

Figure 2.2 Elliot Williams digital painting.
Source: Elliot Williams.

loose, and everything began sliding towards the open door!" Even if you don't know this person, you're going to hang around and hear the rest of that story, right? To get my attention, your portfolio should be like that person. Tell me your *Story*!

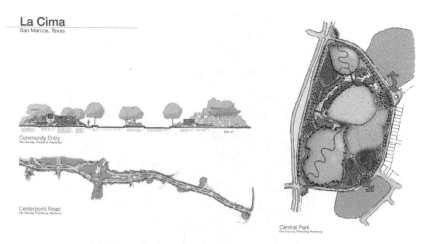

La Cima
San Marcos, Texas

Community Entry

Centerpoint Road

Central Park

Figure 2.3 Wes Gentry internship experience.
Source: Wes Gentry.

STORY: YOUR COVER LETTER

Though a cover letter is not technically a component of your portfolio, virtually every job application you see will require one. Regardless of whether you send one in the email or by separate cover letter attachment, its content is important; it's the best option you have for introducing yourself and your strengths to a recruiter. When you stop and consider just how much information the average job application contains, you can see how difficult it might be for recruiters to weed through it all quickly. Your cover letter provides a concise way for you to introduce yourself, state why you're a good candidate, and answer the question every recruiter asks themselves as they review your submittal; *Why should I hire you?*

From the perspective of a recruiter who reads hundreds of cover letters a year, I can tell you there is no shortage of applicants who just won't be bothered with helping a recruiter answer that question. A typical cover email says something like, "To whom it may concern: I am applying for the position you advertised" or "Dear Recruiter: I saw your ad. I've attached my resume and portfolio. THX !" That's about all I get much of the time.

Did either of those introductions capture your attention? I didn't think so. Did either make a case for why I should consider hiring them? Nope. Introductions like these—and, yes, we get them all the time—are so weak I rarely read them before I move on to the portfolio (and then with the expectation that it will be equally dull). This kind of introduction contributes nothing to your story. To be sure, I do understand that emailing, texting, and tweeting all encourage an "economy of words" that has changed the way most of us correspond with each other. Agreed—few people write letters anymore. I do want to remind you, however, that this letter is not an ordinary letter. You're applying for a professional job. *Do you want to send a letter that looks like a text to a buddy or one that will get a recruiter's attention?* It's your choice. *Write a cover letter that properly introduces yourself to a recruiter.*

Equally unimpressive is an exceedingly long cover letter. Last year, we received an application for a Planner position accompanied by a letter that rambled on and on for three pages about the candidate's expertise with Photoshop and BIM and Rhinoceros; all great software skills, but not at all relevant to the position. This candidate didn't explain why he was writing, describe any relevant skills, or mention any planning experience at all. He got so caught up in describing his software skills that he appeared to have forgotten why he was writing. The rest of the package was equally ambiguous. To his credit, this candidate did take the time to write a personalized letter. Unfortunately, he missed the point of doing so—to make a convincing case for being invited to interview.

Go back to that Planner position I just described and ask yourself what a recruiter trying to fill that position would be looking for. *Do you have experience in large-scale community planning? Can you work in ways that improve collaboration between planners and designers?* Our Planner candidate would have had my ear had he mentioned either of these relevant skills or experiences. Some recruiters feel a long-winded letter shows that you don't respect their valuable time, others just don't have the time to read them. Authorities on the subject say that most recruiters (83%) spend less than one minute reading a cover letter.[1] We're not *all* that restless, but if you want a recruiter to read your letter, it must get to the point quickly. If there's one thing recruiters agree on, it's that your cover letter should be no longer than one page.

So, let's get back to the central question. *Why should I hire you?* There are many ways you could answer this question; not all, of course, will be effective. One applicant recently assured us that he'd be our most dependable employee if hired because he was unemployed and desperately needed the job. Another revealed that she'd recently relocated to our city and sent her portfolio to several local firms. "So far," she said, "none has responded. I sure hope I'll hear from *you.*" While both applicants may have had valuable skills to offer, neither provided any constructive reason for why they would be a good fit in our office. While I'm sure there are employers that may want to help these candidates out, most firms are not looking to hire staff that need help; they are looking for candidates that possess creative skills, will work hard, and will bring value and positive energy to their workforce.

To give you some examples of effective cover letter language, I've drafted four fictitious cover letters that illustrate a range of winning strategies for capturing a recruiter's attention. Let's have a look.

---

[1] "Understanding what employers want in a cover letter." *Society for Human Resource Management.* Web. 17 May 2018. http://www.dummies.com/careers/find-a-job/cover-letters/understanding-what-employers-want-in-a-cover-letter/

The Position

Why would you be a viable candidate for the advertised position? I always enjoy reviewing a submittal from a candidate who has thoroughly researched the position, feels they are a good fit, and is excited by the prospect of working with us. Recently, a planning student sent us an application for a summer internship. She opened her cover letter stating that she was familiar with our work, and she felt her skill set was well-suited for the position. Why? Because she had excellent AutoCAD, M-Color, and GIS skills (all software skills we use regularly for planning projects) and her academic studies were focused on residential planning projects. Her portfolio included a series of project cutsheets that supported her claim that she could plan and render professionally. She also knew that we often hired graduates from her university. In a display of savvy networking, she had discussed the position with her professor (an old friend of mine) who then contacted me and provided an excellent reference. She had done her homework and her submittal was focused on the position and professional. Most other applicants simply provided the minimum required: "I'm applying for your student internship. Here's my portfolio." This candidate's understanding of the position helped her create a unique submittal that secured an interview and got her the job. *Demonstrate why you are a good candidate for the position.*

Check out this cover letter from fictional planner Michelle Bayroot (Figure 2.4). It focuses on why she would be a good candidate for a student intern position.

Your Unique Value

Do you have unique life or work experiences that would make you valuable to a firm? Share them. Student internships are the most relevant job experience you could list, but you may also have engaged in other activities—unique jobs, travel experiences, volunteer positions—that could add depth to your story. During a break from school, I worked as Warehouse Manager for a department store in New Orleans. I handled shipping and receiving, I managed inventory, I packaged products…I was responsible for all sorts of things. One of my most important duties was receiving eighteen-wheelers full of clothing every day—I had to be organized. To improve my organization, I created an improved inventory tracking system to help manage the constantly moving stock. My boss was elated! While that job did little to enhance my design skills, it did wonders for my organizational skills. Those skills, unrelated to my academic pursuits, proved to be transferable skills that design firms need and were instrumental in getting my first job offer.

It's surprising how often I see valuable non-design experience (e.g., store manager, construction supervisor, etc.) on a résumé, yet with no attempt to extol its value in the cover letter. Hey…even recruiters understand that we don't *all* get internships with

MICHELLE BAYROOT

123 CREATIVE DR., Denver, CO 12345 | 555-555-1212 | MBAYROOT@SU.EDU

CreativeCo

11 Main St., Suite 1A
Nashville, TN 37011

Subject: Student Internship

Dear Mr. Smith,

Please accept this letter and attached resume and portfolio as my application for the **Student Intern** position you recently advertised on the APA Job Seekers website for your Nashville office.

After talking with my classmate, Ebb Howward (your Student Intern in 2019), I became very interested in working with you at CreativeCo because of your unique internship program and your thoughtful approach to planning. Our Department Head, Professor Jones, told me he thought that I would be a good fit in your office and suggested that I contact you directly. He added that he knew you personally and would gladly provide a reference this week.

My qualifications for the position include:

- 4th-year Planning student (anticipated graduation; May 2021)
- Large-scale residential planning project experience
- Advanced AutoCAD, GIS, and Adobe Creative Suites skills
- Internship at DesignCo Planning/Nashville (Jan-Aug 2018)
- Director: 2019 State University *Planning Week* Student/Professional Charrette

I am very interested in working with your firm in Nashville, getting involved with the community, and designing memorable places. I hope that you'll give my application serious consideration. If you have questions, I can be reached at 555-555-1212 or email at mbayroot@su.edu.

I appreciate your consideration and hope to hear from you soon!

Sincerely,

Michelle Bayroot

Figure 2.4 Michelle Bayroot cover letter.
Source: Mark W. Smith.

the big-name design firms. The key to using those "ordinary" job experiences to your advantage is knowing how to repurpose them into "valuable" job experience. Transferable skills learned in a non-design position can make you an attractive candidate. *Emphasize any life and work experiences that show your unique value as a candidate.*

This cover letter from fictional designer Fred Olmsted emphasizes positions he has held that would make him a valuable candidate for an interview (Figure 2.5).

Fred Olmstead

123 DESIGNER DR., BROOKLINE, MA 12345 | 555-555-1212 | FOLMSTEAD@SU.EDU

CreativeCo

Attn: Mark W. Smith
11 Main St., Suite 1A
River City TX 12345

Re: Entry Level Designer

Hi Mark:

Having just graduated from The State University, I am now looking for a position as a full-time designer. I visited your website today and noticed an ad for an **Entry-level Designer** for your new River City office.

Recognizing that you've just opened that office, I would like to apply for the position. I worked as Assistant to the Director at the River City Parks Department last year and have a good feel for the city and its park system. I also volunteered with the River City Trail Foundation during my internship and developed working relationships with many of the Foundation's staff. I have excellent freehand graphics and AutoCAD skills, both of which I know you use in your office and will help me to hit the ground running should you hire me. With my local experience and my unique BA/MLA degree combination, I feel I could be a real asset to your new office.

I've attached my résumé and portfolio for your review and look forward to the possibility of interviewing for the position!

Sincerely,

Fred Olmstead

Fred Olmstead

Figure 2.5 Fred Olmstead cover letter.
Source: Mark W. Smith.

The Firm

Why do you want to work in that firm? Hopefully, you're not sending out applications to firms you don't know anything about. You must have a reason for choosing them over all the others, right? It could be because the firm is in your hometown, maybe you want to be associated with a great designer there. Perhaps you just like the work they do. That's what drew me to my first job. My 5th-year design class visited a firm in New Orleans that designed zoos (a passion of mine at the time). The firm occupied the coolest office I'd ever seen (an old plantation house). I was impressed by the people, the office, the work, everything—I knew this was where I wanted to work! The following year, during an interview in that very office, I told the recruiter that the office looked like a wonderful place to work and that I had wanted to work there since our class visit. While I am confident I had the skills they needed that day, I don't think it hurt that I shared that I *really* wanted to work there, too. I got the job. *Be open about your desire to work with that particular firm.*

This cover letter from fictional designer Rey Eemmes makes it clear that the Rey is excited by the possibility of working at this firm (Figure 2.6).

123 Cool Chair Blvd.
Los Angeles, CA 12345
555-555-1212 | reemmes@su.edu
Linkedin.com/in/rey.eemmes

Rey Eemmes

CreativeCo

Attn: Mark W. Smith
11 Main St., Suite 1A
Los Angeles 12345

Re: Student Internship

Good morning, Mr. Smith:

Last fall, my 4th-year design class, led by Professor Jones, visited your offices during our field trip to Los Angeles. I was very impressed by your office and by the work that you and your colleagues are doing. Particularly, I was fascinated with your prototypes for molded plywood furniture for the US Navy.

Professor Smith mentioned that he spoke with you this week and told you that I would be a good fit for your Spring-Summer intern position. I have been working with molded wood construction in conjunction with my capstone project on "Ergonomics in Contemporary Furnishings for Adolescents."

I would be honored to have the opportunity to work in your office. I feel that I'd be a good fit for a student intern in your office and hope that you'll consider me a candidate for the position. My résumé and portfolio are attached for your review. Should you wish to discuss my qualifications further, I'd welcome the opportunity to visit your office for an interview at your convenience.

Sincerely,

Rey Eemmes

Rey Eemmes

Figure 2.6 Rey Eemmes cover letter.
Source: Mark W. Smith.

The Profession

Why do you want to be a designer? Being a designer means different things to different people: it's a job, a career, a lifestyle, it might be your life's purpose. Our industry attracts people who work hard simply because they are driven to be creative, they love what they do, and it's in their DNA. If it's your desire to be involved with something bigger than just getting a paycheck, share that passion in your cover letter. Recruiters want to see enthusiasm in an applicant. In response to an ad for a designer with master planned community design experience, we received a memorable letter from a candidate that, among other things, said, *"My personal and creative interests are focused on developing conscientious communities that integrate humans with their environment in functionally and aesthetically meaningful ways."* I could see this was someone who was passionate about their work. In person, I found this candidate to be every bit the inspired designer I had imagined. *Declare your passion for your profession.*

This fictitious candidate, **Frank Write**, opens his letter by leveraging a personal connection between me and his professor; he understands networking (Figure 2.7). He then provides details about his capstone that are relevant to our firm's work, shows his passion for the profession, and explains why his project experience would make him a good fit in our office.

What do these letters have in common? Each is addressed to me personally, each focuses on the candidate's strengths, each is written with optimism, and they all exude confidence and positivity. In a recent article, "Why Your Résumé Will Be Overlooked Even Though You're Completely Qualified,"[2] author Rachel Montanez reiterates how important it is to use language that carries positive associations in your correspondence. For example, using the phrase, "Dealt with customers," to describe a position in which you interacted with customers carries a negative connotation—it sounds like you didn't enjoy working with customers. Using the phrase, "Managed customer relations," in its place is a more positive way of describing the same experience. *Write in an optimistic and confident voice.*

Kristen Bahler, in an article on writing résumés, "139 Power Words That Will Make Your Résumé Stand Out Immediately,"[3] wrote, "A good résumé is like a magic wand. If you know what you're doing, hiring managers will gravitate in your direction." According to Bahler, to make your cover letter and résumé function like a "magic wand," you should use industry-specific words to describe yourself and your skill set. If you are a team player, for example, use "collaborated" or "worked closely with" to describe that characteristic. If you are creative, try using "visualized" or "illustrated" to communicate your creative capabilities. If you have a strong work ethic, consider using "achieved" or "established." The words you use impact how recruiters perceive

---

[2] Montanez, Rachel. "Why Your Résumé Will Be Overlooked Even Though You're Completely Qualified." Forbes.com. 4 January 2019. Web. 5 January 2019. https://www.forbes.com/sites/rachelmontanez/2019/01/04/why-your-resume-will-be-overlooked-even-though-youre-completely-qualified/#7d1690a5b6a5

[3] Bahler, Kristen. "139 Power Words That Will Make Your Résumé Stand Out Immediately." *Time.com*. 3 January 2019. Web. 5 January 2019. http://time.com/money/5481691/resume-power-words/

Frank Write

123 Frank Write Blvd.
Scottsdale, AZ 12345
555-555-1212 | fwrite@su.edu

CreativeCo

Attn: Mark W. Smith
11 Main St., Suite 1A
Des Moines, IA 12345

Re: Student Internship

Good morning, Mark:

In a conversation earlier this week with Doc Jones here at Southwest College of Design, he mentioned that you have just advertised a Landscape Designer position for your Des Moines office and suggested that I contact you. Knowing you and the work of your firm as well as he does, Doc felt that I might be a good fit for the position and said he'd call you on my behalf. I've also enclosed his letter of recommendation.

My capstone project, "Advancements in Amenity Design for Active Adults," helped me to understand the importance of well-designed amenities to healthy sales velocity and to the long-term health of the residents of large community projects for seniors. Many of my case studies are actually based on an in-depth study of communities your firm designed. I've attached a copy of my capstone so you can review the innovations I have developed. I'd very much enjoy the opportunity to discuss them with you.

I feel that I'd be a good fit as an entry-level designer in your office and hope that you'll consider me a candidate for the position. My résumé and portfolio are attached for your review. Should you wish to discuss my qualifications further, I'd welcome the opportunity to visit your office for an interview at your convenience.

Sincerely,

Frank Write

Frank Write

Figure 2.7 Frank Write cover letter.
Source: Mark W. Smith.

your value as a candidate. *Use industry-specific words to describe yourself and your skill set in a positive tone.*

What if I find a firm I want to work for, but they aren't hiring? So far, we've been talking about firms that are hiring. You may, however, find the perfect place to start your career and discover they aren't hiring. What then? Simple: if you want to work there, request an informational interview. It may feel awkward—even terrifying—to make such a request, but don't let that get in your way. You won't get *anywhere* if you don't ask. Not every recruiter will agree to meet with you, but when they do, the experience can be rewarding for both you and the recruiter. You make a valuable professional connection and get interview practice, the recruiter benefits by meeting available candidates. Who knows…you might even get a job. Design firms often make strategic hires when an exceptional candidate walks in at just the right moment. We may not have an open position today, but an informational interview provides me with a snap-shot of who you are and what kind of employee you might be. That will increase your chances of getting an offer even if we don't have a position today. *Demonstrate your networking abilities and request an informational interview.*

This cover letter from fictional designer Paul O. Sollary illustrates that he recognizes we don't have an open position but understands that networking is a valuable way of making connections and looking for work (Figure 2.8).

Paul O. Sollary

CreativeCo

Attn: Mark W. Smith
11 Main St., Suite 1A
Austin, TX 78700

Re: Student Internship

Dear Mr. Smith:

I am a graduate student of urban planning at Midwest State. After researching design firms in the Austin area that are engaged in Master Planned Community (MPC) design, I found that your firm is very well-known for your MPC work and is involved in several innovative new projects in the area.

My major area of study in school is in Community Planning. I am just finishing my capstone on an innovative new sustainable MPC that relies on solar and wind energy as its primary energy sources. Knowing that your firm is engaged in MPC planning *and* has a solar energy engineering subsidary, I am hoping that your insight on the subject might help me understand this technology better.

If you are open to the possibility, I would greatly appreciate the opportunity to visit your office for an informational interview in the near future. I'll call in the next few days to discuss this further.

Sincerely yours,

Paul O. Sollary

Paul O. Sollary

123 Communal City Blvd.
Arkosanty, AZ 12345
555-555-1212
paul.sollary@su.edu

Figure 2.8 Paul O. Sollary cover letter.
Source: Mark W. Smith.

Oh, and one more thing; ask for the position! I occasionally get a poorly written email saying something like, "Hey, here's my portfolio." You'll have to do better than that. Do you just want me to have a copy of your portfolio or are you really looking for a job? You could say it's implied that you want a job since you sent the email, but that's not good enough for me. You must go through the motion and ask for the position. It's a bit like one of those old Hollywood movies where the handsome high school football quarterback really likes the head cheerleader but is too shy to talk with her. And she likes him, too. Unfortunately, he doesn't go on a date with her because he's afraid to ask her out. Don't be like that football player. *Ask for the position!*

The Cover Letter: Sidebar Checklist

- ☐ Write a cover letter that properly introduces yourself to a recruiter.
- ☐ Demonstrate why you are a good candidate for the position.
- ☐ Emphasize any life and work experiences that show your unique value as a candidate.
- ☐ Be open about your desire to work with that particular firm.
- ☐ Declare your passion for your profession.
- ☐ Write in an optimistic and confident voice.
- ☐ Use industry-specific words to describe yourself and your skill set in a positive tone.
- ☐ Demonstrate your networking abilities and request an informational interview.
- ☐ Ask for the position!

STORY: YOUR RÉSUMÉ

I don't mean to be blunt here but reviewing résumés all day can get tedious. Many applicants think of their résumé as a document that conveys only facts: education, work experience, degrees. It's just a list, right? That's true; recruiters do need a concise way to confirm you are qualified for the position and your résumé facilitates that. What many applicants overlook, however, is the opportunity to present a richer story, to go beyond just proving they have the minimum qualifications and show some creativity. You're a designer; it's OK to get creative with your résumé.

For such a creative group, designers are surprisingly conservative when it comes to résumé design. Many of the résumés I receive look as if they were designed by attorneys (I'm not bashing attorneys. I work with many brilliant attorneys, but it's a fact—their résumés are rarely visually creative). While the credentials and qualifications may be there, there is a conspicuous lack of concern for unique appearance (Style) and content (Story). Your résumé presents yet another opportunity for you to show your creativity. *Communicate your creativity through unique résumé design and content.*

Assume for a moment that we are looking to hire an Architect with a Bachelor of Architecture degree, AutoCAD and Lumion skills, and internship experience. We've just received a new batch of applicants and I'm reviewing a résumé from fictitious applicant Dan Designer (he's fictitious, of course, but his résumé is modeled after a recently submitted résumé) (Figure 2.9). There is so much wrong here: visually bland, poor formatting, no work chronology, misspelled words. I could go on, but I want to focus on *Story* here. This résumé provides no sense of *who* Dan is (except that he's obviously unconcerned about the quality of his résumé); it's just data. After reviewing it, we conclude that Dan *might* be a minimally competent designer with the required qualifications, but the résumé does nothing to highlight any unique skills or strengths. A recruiter might still be asking: *Is he creative? Is he a leader? Is he collaborative?* Based on what's provided, it's unlikely that we would ever shortlist him for an interview. We typically don't hire minimally competent employees—we hire the best designers we can find. A few enhancements, such as providing more detail about his degree,

Dan Designer
dan.designer@acmeemailco.com   555-123-1111

Objective
hoping to obtain a positoin as designer in a successful design firm and apply my education and skills

Selected Skills and Accomplishments
- Microsoft Ofice Suite
- AutoCAD
- Lumion

Work Experience
Acme Auto Parts (Round Rock, TX)
- < Picked up parts at wholesaler and drove to buyer
- < Scheduled deliveries

Cashier: Mama's Restaurant (Austin, TX)
- < Dealt with customers, washed dishes, bussed tables

Intern: Acme Design (Austin, TX)
- < Drafted
- < Prepared takeoffs and cost estimates
- < Visitd construction sites

Education:
Austin City High School; Austin TX (graduated 2010)
The Design University/Austin, TX: Bachelor of Architecture (2019)

Personal:
Age: 24
Height: 5'-9"
Weight: 160

Hobbies:
Playing video games with friends
Java and HTML Coding

Figure 2.9 Dan Designer poorly prepared resume.
Source: Mark W. Smith.

software skills, and internship, deleting irrelevant personal data and hobbies, adding work experience chronology, improving the overall graphic design, and spellchecking might have made this résumé significantly more impactful.

Fortunately, there are many ways for you to enhance the story your résumé tells. For starters, you could include a *Headline Summary*—your elevator pitch. A well-written headline summary, such as this one by fictitious designer Frank Write, succinctly introduces who you are and identifies your strengths (Figure 2.10). If I read nothing else in your résumé, your summary should give me a sense of what kind of candidate you are. Your summary should also be tweaked to match every firm you write to. Recruiters will be more interested in you if it's clear that you've targeted their firm, rather than mass mailed your résumé to every firm in town. *Write a headline summary that highlights your strengths.*

FRANK WRITE

1867 Cherokee Red Blvd., Scottsdale, AZ 85259
P: 555-555-1212 | E: fwrite@su.edu | LI: linkedin.com/in/frank-write

SUMMARY

Detail-oriented architectural designer with multiple student internships and well-developed conceptualization skills. Experienced project team leader and effective collaborator with advanced contract document production capabilities. Excellent writing and photography skills. I thrive in an office environment where I can take responsibility and get things done.

SKILL SET

Software:	AutoCAD • Revit • Adobe Creative Suite • Lumion • MasterSpec
Handcraft Skills:	Advanced Freehand Graphics • Technical Writing • Photography • Model Building

EXPERIENCE

ACME ARCHITECTURE; Denver, CO
Student Intern Jan-Aug 2018

Reported to Design Director of mid-size architectural design firm with focus on mixed-use and multi-family residential design market throughout the Midwestern US.

- Prepared Construction Documents
- Managed AutoCAD files
- Attended in construction site visits.
- Prepared Lumion photorealistic renderings for marketing department

DARN GOOD DESIGN; Colorado Springs, CO
Student Intern Summer 2019

Hired to support company's production team in the planning and design of single-family residential-for-rent communities along the Front Range.

- Prepared construction drawings and planning documents with AutoCAD and M-Color
- Assisted Principal-in-Charge with design of firmwide marketing collateral

EDUCATION

THE ARIZONA UNIVERSITY/ SCHOOL OF DESIGN; Phoenix, AZ
Bachelor of Architecture   Anticipated Graduation 2021

Honors & Activities
Dean's List: 2018-2020
Recipient: Usonian Intern Scholarship (2018), Arcological Research Grant (2019)
President of AU/AIA Student Chapter
Director of 2019 Student Workshop
Cumulative GPA: 3.47

Figure 2.10 Frank Write headline summary.

Source: Mark W. Smith

Let's take a quick look at the language you might use in your résumé. In addition to the required qualifications and credentials, the typical job ad contains words like *leader*, *motivated*, *flexible*, or *collaborative* to describe the qualities employers seek in a candidate. In recruiting parlance, these are *Key Words*. By repeating key words (assuming you possess those attributes, of course) from the ad in your résumé, you better align yourself with the position and the firm. While this might seem subtle, it can help to differentiate you from other candidates. *Incorporate key words from the job posting into your résumé.*

Another way to add depth to your résumé is to share details about valuable life experiences, such as military service, volunteer activities, or membership in organizations. A few years ago, we received an application from a designer who was temporarily working in a theater while she searched for a full-time design position. While she had all the required credentials, what really stood out was the diversity of her life experiences; landscape designer, graphic designer, administrative assistant, set designer, ticketing manager, Peace Corps Volunteer. This résumé painted the picture of a truly versatile individual; it caught my eye immediately. During her interview, I could tell that she was intensely optimistic, eager to learn, and willing to tackle new challenges—all qualities we look for in a candidate. Though her academic credentials were like those of other candidates we were considering, her unique personal qualities and experiences helped her stand out; she was clearly the best candidate. We hired her and she quickly proved our assessment of her abilities to be spot on. *Share life experiences that contribute to your story and are relevant to the position.*

This leads me to an especially key point about résumé content: honesty. Be completely honest with *everything* in your résumé. One false claim can end your chances of being interviewed or, worse, cost you a job. I once had the pleasure of working with a designer who came to our firm with a résumé loaded with advanced degrees, awards, and work experience with some of the best design firms in the world. Some of his designs had even been patented! Overall, he was talented and pleasant to work with. Shortly after he joined us, however, our human resources department did some additional background checking and discovered that one of his degrees was fictitious and his entire résumé quickly unraveled after that. Most of his education, awards—even the patents—proved to be fake news. He was fired immediately.

In those days, it was time-consuming to perform background checks and few employers were thorough about it. Things have changed. Today, we can perform internet searches, visit social media, call references, and verify degrees and registrations—all within minutes. A search might produce a fabulous LinkedIn profile, or it might reveal a Facebook page someone is not so proud of. What does *your* social media profile look like? In addition to passive verification, you may also be asked to consent to a formal background check before you get an offer. I just read a story about a woman from Australia[4] who was convicted of deception, dishonesty, and abuse of public office for lying on her résumé. This was an extreme case, but the story underscores the importance of stating your credentials accurately. *Accurately portray your credentials and experience on your résumé.*

Finally, design your résumé to work in harmony with your cover letter and portfolio. Your package should effectively communicate your "brand." Those of you in graphic design already get this, but it applies to everyone in a creative industry. Just as a company is a brand or automobile is a brand, YOU are a brand. Consider the way movie stars manage their images. They act only in certain genres of movies, they wear particular clothes, they support specific social causes. Everything they do is designed to maintain a carefully crafted image and their acting portfolios reflect that image. Few designers achieve the high-profile kind of brand that big-name actors have, but you should nevertheless be working to develop your brand.

Graphic designer **Eric Andrews** (Austin Community College: Associate of Applied Science in Visual Communication/Graphic Design Specialization, 2018) designed his résumé to work very closely with his portfolio cover (Figures 2.11 and 2.12). He carried his cover's striking red background and custom logo into his résumé to keep our attention, then used the bold accent color in custom bullets that lead us to his experience and skills. Choosing to keep his résumé separate from his portfolio, Eric provided a link to his website where recruiters can download it. Eric's obvious effort to carry his bold graphic theme throughout his portfolio, résumé, and website makes a clear statement about what kind of designer he is.

I consider my personal brand to be clean and contemporary. I designed my résumé to reflect that brand and I update it periodically as my personal aesthetic changes. Given all the years I've practiced, I could easily fill a three-page résumé, but I didn't. Because my brand also suggests restraint, I've limited it to one page (Figure 2.13). The result is focused, legible, and uncrowded, my credentials are organized, and it immediately communicates what kind of designer I am. This didn't just happen; I've revised and refined this résumé many times during my career. Telling your story in a résumé takes work—whether you're just entering the profession, or you've been at it for years. Put in the time to really understand your story and design your résumé to communicate it as clearly as possible.

Think of your résumé as a "snapshot" that illustrates, at a glance, everything you bring to the table; it's not just data. In addition to sharing your accomplishments and skill set and academic career, it must share something unique about you—your *Story*—to be an effective job-hunting tool. *Design your résumé to work closely with your cover letter and portfolio to communicate your brand.*

---

[4] Cheung, Eric. "A Woman Lied on Her Résumé to Land a $185,000-A-Year Job. Now She's Going to Jail." CNN.com. 4 December 2019. Web. 14 December 2019. https://www.cnn.com/2019/12/04/australia/australia-woman-jailed-fake-resume-intl-hnk-scli/index.html

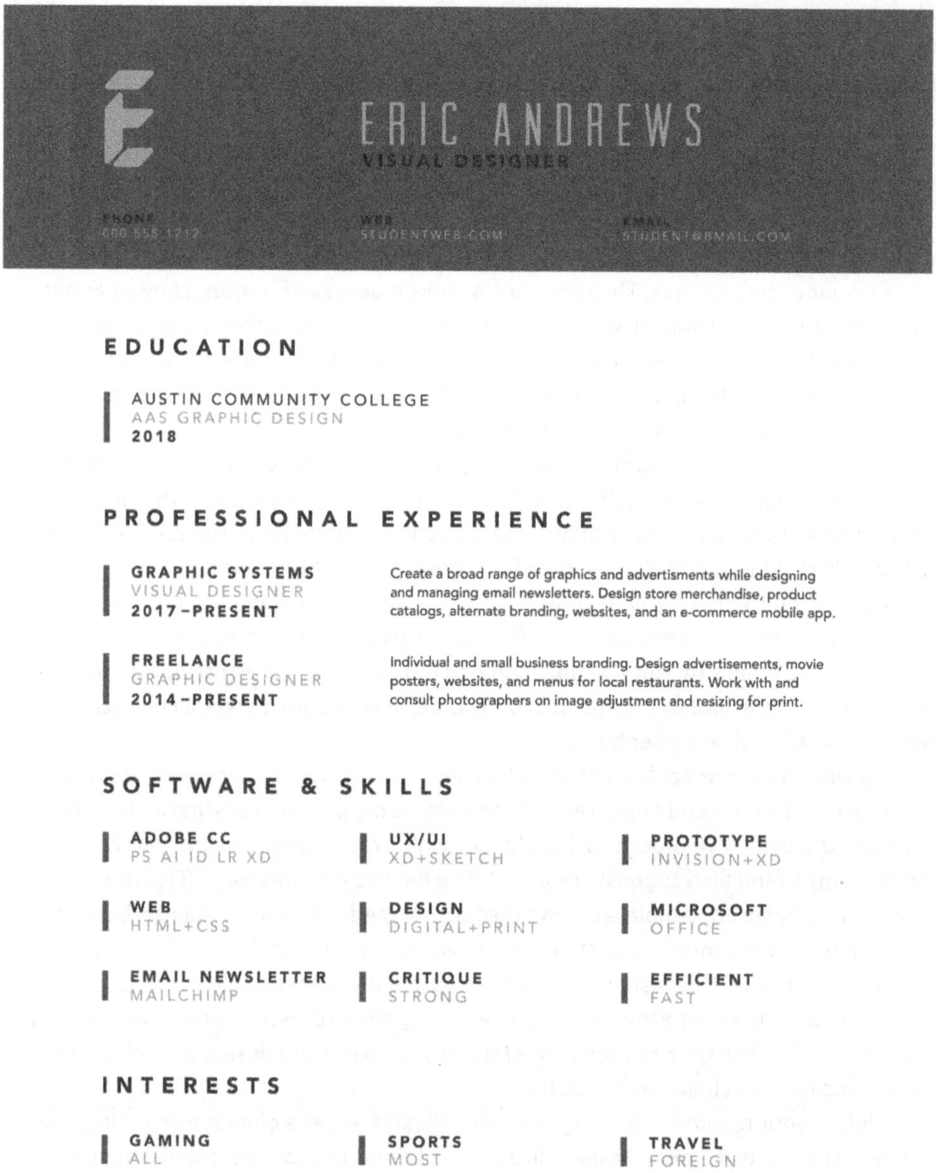

ERIC ANDREWS
VISUAL DESIGNER

PHONE
000 555 1212

WEB
STUDENTWEB.COM

EMAIL
STUDENT@MAIL.COM

EDUCATION

AUSTIN COMMUNITY COLLEGE
AAS GRAPHIC DESIGN
2018

PROFESSIONAL EXPERIENCE

GRAPHIC SYSTEMS
VISUAL DESIGNER
2017–PRESENT

Create a broad range of graphics and advertisments while designing and managing email newsletters. Design store merchandise, product catalogs, alternate branding, websites, and an e-commerce mobile app.

FREELANCE
GRAPHIC DESIGNER
2014–PRESENT

Individual and small business branding. Design advertisements, movie posters, websites, and menus for local restaurants. Work with and consult photographers on image adjustment and resizing for print.

SOFTWARE & SKILLS

ADOBE CC
PS AI ID LR XD

UX/UI
XD+SKETCH

PROTOTYPE
INVISION+XD

WEB
HTML+CSS

DESIGN
DIGITAL+PRINT

MICROSOFT
OFFICE

EMAIL NEWSLETTER
MAILCHIMP

CRITIQUE
STRONG

EFFICIENT
FAST

INTERESTS

GAMING
ALL

SPORTS
MOST

TRAVEL
FOREIGN

Figures 2.11 and 2.12 Eric Andrews coordinated graphics.
Source: Eric Andrews.

Figures 2.11 and 2.12 (*Continued*).

Source: Eric Andrews.

The Résumé: Sidebar Checklist

- ☐ Communicate your creativity through unique résumé design and content.
- ☐ Write a headline summary that highlights your strengths.
- ☐ Incorporate key words from the job posting into your résumé.
- ☐ Share life experiences that contribute to your story and are relevant to the position.
- ☐ Accurately portray your credentials and experience on your résumé.
- ☐ Design your résumé to work closely with your cover letter and portfolio to communicate your brand.

123 Design Dr., Austin, TX 12345, 555/555-1212, mwsmith007@mywebsite.com

PROFILE

Registered Landscape Architect with 35+ years of private-sector practice focused on landscape architecture in the Continental U.S.

- Diverse design and project management experience w/ construction valued to $30M
- Specialist in design conceptualization and the creative process
- Advanced hand and digital graphics capabilities
- Advanced marketing, human resources, administrative, and financial proficiency

PROFESSIONAL HISTORY

Vice-President [2002-present] *RVi Planning + Landscape Architecture,* Austin, TX
Associate Principal [2000-2002] *Land Design Studio,* Austin, TX
Senior Associate [1998-2000] *EDAW,* Atlanta, GA
Director of Landscape Architecture [1986-1998] *Cooper Carry,* Atlanta, GA
Associate/Project Manager [1984-1986] *Steve Domigan & Assoc.,* Austin, TX
Project Manager [1980-1984] *Design Consortium,* New Orleans, LA

EDUCATION

Louisiana State University, Bachelor of Landscape Architecture

REGISTRATION

Registered Landscape Architect
CLARB (Council of Landscape Architectural Review Boards) Certification

MEMBERSHIPS

American Society of Landscape Architects

AWARDS

Leadership Development Award (ASLA National)
Distinguished Service Award (ASLA/Georgia)
Merit Award: Newsletter Editor (ASLA/Georgia)
1st Place: Newsletter Design Competition (ASLA/Texas)

PROFESSIONAL ACTIVITIES

Organizer: Annual UT/ASLA Student Portfolio Review (2008-present)
Speaker: LSU Professional Practice Series (2005-present)
Speaker: Texas A&M Professional Practice Series (2013-present)
Committee Member: CLARB LARE Digital Cut Score Committee (2012)
Speaker: *Art in the Classroom* Program, Round Rock ISD (2003-2012)
Editor and Staff Writer: ASLA Newsletter: ASLA/GA Chapter (1989-1995)
ASLA Newsletter Sponsorship Chair; GA Chapter/ ASLA (1993-1998)
ASLA National Conference Program Committee/Atlanta; ASLA (1997)
Chair: ASLA Student Mentor Committee; ASLA/GA Chapter (1993-1994)

Figure 2.13 Mark W. Smith personal brand.
Source: Mark W. Smith.

STORY: YOUR PORTFOLIO

A design portfolio is, of course, an archive created for the purpose of storing completed design work and organizing it in such a way that it enables an effective presentation; that's its functional role. So how can you use a portfolio to convey your personal qualities—your *Story*? If you stick with the traditional components of a portfolio—cover, résumé, project cutsheets—you'll find your ability to tell your story through your portfolio may be limited. There are, however, several "optional" portfolio components that can help you tell a much richer story. There are many options, such as a *Cover, Table of Contents, Personal Biography, Project Experience Map, Project List,* or *Design Philosophy*, that can contribute a much higher level of personalization to your portfolio. Which of these you choose to include in your portfolio depends on what makes *your* story unique.

As you inventory your work, look for anything distinctive that will help you stand out from your classmates. You're not looking to just fill your portfolio up; you're looking for high quality content that will convey your unique qualities. If you are a highly organized individual, a *Table of Contents* might be a useful tool for revealing that soft skill. A candidate with extensive travels, volunteer experiences, or a captivating personal journey might find a *Personal Biography* useful. If you have diverse project experience in a variety of places, a *Project Experience Map* or a *Project List* might help you illustrate that. If you want to share a little about what inspires your creativity, a *Design Philosophy* would be useful. If you consider that few students include *any* of these components in their portfolios, you can see why they can help you create a unique portfolio. *Develop optional portfolio content to tell a richer story.*

Let's take a closer look at each of these optional portfolio components.

Cover

"They" say you can't judge a book by its cover. Don't buy a word of that adage; your cover is the first thing a recruiter experiences as they open your portfolio, and it *does* impact how they perceive your work. It is valuable real estate when it comes to telling your story. Think of a well-designed cover as the rough equivalent of dressing professionally for an interview. As a recruiter opens your PDF (i.e. meets you for the first time), your cover splashes onto the monitor and (hopefully) makes a favorable impression about you that will naturally draw them in and help them get comfortable with you.

While many candidates do go the distance and design stunning portfolio covers, others seem to think of designing a cover as something of a bother. Some candidates don't bother to design a cover at all. When you send a portfolio without a cover, you're sending what amounts to a bunch of projects, cobbled together and figuratively "dumped" on the recruiter's desk; a book without a cover. A coverless submittal makes a weak opening statement about your interest in the job, your ability to present yourself effectively, and your creative abilities. Hear me now—every design portfolio MUST have a well-designed cover!

For the balance of portfolio submittals—those that do have covers—many arrive with bland generic covers that say absolutely nothing about the candidate. Consider this fictional cover (Figure 2.14) (it's not *totally* fictional; I just received one just like it) with "Portfolio" boldly (and unimaginatively) stamped across the page. Yes, it's obviously a portfolio, but that's all. It communicates nothing about its owner except that he or she did not care enough to put any creative effort into the cover of a document that represents the whole of their academic career. It might as well not have a cover at all.

Figure 2.14 Unidentified Portfolio.
Source: Mark W. Smith.

I repeat; a poorly designed cover is a poor introduction. It's not an effective way for someone seeking employment in a creative industry to open the conversation. You *do* want recruiters to have a strong first impression of you as they open your portfolio, right? There are so many great ways to achieve this! You could design a cover that spotlights your personal logo. Perhaps it incorporates imagery from your award-winning student project. Whatever you do, create something that makes a clear statement about you, the designer, and your abilities. Great websites have cool home pages. Great movies have riveting opening scenes. Great design portfolios have well-designed covers. *Design a portfolio cover that identifies who you are and makes an immediate statement.*

So, what should a portfolio cover that tells your story look like? Let's look at a few examples. Graphic designer **Rebekah Lynne Spence** (Louisiana State University: Bachelor of Fine Arts in Graphic Design, 2018) designed a cover that communicates both her brand *and* her style (Figures 2.15 and 2.16). Because she prefers hand-written typography over digital fonts, her logo is completely hand-rendered. The bold black strokes and graceful loops communicate a playful, yet precise, graphic quality that runs through *all* her work. The logo is centered in white space and grabs our attention immediately; there are no distractions on this cover. She added the yellow "eye" for accent and because she is drawn to eyes as subject matter; another personal choice. Rebekah told me that since she began painting as a young girl, she has been drawn to eyes and, to this day, still "plays around with them" in her art. Why black and yellow? She chose these colors because those are her favorite colors, but they also have a functional role. Used with black, yellow immediately catches the eye, making it an excellent choice for drawing attention to something. Wisely, Rebekah uses color with restraint on her cover, then repeats it on each project cutsheet (seen here in her "The Dirty Hipster's Guide to Nashville's Greatest Record Shops") for continuity throughout her portfolio. Rebekah's cover displays her abilities as a talented graphic designer *and* reveals her skill as a storyteller; a highly effective way to open a conversation with any recruiter. *Design a portfolio cover that puts your creative strengths on display.*

Figure 2.15 Rebekah Lynne Spence creative portfolio cover.
Source: Rebekah Lynne Spence.

THE DIRTY HIPSTER'S GUIDE TO NASHVILLE'S GREATEST RECORD SHOPS
Font: Niveau Grotesk & hand-lettering

The Dirty Hipster's Guide to Nashville's Greatest Record Shops is a tour-guide book that takes the reader through Nashville's most unique, popular, and incredible record shops.

I used Adobe Illustrator and InDesign to layout each page in a fashion that complimented the shop's individual personalities.

Each spread uses vector illustrations, photography, and typography for the whole composition. The book is accordion-style bound with records used as both the front and back cover.

Figure 2.16 Rebekah Lynne Spence coordinated cutsheet.
Source: Rebekah Lynne Spence.

Sally Kronsnoble (Austin Community College: Associate of Applied Science in Visual Communication/Graphic Design Specialization, 2019) exercised exceptional restraint in the design of her portfolio cover (Figures 2.17 and 2.18). Only her signature "Crown" logo and the title, *Sally Kronsnoble Design*, appear on the cover; the rest is white space. Though quite small, her logo represents a lot. As Sally was developing her brand, she wanted to create a logo that would incorporate her surname; Kronsnoble. As she put it, "I was after something fierce and elegant." "Krons" translates to "crown," an icon she had, coincidentally, already been using for her personal work. Typically printed in black, she sometimes adds gold foil for emphasis for special projects. As a bonus, the crown can be broken into individual elements that are used for other branding purposes, such as on the back of her business card. Sally has confidently combined a unique logo and white space to create a cover of great simplicity. As we open her portfolio, we can see that she carries this elegant, yet reserved, style right into her work. For her "Fleet" project, Sally uses white space to maintain the focus on her work and to create continuity with other work in her portfolio. The simplicity of this cover makes for a quiet, yet powerful, opening statement.

SALLY KRONSNOBLE
DESIGN

FLEET
Brand Identity, Illustration, Typography

Fleet is a local, one woman owned and
operated company that creates custom
cycling bags. Each bag is created for the
customer's particular aesthetic and usage,
so I had the brand reflect the blank slate
quality that each idea starts as. There is
also a focus on sustainability within the
company that I translated into the material
used within the various collateral.

Figures 2.17 and 2.18 Sally Kronsnoble corrdinated portfolio cover and cutsheet.
Source: Sally Kronsnoble and gumuszeybek/Shutterstock.

Graphic designers aren't the only creatives who strive for an uncluttered look for their portfolio cover. Architectural designer **Alex Yen-Jung Wu** (University of Texas at Austin: Bachelor of Architecture, 2017) adopted a "less is more" approach for his cover design as well (Figures 2.19 and 2.20). Alex's cover contains only his name boldly positioned in the center, the title *Portfolio*, and the date, all centered in white space. Two thin horizontal lines bracket and subtly draw attention to his name. The simplicity

Figures 2.19 and 2.20 Alex Yen-Jung Wu portfolio cover.
Source: Alex Yen-Jung Wu.

AUSTIN HIGH SPEED RAIL STATION

Design VI · Spring 2015
Critic: Danelle Briscoe

Figures 2.19 and 2.20 Alex Yen-Jung coordinated graphics.
Source: Alex Yen-Jung Wu.

of this design—a signature of Alex's style—is applied effectively to each of his project cutsheets (seen here in his *Austin High Speed Rail Station* project) and visually ties his portfolio together. Alex's cover design is reserved, yet very professional. *Use white space for emphasis.*

Paul Yoder (University of Cincinnati: Bachelor of Urban Planning, 2020; University of Cincinnati; Bachelor of Community Planning, 2021) designed his portfolio cover to impart clues about his chosen profession *and* himself (Figure 2.21). As an urban planner, he is passionate about the urban fabric and selected an image of a regional roadway network to represent that passion. Though literally a map, when rendered in white and orange, the pattern takes on a bright abstract quality that draws us in for a closer look, all the while whispering in our ear, "Paul is a planner." Surely, you've guessed the location by now. Cape Cod, as viewed from 100 miles above the earth. *Why?* It wasn't a random selection; Paul has a story to tell. As a child, his late father (a Merchant Marine) often took the family sailing in Cape Cod Bay. As Paul puts it, "The experiences were vivid, and I'll always cherish Cape Cod for that." Paul loves boats, he loves to sail, and he loves Boston. A cover like this just *begs* a recruiter to get engaged and ask about it. When that happens, Paul is presented with an opportunity to tell a story that gets the conversation started and provides a smooth segue into his portfolio content. *Make a personal and professional statement.*

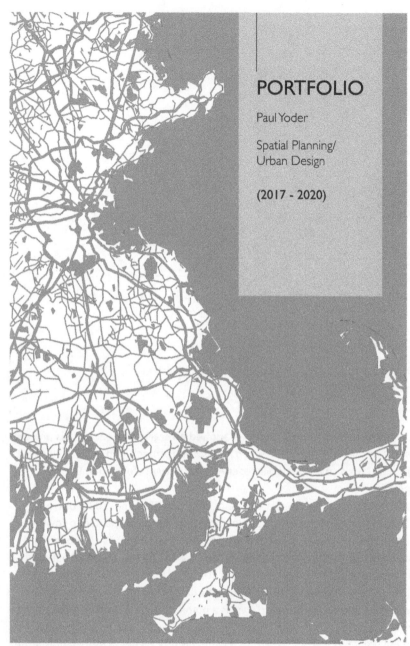

PORTFOLIO

Paul Yoder

Spatial Planning/
Urban Design

(2017 - 2020)

Figure 2.21 Paul Yoder portfolio cover.
Source: Paul Yoder.

For her portfolio cover, **Manasa Hegde** (Texas A&M University: Bachelor of Landscape Architecture, 2018) also used color in a bold way. Manasa superimposed a stylized black-and-white rendering of her *Enchanting Groves Park* pergola design over a brilliant watercolor-style background (Figures 2.22 and 2.23). Titled simply, *Manasa Hegde: Landscape Architecture Portfolio (2017–2018)*, Manasa's use of color is artful and eye-catching, and the bold pergola design gives the viewer just a taste of her design prowess. Her portfolio cover serves as a "teaser." *What is this interesting circular structure?* Well, you'll just have to look inside to find out. Manasa has used a highly effective technique; visually linking her portfolio cover design to her portfolio content to draw the viewer in to learn more. *Link your cover design to your content to draw the viewer in.*

Figure 2.22 Manasa Hegde portfolio cover link to content.
Source: Manasa Hegde.

5. Healing Garden-- Central Plaza

Key Plan

This is the center of the healing garden. It has a beautiful wooden pergola which provides shade to the benches. There is a green lawn in the center with a small fountain. This space can be used for events.

Key Plan

6. Healing Garden-- Aqua therapy

The aqua therapy space of the healing garden has a shallow pond which is 3' deep. A wooden deck extends into the pond for seniors to relax and enjoy the pond. Rock edge gives it a natural look.

Figure 2.23 Manasa Hegde coordinated cutsheet.
Source: Manasa Hegde.

Haley Meeks (University of Georgia: Bachelor of Landscape Architecture, 2018) designed a soft impressionistic image of an antebellum plantation framed by magnolia trees for her cover (Figures 2.24 and 2.25). The image is rendered in muted earthy tones and left slightly out of focus—both striking and artistic. The title, *Haley Meeks: Landscape Architecture Portfolio*, is printed tastefully in the lower corner. As I reviewed Haley's portfolio, I learned that the image is representative of where she grew up; she is from Georgia where southern magnolias and antebellum architecture are part of everyday life. On the contact/résumé page that follows, she subtly carried the cover color and font through to her résumé to continue the theme. Haley concluded her portfolio with a *Design Philosophy* that speaks to regional influences and southern design values. It's a nicely developed package. It left me with the feeling that Haley is creative, has a great appreciation for her roots, and put a lot of thought into her presentation.

HALEY MEEKS

haleym@gthatmail.com
123.555.1212

EDUCATION

University of Georgia
College of Environment + Design
Bachelor of Landscape Architecture
Historic Preservation Certificate
Anticipated Summer 2018

WORK EXPERIENCE

Cold Creek Nurseries; Aiken, South Carolina
Landscape Design Intern
Summer 2015

Northway Landscaping; Atlanta, Georgia
Landscape Architecture Intern
Summer 2017

SKILLS

Microsoft Suite | Photoshop | AutoCAD
SketchUp | InDesign | Illustrator
Hand Rendering

Figures 2.24 and 2.25 Haley Meeks portfolio cover.
Source: Haley Meeks.

It's been many years since I shared my own student portfolio with anyone, but I feel compelled to show it now just to make a point. I was *very* architecturally oriented while in school and I was determined to create a technical look for my portfolio that would reflect that interest (Figure 2.26). I hand-drafted a retaining wall detail, then photographically enlarged it 300%. I ran the resulting negative through a blueline machine

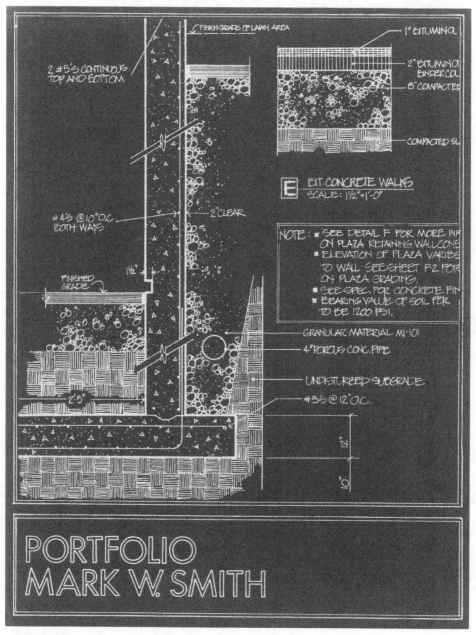

Figure 2.26 Mark W. Smith student portfolio cover.
Source: Mark W. Smith.

(remember, this was the 1970s) to create the look of an old blueprint. I titled it simply, *Portfolio, Mark W. Smith*, all hand-inked in Helvetica Outline with a Leroy lettering set (What is a Leroy lettering set? Google it!). Looking at it all these years later, it feels a little busy and old-fashioned. At the time, however, I utilized current technology to create a cover that would say something unique about me: I was a good draftsperson, I lettered well, and I was creative. *Share your personal influences in the design of your cover.*

In the years since I designed that first student portfolio, I have updated my portfolio numerous times to reflect my constantly shifting views on the profession and my growing body of experience. In the most recent iteration, I simplified the design and added a freehand concept plan to reflect my more "artful" side (Figure 2.27).

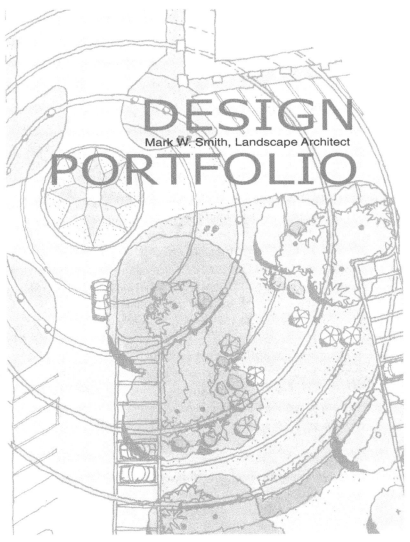

Figure 2.27 Mark W. Smith professional portfolio cover.
Source: Mark W. Smith.

I screened the image back to give only a hint of the artwork and create a background that wouldn't visually compete with the title. The title, *Design Portfolio, Mark W. Smith, Landscape Architect,* clearly identifies me and what I do. To help tie the various elements of my portfolio together, the title font incorporates the same accent color used on my résumé and project cutsheets. Just a glance tells a recruiter who I am, what I do, and gives them just a hint of what kind of designer I am.

Table of Contents

Almost every document we read—books, magazines, websites—contains a *Table of Contents* (TOC) or navigational menu of some kind. And for good reason. A TOC provides a framework that helps a writer get organized and it serves as a "road map" that gives readers a high-level understanding of a document's content. *Jeez, I'm not writing a book. Why do I need a table of contents for a design portfolio?* Because you, too, should be organized and working to lead recruiters through your portfolio and help them see the big picture. But it's not all functionality; a TOC can also endow your portfolio with several less tangible yet valuable benefits. Using a TOC makes a great first impression on a recruiter, as well as demonstrating your organizational abilities, attention to detail, and thoroughness. While these benefits are subtle, subtle touches are meaningful in the world of portfolio design. I can tell you, from my own perspective, that reviewing a well-organized portfolio is *much* more enjoyable and understandable than fumbling through a disorganized stack of project cutsheets.

Graphic designer **Dakota Baños** (Louisiana State University: Bachelor of Fine Arts in Graphic Design, 2020) focused on the use of bold graphic design and color to tell her story. As you'll see in Chapter 3, Dakota's portfolio cover design was intended to provide insight into her personality. To carry that into her portfolio, Dakota drew on her cover's color palette to create a vivid TOC that assigns a signature color to each project (Figure 2.28). As we navigate her portfolio, we find that each project includes a title page emblazoned with this coordinated index number and colored bar. This TOC introduces us to Dakota's bold graphic style and helps us to clearly understand her portfolio's organization.

Architectural designer and interior designer **Jessica King** (University of Texas at Austin: Master of Architecture, 2017; University of Tennessee/Knoxville: Bachelor of Science in Interior Design, 2015) developed a TOC that both communicates professionalism and effectively organizes her work (Figures 2.29 and 2.30). Jessica created a numerical sequence for her projects which she carries over to the title page of each project and then on to the project cutsheet itself. She repeats the entire index, but only the name of the current project is fully legible; all others are shaded back. This repetition on each page subtly keeps the reader oriented and visually ties the portfolio together. While we don't necessarily learn anything personal about Jessica's story from her TOC, we do understand that she is extremely organized and has an eye for detail.

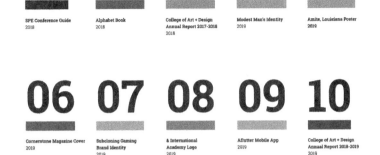

01
SPE Conference Guide
2018
02
Alphabet Book
2018
03
College of Art + Design
Annual Report 2017-2018
2018
04
Modest Man's Identity
2019
05
Amite, Louisiana Poster
2019
06
Cornerstone Magazine Cover
2019
07
Subcloning Gaming
Brand Identity
2019
08
& International
Academy Logo
2019
09
Aflutter Mobile App
2019
10
College of Art + Design
Annual Report 2018-2019
2019

Figure 2.28 Dakota Baños' TOC.
Source: Dakota Baños.

01 learning lounge
02 ridge house addition
03 four chaplains memorial
04 an oblique intermission
05 joe & norma jeane
06 to you from me
07 process composed
08 east austin production studio
09 bienville. we're home.
10 photography
graduate work/ university of texas at austin
ridge house addition.....p13
an oblique intermission.....p33
process composed.....p59
east austin production studio.....p72
undergraduate work/ university of tennessee, knoxville
learning lounge.....p3
four chaplains memorial.....p23
joe & norma jeane.....p41
competitions/ 2013-15
curtains.....p51
bienville. we're home.....p85

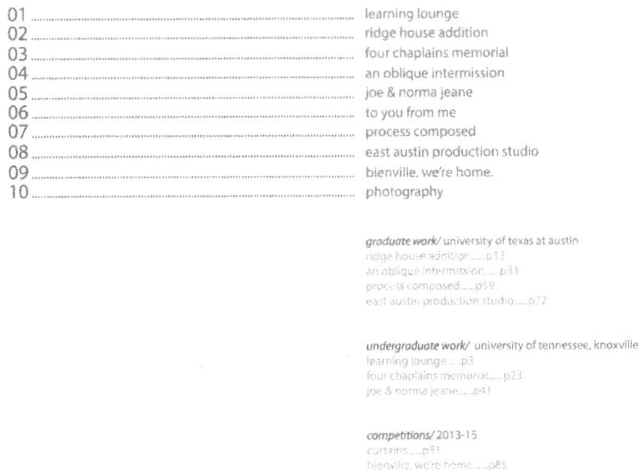

Figure 2.29 Jessica King TOC.
Source: Jessica King.

date/ spring 2013
instructor/ michael benedikt
institution/ university of texas at austin
course/ arc 394-395

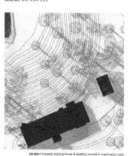

Figure 2.30 Jessica King link to TOC.
Source: Jessica King.

Like Jessica, architectural designer **Alex Yen-Jung Wu** (University of Texas at Austin: Bachelor of Architecture, 2017) chose to design his *Contents* page as an extension of his portfolio cover (Figure 2.31). For structure, he grouped his work into four categories (Architecture + Urban Design, Fabrication, Professional, Résumé) that provide a high-level overview of his portfolio content. He then provided the name of each project and identified the associated class, date, and professor. With this organized introduction, the viewer is oriented to Alex's work and can easily navigate the portfolio.

Landscape designer **Clara Restrepo** (University of Texas at Austin: Master of Landscape Architecture, 2019; University of Texas at Austin: Master of Architecture, 2017; Pontifica Bolivariana University: Bachelor of Architecture, 2010) created a visually simple *Contents* page that quickly orients the viewer to her portfolio's content and makes a smooth transition to the project cutsheets that follow (Figure 2.32). The simplicity of this design and reliance on white space reveal the clarity of her design style. The inclusion of her personal biography on this page also gives the recruiter a glimpse of her *Story* by expressing her personal inspirations and goals.

KARL MARX ALLEE 30 – INTERRELATIONAL COMMUNITIES
Advanced Design · Berlin · Spring 2019 · Barbara Hedri

AUSTIN HIGH SPEED RAIL
Design VI · Spring 2018 · Danelle Briscoe

VERTICAL MONASTERY
Advanced Design · Spring 2018 · Marlon Blackwell

SERIAL STOOLS
Prototype Seminar · Spring 2017 · Igor Siddiqu

OBJECTS 1, 2, 3
Design V · Fall 2014 · Kory Bieg

ROYAL COLLEGE OF ART
Tutor: Godwin · Redbo · NYC

ONLINE

Figure 2.31 Alex Yen-Jung Wu TOC.
Source: Alex Jen-Jung Wu.

CONTENTS

Around 30 years ago the city of Medellin, Colombia began to develop its public spaces and cultural infrastructure. Growing up there, I saw how urban design and public spaces can reduce social inequalities and violence, which has inspired my career.

In my studies and professional work, I have sought to approach the challenges of urban development from a practical and technical perspective, combining architecture, landscape design, and ecology. I love to work with form, the design of habitats, the representation of reality through art, and the sculpture of physical and digital models. My goal is always to create spaces that encourage interaction and support a healthy, beautiful life, whether in the public sphere or in private residences.

It would be a great joy to have an opportunity to join an office that fulfills my professional goals and values, as a designer who wants to help build communities by creating vibrant and sustainable places.

Figure 2.32 Clara Restrepo TOC.
Source: Clara Restrepo.

In summary, a *Table of Contents* is a valuable component of design portfolio infrastructure that plays both a functional *and* an aesthetic role. A TOC will help you organize your portfolio and create a structure that will make navigating your portfolio more enjoyable. At the same time, it communicates to a recruiter that you are an individual who cares about clarity and understands the value of making an organized presentation—all part of telling your story. *Use your Table of Contents to guide the recruiter and to make a statement about yourself and your organizational skills.*

Personal Biography

Another portfolio component that can help you tell your *Story* is a *Personal Biography*, often called an *About Me* page. This one has obvious value, yet few students take the time to create one. A personal biography should be concise, just long enough to help the recruiter understand who you are. It might describe your influences (*As a child, I lived in a small community where all the residents were artists*) or your motivations for being a designer (*my best friend's mom was an architect and inspired me to be like her*). Maybe it simply expresses how excited you get at the prospect of creating something. Try to capture the essence of that inspiration and put it into words.

Graphic designer **Rebekah Lynne Spence** (Louisiana State University: Bachelor of Fine Arts in Graphic Design, 2018) uses her online *"About"* page, simply titled, "Hey Ya'll," to tell us about some of the natural and cultural influences that shaped her as a child and to share that she knew she would be an artist by the time she was 5 years old. Just the informal title of this page gives us some insight into Rebekah roots, doesn't it? Her story and the accompanying photo, showing Rebekah enjoying nature, paint a wonderful picture of an inspired and vibrant artist, an image that is consistent with the work contained in her portfolio (Figure 2.33).

Figure 2.33 Rebekah Lynne Spence personal biography.
Source: Rebekah Lynne Spence.

Landscape Designer **Haley Meeks** (University of Georgia: Bachelor of Landscape Architecture, 2018) created an untitled personal bio for her portfolio that makes it clear that she is passionate about her profession and concerned about the environment. Visually, it subtly carries over the color theme and font from her portfolio cover. It tells us that she loves life, has a big heart and a big laugh, is a singer, loves pink, and has a puppy named Scarlett (Figure 2.34). When I read her bio, I immediately get the picture of someone who is passionate about what she does and would be enjoyable to work with!

Hey, y'all! My name is Haley Elizabeth Meeks,
and I am from the small town of Waynesboro, Georgia.
I am fervently passionate about landscape architecture and all it encompasses.
I believe that successful design is thoughtful, functional, and passionate.
I believe in the coexistence of the natural and built environments,
and thata cultural landscapes and their preservation play a vital role
in knowing who we are as a society.

When I am not practicing my rendering or researching cultural landscape sites,
I am either singing or playin with my puppy, Scarlett.
I love life, my favorite color is pink, and I have a big heart and an even bigger laugh.

Figure 2.34 Haley Meeks personal biography.
Source: Haley Meeks.

Interior Designer **Brandi Reed** (Louisiana State University: Bachelor of Interior Design, 2021) designed her *About Me* page to answer that universal question about candidates, "Who is she?" Her portrait photo gives us the feeling that Brandi is a cheerful person, the graphic design is bright and bold, and her narrative is professional and optimistic (Figure 2.35). Put it all together and it does an excellent job of helping a recruiter understand what kind of person Brandi is and what she might be like to work with. *Help the recruiter get to know who you are with a personal biography.*

ABOUT ME

Brandi Reed is a 3rd year Interior Design student at Louisiana State University. Her passion for design started young, with painting and drawing, and has flourished into a life-long love for Interiors and Architecture. At the age of 18, she started her own design business to keep her creative mind flowing. She generates original ideas for clients that are looking for effective, functional, and long-lasting designs. Brandi's goal as an interior designer is to create healthy livable spaces that provide a sense of comfort and function. She focuses on environmental design, and heavily values Biophilic Design principles. Upon graduation, she plans to obtain her Master's Degree in Architecture and further her understanding of innovative design solutions.

WHO IS SHE?

Figure 2.35 Brandi Reed about me.
Source: Brandi Reed.

Design Philosophy

In my perfect world, every student portfolio would contain a *Design Philosophy*. A design philosophy tells me that you're more than just a problem solver; it shouts, "I'm a designer!" Again, few students take the time to write one. I suppose that's understandable; writing a design philosophy challenges even the best of designers. But don't let that stop you from trying. As I've already pointed out, providing supplemental information that helps a recruiter better understand who you are sends the message that you are a candidate that goes the extra mile.

Where do I start? A great place to start is to look at what other designers have done. A Google search for "Design Philosophy" will reveal everything from simple one-liners to multi-page essays. While there is no *right* way to do this, I feel that the more succinct a design philosophy is, the better. If it's so esoteric that you lose your audience, it will be of little value. That said, look for examples that get to the point quickly. One of the first design philosophies I learned did just that; it was just three words long, penned by architect Louis Sullivan. Sullivan felt that the external form of a building should be determined by its intended purpose. In his essay, "The Tall Office Building

Artistically Considered."[5] he published his now-famous axiom, "Form follows function." It's clear, concise, and easy to understand. It was effective because it guided his design thinking and his clients understood that the form of his building designs would also reflect their function. *Write a design philosophy to provide the rationale for how you approach your work.*

As you set out to write your design philosophy, be honest. Let's say your design philosophy is, "Good design must have purpose." If everything you design is layered with ornamentation that serves little purpose, your work isn't really aligned with your philosophy. Alignment is important because your design philosophy is an intellectual mindset intended to guide you through the design process and help others understand how you work. Architect Ludwig Mies van der Rohe, a pioneer of modernist architecture, was guided by a philosophy of distilling a building's design into its simplest form. The simplicity of his design philosophy, "Less is more," makes it memorable and easily understood. Just a glance at van der Rohe's completed work reveals that his built work agrees with his design philosophy.

As I began my first full-time design job, I was deeply influenced by the work of another talented designer, Dieter Rams. Rams's design philosophy impressed me as being both intellectually sound *and* practical. During his tenure as consumer products designer for Braun AG, Rams wrote what he called, "10 Principles of Good Design."[6] Though I found all ten of Rams's principles to be most inspiring, one stood out as being particularly thoughtful: "Good design is honest." This aspect of Rams's philosophy required that his designs honestly represent their intended function. Virtually every product Rams designed while at Braun, ranging from electronics to kitchen appliances to furniture, stayed true to this philosophy. *A design philosophy must be aligned with your actual design output.*

Are you kidding? … those philosophies were written by legendary designers! I'm just a student. That's true, but a student is just as capable of developing a meaningful design philosophy as a professional. It may sound daunting but all you're really trying to do is describe how you approach design. It may be that you're concerned about the planet, and you design with a goal of improving sustainability? Perhaps you focus on designing to meet the client's needs? Maybe you are artistically inclined and want to make a bold and artistic statement? Don't make it harder than it is; the best design philosophies are the simplest. Here are a few student examples that are very straightforward and capture the spirit of the designer's work.

Kaitlin Craig (Texas Tech University: Bachelor of Landscape Architecture, 2017) wrote a simple and optimistic design philosophy, telling us that her approach to design goes deeper than just solving design problems; she strives to create places for people that are memorable, purposeful, and will have positive impact on all who use them.

---

[5] Backman, Maurie. "The Meaning of 'Form Follows Function.'" *Thought.com*. 14 November 2018. Web. 24 November 2018.

[6] "The Power of Good Design: Dieter Rams' Ideology, Ingrained within Vitsoe." *Vitsoe.com*. 2018. Web. 24 November 2018.

Kaitlin's philosophy is to-the-point and easily understood. Her philosophy, located on the first page of her portfolio, ensures that recruiters will understand her approach before they see any of her work. To give it an individualized touch, Kaitlin inserted a nicely composed photo of herself and closed it with her artful signature (Figure 2.36).

Landscape Architecture is creating places that are memorable. Believing in the product we provide will withstand a lifetime, not only because it is structurally sound, but also because the landscape has a meaningful purpose. Designing places that positively impact the people and the environment surrounding them. Places where we can live our day-to-day life and look forward to a new day. With this mentality comes the promise of innovation that will lead to a livelier future.

- Kaitlin Craig

Figure 2.36 Kaitlin Craig design philosophy.
Source: Kaitlin Craig.

Some design philosophies are meant to be motivational. **Emily Bell** (Clemson University: Bachelor of Landscape Architecture, 2019) introduced her portfolio with, "That's just the way it is" (Figure 2.37). Rather than being an expression of resignation, Emily sees this familiar saying as a personal challenge; a motivational starting point in her design process that says, "No…it doesn't have to be that way!" Emily feels that, as designers, we have a responsibility to do better, to improve on the status quo. I like that she also used this page as opportunity to continue the display of her photographic and graphic design skills—something she integrates nicely throughout her portfolio—and to repeat the unique signature "yellow highlighter" from her cover for special emphasis.

Some design philosophies are more procedural in nature; they tell us how the designer approaches design. In her philosophy, **Brittany Geist** (Louisiana State University: Bachelor of Landscape Architecture, 2009) wrote, "I listen, observe, study, draw, present, and repeat until the story comes to life" (Figure 2.38). I like this design

Figure 2.37 Emily Bell design philosophy.
Source: Emily Bell.

Figure 2.38 Brittany Geist design philosophy.
Source: Brittany Geist.

philosophy because of the active voice it is written in; we can easily visualize *how* Brittany thinks as she works to bring life to a design. I can just see Brittany sitting at her drafting table late at night, tracing paper all over the floor, working through concept after concept until she arrives at that perfect design solution. By adding a nicely composed photo of herself and complete contact information, Brittany provides a highly personalized introduction to her portfolio. We now know who she is.

Roger Montelongo (Texas State University/San Marcos: BS Geography: Urban and Regional Planning, 2016; University College London: MSc Urban Design and City Planning, 2008) opens his portfolio with a design philosophy that introduces us to the planners who have influenced and helped him recognize the importance of planning for people in the public realm. Roger's *Design Manifesto* states, "It is our duty to harmonize People + The Built Form and make places suitable for all." His core design philosophy, "Urban Design is Placemaking," is visually supported by a simple Venn diagram illustrating Urban Design occurring at the intersection of People and Built Form (Figures 2.39 and 2.40). Taking it one step further, Roger created a series of renderings that boil this concept down to its simplest terms: People + Space + Form = Urban Design. Collectively, his Manifesto and the accompanying renderings give us a clear picture of how Roger approaches his work.

Like Roger and many other designers, I too have been influenced and inspired by the work of many others—some famous, some not-so-famous— throughout my career. Over the years, I've attempted to put my own philosophy into words many times and, like many of you, found it to be quite a challenge. Just as I come up with something that I feel captures my philosophy, a change in my worldview causes me to second-guess it and I end up tweaking it more. It's never finished! As frustrating as that may be, I've come to accept this evolution as part of a designer's learning curve; we're *always* learning.

Though design trends come and go, and my own design process continues to evolve, my personal design philosophy has remained, from the beginning, constant in three core areas:

1. **Good Design is Contextual**: It must recognize its relationship to its surroundings and work to harmonize with them.

2. **Good Design is Meaningful**: Its built form must express its intended meaning openly and is meaningful to its users.

3. **Good Design is Purposeful**: Its purpose and function are visible to users, and they easily understand how to engage with and use the end product.

If we take these three statements and combine them into a single statement, my design philosophy could be stated as: *Good design integrates context, meaningful form, and a sense of clear purpose.*

There are no revelations here; it's a straightforward statement that helps me stay true to my core values and, when necessary, express them to others so they understand where I'm coming from as a designer. While it is possible to have a successful design career without ever developing a design philosophy, I believe it's worth the

As an Urban Designer, my design principles and philosophy have been highly influenced by American Urban Activist **Jane Jacobs** and Copenhagen Architect **Jan Gehl**, who both highlight the importance of people in the public realm.

It is the combination of **Human Science + Architecture/Design** that formulates Urban Design. It is the act of critically analyzing how people use spaces and enhance them for maximum use.

It is our duty to harmonize **People + The Built Form** and make places that are suitable for all. We need to activate outdoor spaces that are suitable for the youth to the elder.

The three main components in urban design are the **People, Space, + Urban Form**. As Urban designers, we must work together with city planners, architects, engineers, council members, and the public to formulate unique spaces that will enhance people's lives and solve place specific urban issues.

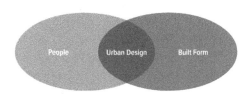

Urban Design is **Placemaking**
It is human instinct to gravitate towards other people. While there are necessary trips one must take (school or work), Optional and social activities need to have favourable conditions to engage more people to use space. The act of placemaking is the most critical element in Urban Design.

Urban Design is **People**
Cities should be planned for people and move away from the car centric ideology most American, Australian, European Suburbs and developing countries carry. In a world of rapid urbanization, it is critical to reclaim the streets for human activities.

Urban Design is **Space**
Spaces between buildings should be the primary focus of any design intervention. It should act as the placemaking element that brings together people + form. Enhancing outdoor environments will increase human activities and the benefits it carries.

Urban Design is **Form**
Buildings should be seen as a secondary component in any design intervention. The problem with architects is that they focus on the building itself without social implications. A building working harmoniously with space will better enhance the human experience.

Figures 2.39 and 2.40 Roger Montelongo design philosophy.
Source: Roger Montelongo.

effort to sit down and get your thoughts on paper. Regardless of how well developed a student's design philosophy may or may not be, I am ALWAYS impressed by a student who willingly takes on this challenge. Give it a shot!

Project Experience Map

A *Project Experience Map* is another component that can enhance your standing as a candidate. If you are well-traveled or have had internships or jobs that gave you project experience in multiple places, you might consider placing a map that shows off your "worldliness" in your portfolio. Briefly, a project experience map reveals your global awareness and desire to fully explore the built environment—both attributes that many recruiters find valuable.

Originally from New York City, **Luca Smith Senise** (University of Texas: Bachelor of Architecture, 2016) is a particularly well-traveled designer. To help recruiters visualize this part of his personal and professional story, Luca created a *Global Context* map that identifies where he has lived, where he attended school, and the locations of projects he's worked on throughout the world (Figure 2.41). One look at this map and it's obvious that Luca is a worldly designer. Each point on the map is accompanied by a description that provides details about Luca's experience and relationship to each. The project cutsheets that follow in his portfolio provide confirmation, through photos and descriptions, of Luca's truly international perspective.

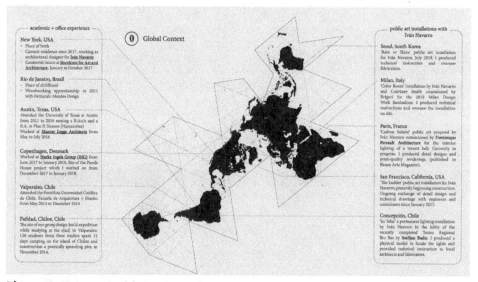

Figure 2.41 Luca Smith Senise project experience map.
Source: Luca Smith Senise.

Eric Garrison (Texas Tech University: Bachelor of Landscape Architecture, 2002) is also a well-traveled designer. To ensure that recruiters see that quickly, Eric created a *Project Distribution* map that shows us where he has project experience

(Figures 2.42 and 2.43). Eric added a *Project List* on the following page to provide the name and location of every project he's been involved with and to make a smooth transition to his project cutsheets. Like Luca, we can see that Eric is well-traveled and has experience in a variety of interesting places. On a purely graphic note, it's worth pointing out here that the color Eric used for this map is the same color he uses for accent and continuity throughout his portfolio.

Figure 2.42 Eric Garrison project distribution map 1.
Source: Eric Garrison.

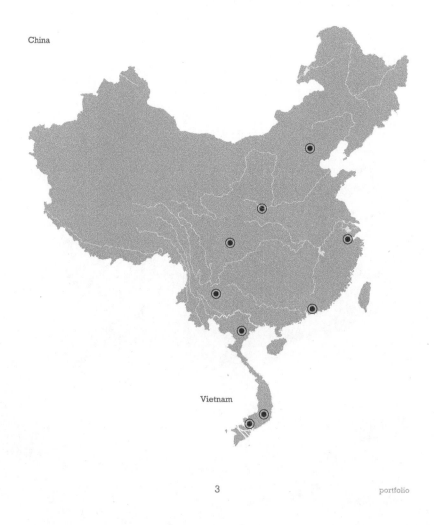

China

Vietnam

3   portfolio

Figure 2.43 Eric Garrison project distribution map 2.
Source: Eric Garrison.

Though it's unlikely you'll be doing much globetrotting as an entry-level designer, most recruiters know that well-traveled designers have a broader design perspective than their less-traveled peers. They also know that, once you have some project experience under your belt, your willingness and desire to travel will make you a great candidate for some of those far-flung design projects that every office seems to land occasionally. Good designers, by nature, tend to explore, study, and enjoy working on projects in a variety of different locales. If you have travel and work experience that makes you a more worldly candidate, make it known. *Create a Project Experience map to show your global awareness.*

Project Cutsheets

Now that I've reviewed your résumé, table of contents, design philosophy, and project experience map, I should be so pumped by what I've seen that I just *must* learn more about you. I start thumbing through your project cutsheets, looking for signs of the skill set and the future potential that we have been looking for in our next hire. This is where I hope to find evidence of the knowledge, skill set, and project experience that you've been accumulating while in school.

What should I place in my project cutsheets? Project information, right? Yes, but to a limited degree. Most project cutsheets contain way too much project data and not enough information about the designer and their skill set. A typical project description might say something like:

> Situated on a beautiful 27-acre coastal site in Florida, this luxury resort was designed to appeal to vacationers from the Midwest. Developed around a midwestern "Farmhouse" concept, the design incorporates sophisticated farm style and is organized around a network of indoor and outdoor family gathering spaces.

While that may summarize the project well, it says nothing about *you. What did you do on this project? Were you the team leader? Did you produce all the graphics? Did it win any awards?* While that project may very well be on a beautiful coastal site, recruiters are going to be more interested in what you contributed to the project than in the project's details. The project description could easily be re-worded to provide more information about your contributions, as follows:

> Situated on a beautiful 14-acre coastal site in Florida, this luxury resort was designed for vacationers from the Midwest. I collaborated with two students from our architecture and engineering programs to develop a site plan that incorporated a sophisticated "Farmhouse" style, was respectful of its coastal location, and solved the site's severe erosion problems. Our solution revealed the importance of effective collaboration. My role included the preparation of a site analysis, development of the conceptual site plan, and final Lumion renderings.

Provide a brief description of the project, then focus on the skills that made the project a success and what you learned. Some students talk about collaboration to show they can work with others. Some describe how they developed the project's concept to emphasize their conceptualization skills. Still others describe the skills they used on the project to show the diversity of their skill set. *Create project cutsheet content that highlights unique details of your story.*

Elliot Williams (Texas A&M University: Bachelor of Landscape Architecture, 2016) created the cutsheets for his *Kenya Designs* (a proposed school) project using several of these techniques to tell his story. He opens with two images of the school nestled into the landscape (Figures 2.44–2.47). The very concise description tells us that it was an individual and a team project, that he created the model, and that he produced the work using Maya and Photoshop software. As we turn the page, we see additional images that help us understand how the structure might look from different angles and at night. Elliot's cutsheet makes it clear that he is collaborative, talented at 3D visualization, and is a wonderful illustrator. If that weren't enough, Elliot provides an additional "Maya Modeling" cutsheet to show the full range of his Maya software capabilities. As we flip to his next project, *Energy Corridor*, he lists a separate set of skills—team leadership, building design and bridge aesthetics, and Rhino capabilities—used on the project. While each of Elliot's cutsheets tells a different story, collectively, they tell a story of a talented and capable designer who is eager to learn new tools and skills—the kind of candidate every recruiter looks for.

For her "Natalia Tenedor, Hypopressives Trainer" project, **Marta Vizcarro** (Universitat de Vic-Universitat Central de Catalunya: Visual Communications-Graphic Design A.A.S., Graphic Design; 2017; Bachelor of Science, 1999) developed a series of freehand sketches (Figure 2.48) that show how she approached the design challenge, then refined the design and applied it to her final "Hypopressives Benefits" poster (Figure 2.49). Marta shows us how she works through a design problem and reveals important graphic design skills in just two cutsheets.

As we can see in these examples, there are many ways you can use project cutsheets to communicate your character, your skill set, and your design intelligence to a recruiter. Stop and think about what your cutsheets are saying about *you*, rather than using up all that space focusing on the *project*. Don't ramble on about project details, focus on what you can do! Here are a few descriptive statements I've seen in project cutsheets lately that I feel achieved this goal well:

- I developed a system that improved my project team's efficiency and streamlined our production time dramatically. We completed our project ahead of schedule.

- I used a new presentation technique that helped my professor and classmates better understand my concept. I received the Student Chapter Honorable Mention award for the project.

- My design concept creates a safe outdoor space that makes the user experience more pleasurable and reduces the need for more conspicuous security measures.

- The project team selected me to be Project Manager because of my strong organizational skills.

- I combined my freehand capabilities with new experimental software to develop a more natural rendering technique.

KENYA DESIGNS

team project & individual

Worked with team to design
School & make model. Image
created by Elliot.

Modeled & rendered tower design
in Maya. Placed within landscape
with Adobe Photoshop.

School entrance

5

Figures 2.44 Elliot Williams skills described in cutsheet.
Source: Elliot Williams.

Towers amidst open landscape

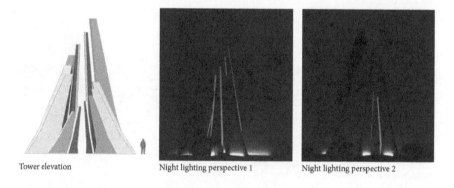

Tower elevation   Night lighting perspective 1   Night lighting perspective 2

6

Figure 2.45 Elliot Williams skills illustrated in cutsheet.
Source: Elliot Williams.

Stone perspective 1

Intersection of e & w

Structure lighting

MAYA MODELING

various personal projects

Elliot enjoys learning modeling
and rendering programs. He is
fascinated with how light plays on
objects and how people perceive
reality.

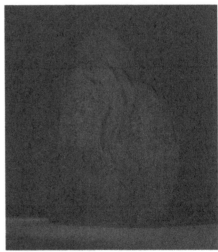

Stone perspective 2

13

Figure 2.46 Elliot Williams additional skills illustrated.
Source: Elliot Williams.

1.Apartments & retail   2.Pedestrian bridge   3.I-10   4.Plaza   5.Transit center   6.Detention pond   7.Convention center

ENERGY CORRIDOR

design leader of 4 member team

Addicks Park & Ride is located in Houston's Energy Corridor. The objective was to create an iconic center for business & innovation. Addicks is currently a large surface parking lot. We preposed converting the surface parking into a parking structure connected to a conference center. A pedestrian bridge connects business & homes divided by I-10.

- Guided team members in general design decisions.
- Developed conference building & bridge aesthetics.
- Modeled bridge, conference center, & surrounding buildings in Rhino.
- Produced all graphics shown.

Curvilinear building concept

Sharp building concept

7

Figure 2.47 Elliot Williams skills learned described.
Source: Elliot Williams.

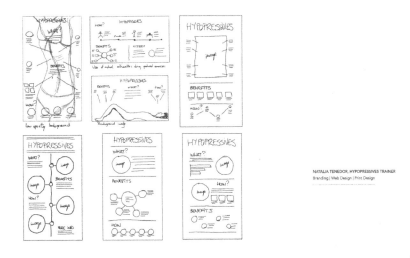

Figures 2.48 and 2.49 Marta Vizcarro process sketches.
Source: Marta Vizcarro and Natalia Tenedor.

- On this project I learned ...
- The biggest challenge on this project was ... and this is how I solved for the problem.

Describe the unique skills, tools, methods used to make the project a success; don't focus on project data.

In addition to well-written descriptive text, a good cutsheet must incorporate your best imagery. Using substandard graphics suggests that you aren't concerned with the details. We recently received a submittal from a candidate who appeared to be well-qualified for the position we were advertising. He had great credentials, good grades, and an excellent internship the year before. Unfortunately, his portfolio was full of poor-quality graphics. Most of the images were low resolution and poorly cropped. The text was barely legible. The result: though I could easily see he was capable of good design, the visual quality of his portfolio was terrible. As I reviewed the range of potential candidates with my partners, their response to this candidate's portfolio was uniform: "He's got great credentials, but his graphics are dreadful. It doesn't look like he cares about the quality of his work." For obvious reasons, he never made it to our interview shortlist. Carefully select every graphic you use in your portfolio. If it's weak, make it better or use another image. *Incorporate only your very best imagery.*

You should also use your cutsheets to illustrate *how* you work. Design is much more than just the finished product; it's an iterative process. As I review your work, I want to know that you understand the design process and how to use it to solve design problems. That's what I'm hiring you to do, right? Showing only finished graphics won't help me understand how you work. Include some of those design process doodles and concept sketches you prepared as you worked through the design; show how you think. Redraw them if you must but remember—it's OK if they're a little messy.

To demonstrate his design conceptualization process, **Zheng Lu** (Texas A&M University: Master of Landscape Architecture, 2011) included the series of concept studies he prepared for his *Madisonville Downtown Plaza* project (Figure 2.50). He opens with a description of the project, a freehand sketch, and a nicely rendered aerial perspective. In the pages that follow, he progresses from an early concept plan drawn over the base plan and sketches drawn over photographs to a series of more refined plans and elevations (Figures 2.51–2.53). He closes with a perspective view of the plaza that gives us a good feeling for what the built plaza might look like (Figure 2.54). In just five pages, this series of sketches and renderings provides great insight into the design process Zheng utilizes as he works.

Sometimes, you don't need to take your ideas all the way to photorealistic 3D visualization; you just need to be comfortable exploring. Here, **Brandi Reed** (Louisiana State University: Bachelor of Interior Design, 2021) has created a cutsheet called *Exploration of Natural Materials* that is intended to show her exploration of the relationships between various building materials. It's rough and to-the-point (Figure 2.55). What makes it interesting to me is the way she blended freehand sketching, photography, and Photoshop to create a quick study; it shows her ability to work quickly at a conceptual level. *Show your mastery of the design process.*

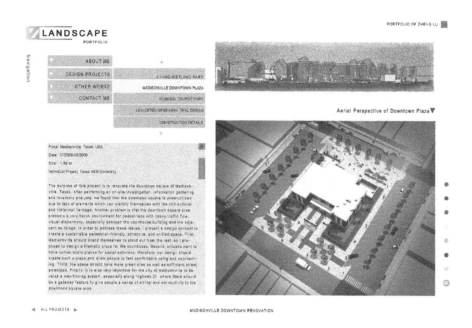

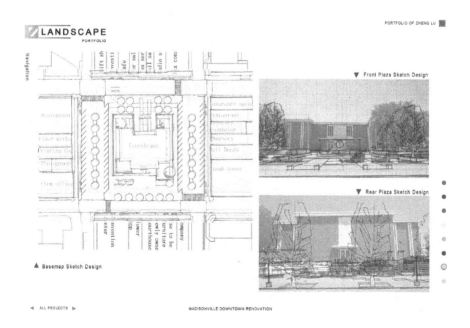

Figures 2.50–2.51 Zheng Lu design process.

Source: Zheng Lu.

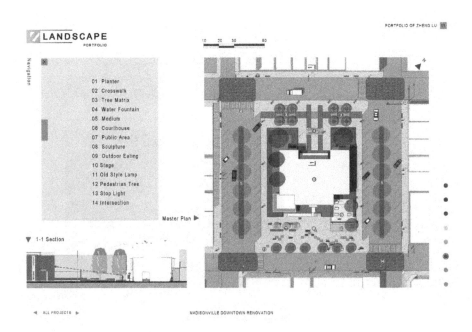

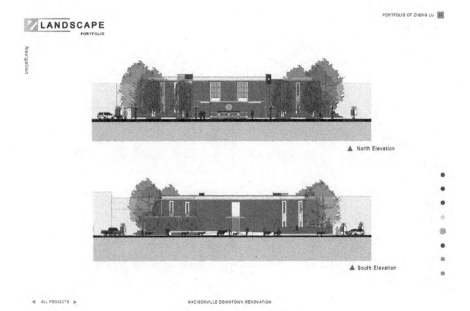

Figures 2.52–2.53 Zheng Lu design process.
Source: Zheng Lu.

LANDSCAPE
PORTFOLIO

Navigation

Front Plaza Perspective ▲

◄ ALL PROJECTS ►   MADISONVILLE DOWNTOWN RENOVATION

Figures 2.54 Zheng Lu design process.
Source: Zheng Lu

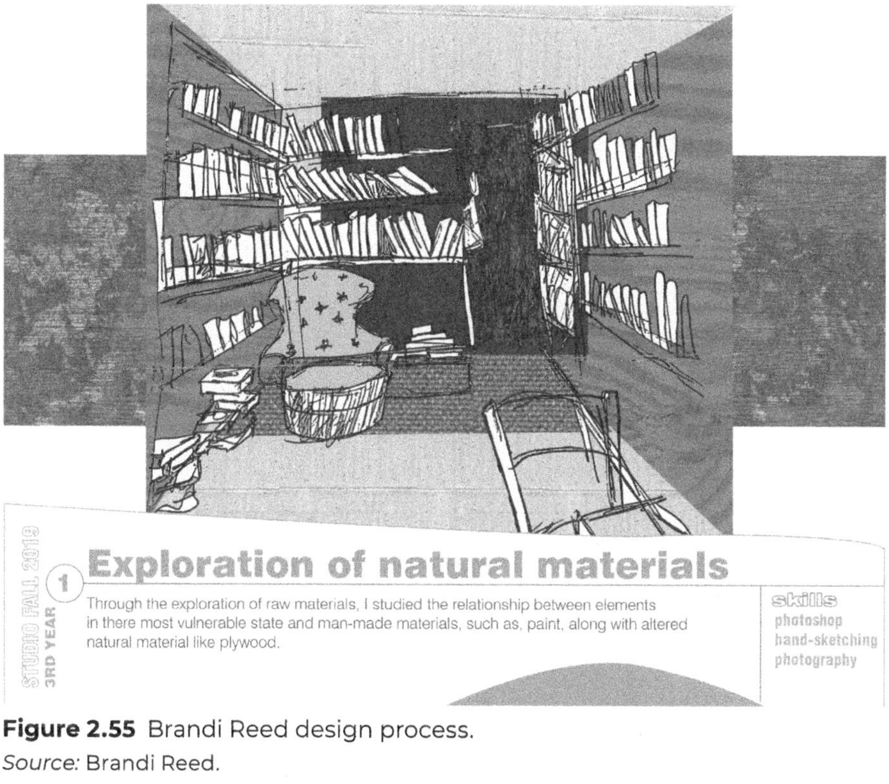

STUDIO FALL, 2018
3RD YEAR
(1)

Exploration of natural materials

Through the exploration of raw materials, I studied the relationship between elements in there most vulnerable state and man-made materials, such as, paint, along with altered natural material like plywood.

skills
photoshop
hand-sketching
photography

Figure 2.55 Brandi Reed design process.
Source: Brandi Reed.

Your cutsheets are also a place to show the full range of media you are comfortable working with. Though I'm sure you've already listed your relevant skills on your résumé, providing visual evidence is much more convincing than one of those "Digital Skills" infographics everyone is using these days. It's not unusual to see student portfolios in which every cutsheet contains only a CAD plan. How many CAD plans do I need to see to understand that you are CAD-proficient? A much more effective approach is to distribute evidence of your skill set throughout your portfolio. Each cutsheet should display a distinct set of skills. One project might highlight your Lumion capabilities, the next might present your AutoCAD skills, and another could show off your freehand drawing skills. In addition to highlighting your skills, this approach adds visual diversity and makes your portfolio much more interesting to review.

Jessica King (University of Texas at Austin: Master of Architecture, 2017; University of Tennessee/Knoxville: Bachelor of Science in Interior Design, 2015) used a variety of freehand sketches to exhibit her conceptualization process, then works through a series of refined digital plans, sections, axons, and photorealistic renderings to illustrate her *Hybrid Program* project (Figures 2.56–2.60). Collectively, these images help us to see that Jessica is creative, has a full understanding of the design process, and utilizes a full range of conceptualization tools to develop her ideas fully.

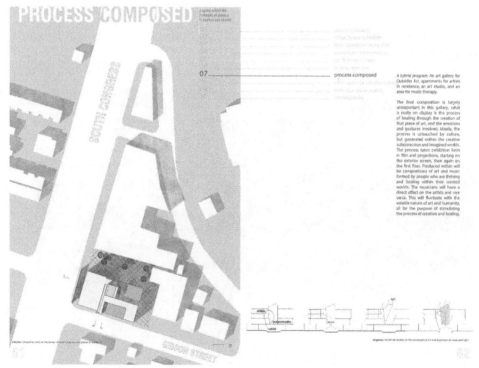

Figures 2.56–2.60 Jessica King design conceptualization process.
Source: Jessica King.

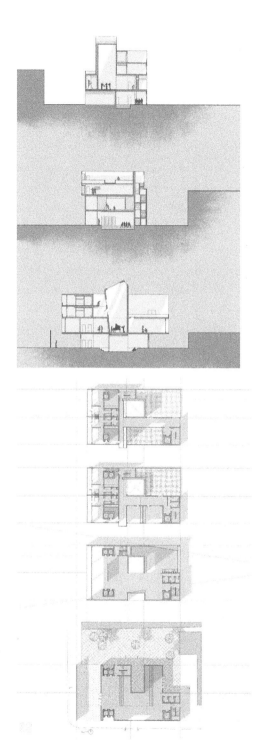

The integration of art and music is most saturated in the studio space. The volume containing the music therapy practice space is shaped in an ideal form and in concrete material for maximizing sound. While the ensuing music and its effect is most recognizable in the studio space, it has reaches in several areas of the building, including the film area on the floor below and the pin-up atrium space on the floors above. The arrangement of the program in section is meant to allow for the transition of art in its different stages (production, critique, and display), as well as the flow of sound and light in varying volumes throughout the building. This creates visual and auditory connections between the public and the private, providing glimpses of the artist's personalities without formal interactions.

Figures 2.56–2.60 (*Continued*).

Source: Jessica King.

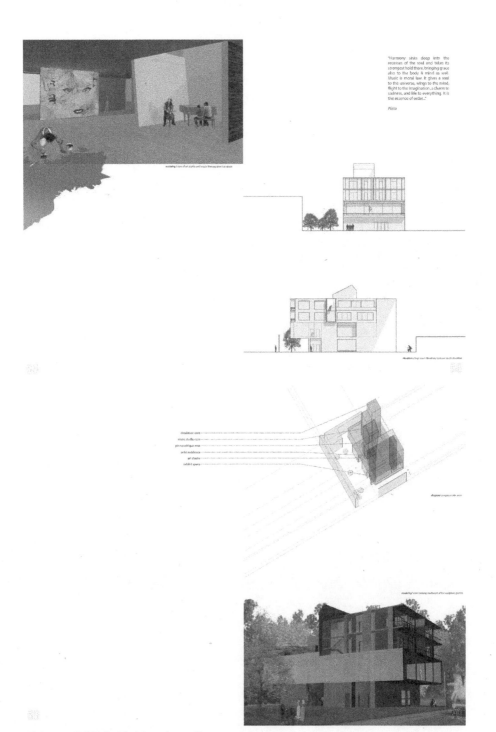

Figures 2.56–2.60 (*Continued*).
Source: Jessica King.

Another way to show your diversity of skills is to create cutsheets that display nothing but your personal skill set. Landscape architecture student **Zheng Lu** (Texas A&M University: Master of Landscape Architecture, 2011), also an accomplished artist, devoted a full section of his portfolio to *Other Works* in which he placed cutsheets that display his broad range of drawing, painting, graphic design, and photography talents (Figures 2.61–2.65). Any recruiter reviewing Zheng's work would be tempted to imagine how they might employ some of these skills to enhance their firm's design and production capabilities.

Over the course of my own career, I've done a considerable amount of creative work on the side. I've been commissioned to design greeting cards (seen here in "Greeting Cards") (Figure 2.66), business cards, pen & ink architectural renderings (shown here in "Freehand Drawing") (Figure 2.67), sold photography, and written newsletter articles, blogs, and reports. To show off this versatility, I created a cutsheet for each skill set. Even though I've only interviewed for Landscape Architect positions throughout my career, these cutsheets have created wonderful talking points during virtually every interview.

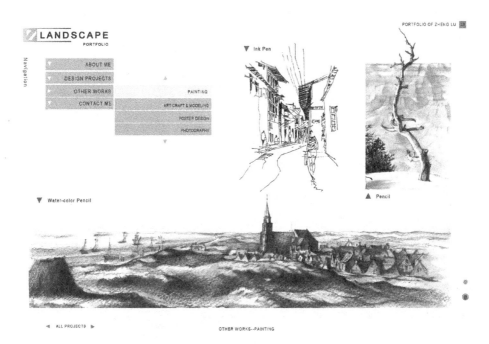

Figures 2.61–2.65 Zheng Lu other works.
Source: Zheng Lu.

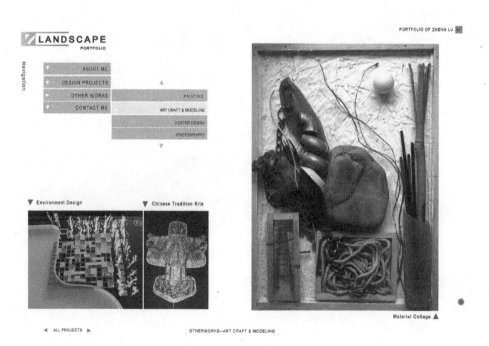

Figures 2.61–2.65 *(Continued)*.
Source: Zheng Lu.

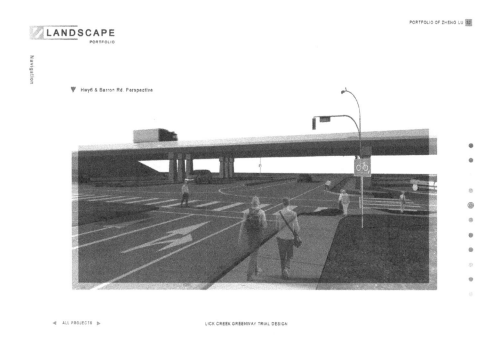

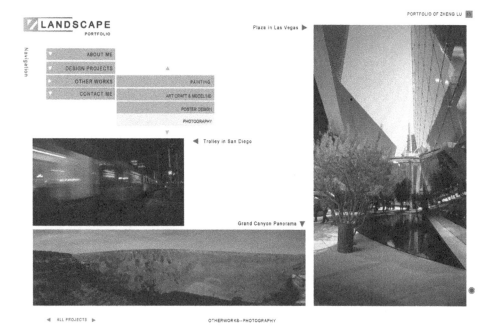

Figures 2.61–2.65 (*Continued*).
Source: Zheng Lu.

Greeting Cards

Mark Smith has been creating personalized greeting cards for every occasion since 1975. These cards are individually designed, hand-drawn in pen & ink, and rendered as an original artwork. Many are pen & ink originals, others have been reproduced by scanning, silkscreen, and copier.

Figures 2.66 and 2.67 Mark W. Smith other works.

Source: Mark W. Smith.

Freehand Drawing

Pen and Ink and freehand sketching has been a personal passion of mine since childhood and is now a sideline business. Many of my works have been silkscreened, lithographed as limited edition prints, or sold as originals. Typically architectural in nature, my work strives to document historic architectural detail as accurately as possible. My preferred media is rapidograph and india ink, with an occasional Prismacolor or watercolor wash.

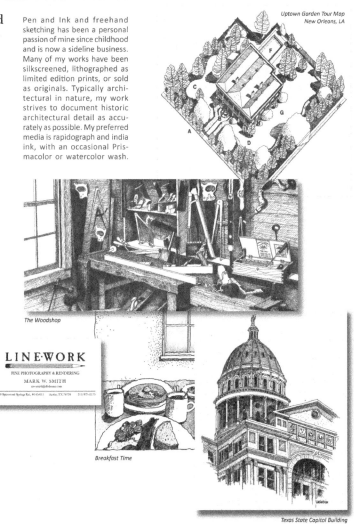

Uptown Garden Tour Map New Orleans, LA

The Woodshop

Breakfast Time

Texas State Capitol Building

Figures 2.66 and 2.67 (*Continued*).

Source: Mark W. Smith.

Most design students also have a variety of competition entries, capstone reports, and theses that may be difficult to share during an interview due to their bulk and complexity. A more effective way to handle these kinds of material is to insert imagery and brief descriptions from each on a separate cutsheet. **Eric Garrison** (Texas Tech University: Bachelor of Landscape Architecture, 2002) created a separate "Collateral" section for his portfolio in which he inserts photos of reports and other written documents he's prepared (Figure 2.68). This eliminates the need to haul a big stack of

Collateral

Los Altos site analysis booklet

ericgarrison 78

Figure 2.68 Eric Garrison collateral.
Source: Eric Garrison.

reports to the interview and gives the recruiter a sense of the range of his technical writing and production capabilities. *Use your project cutsheets to illustrate the variety of media you are comfortable working with.*

There's one last point I'd like to make; your portfolio is a design project, too. Just like every other design project you've worked on, your portfolio must be well-organized if it is to tell your story effectively. All too often, I see student portfolios that lack visual cohesiveness. This is usually because every project was done at a different time and in different formats. Often, the presentation boards have simply been reduced and dropped into the portfolio to avoid the hassle of reformatting them. While each project may be well-designed and attractive, the lack of continuity between pages creates an inconsistent viewing experience. Please don't take short cuts here—reformat *every* project you include in your portfolio and create a consistent thematic organization that ties your work together all the way through. This extra effort will show recruiters that you understand the importance of making a professional presentation. *Design your portfolio around a theme that creates visual continuity front to back.*

The Portfolio: Sidebar Checklist

- ☐ Develop optional portfolio content to tell a richer story.
- ☐ Design a portfolio cover that identifies who you are and makes an immediate statement.
- ☐ Design your portfolio cover that puts your creative strengths on display.
- ☐ Use white space for emphasis.
- ☐ Make a personal and professional statement.
- ☐ Link your cover design to your content to draw the viewer in.
- ☐ Share your personal influences in the design of your cover.
- ☐ Use your Table of Contents to guide the recruiter and to make a statement about yourself and your organizational skills.
- ☐ Help the recruiter get to know who you are with a personal biography.
- ☐ Write a design philosophy to provide the rationale for how you approach your work.
- ☐ A design philosophy must be aligned with your actual design output.
- ☐ Create a Project Experience map to show your global awareness.
- ☐ Create project cutsheet content that highlights unique details of your story.
- ☐ Describe the unique skills, tools, and methods used to make the project a success; don't focus on project data.
- ☐ Incorporate only your very best imagery.
- ☐ Show your mastery of the design process.
- ☐ Use your project cutsheets to illustrate the variety of media you are comfortable working with.
- ☐ Design your portfolio around a theme that creates visual continuity from front to back.

Let's wrap it up where we started this conversation; *So...tell me a little bit about yourself.* The key to effectively telling your story in a portfolio lies in answering this basic interview question. And that is what your portfolio must do if it is to secure an interview for you. In your absence, it must speak boldly on your behalf to convince a recruiter that, beyond just being qualified, you are a candidate they absolutely must get to know better.

As you prepare to tell your *Story*, remember just one thing...*recruiters don't recruit portfolios, they recruit people.* Sure, the recruiting process we use is designed to help us efficiently evaluate candidates and separate those who are qualified for the position from those who aren't. But, in the design industry, we aren't hiring *robots.* After all the qualifications and credentials have been reviewed, we still need to know who you are and determine if you'd be a good fit for our firm. And so, when it comes down to shortlisting otherwise equally qualified candidates for interviews, those with unique stories, as told through their portfolios, rise above all the project data and groovy graphics, and help us connect with them as *people.* They are the ones that will be called for an interview.

As you prepare for graduation, just know that you are entering a creative, yet fiercely competitive, industry. Being qualified simply gets you in the queue. Being creative with your story and understanding how to share it confidently and effectively with others will get you to the head of the line.

Chapter 3
Define Your Style

So … how would you describe your style?

Honestly, what are the odds of anyone ever asking you this question in an inter-view? The odds are low, at best. In fact, during my lengthy career, no recruiter has ever asked me that question. *Well, then why did you bring it up?* Because, even without the prospect of ever having to answer this question in an interview, you should have some understanding of what makes your creative work uniquely yours.

This "understanding" is more important than you might think. Knowing what is distinctive about how you express yourself creatively is central to your identity as a designer. And it's an equally important part of creating your design portfolio. Without style, a designer is little more than a problem-solver. Without style, your portfolio will look like one produced by all those "problem-solvers" who simply clamped a bunch of projects together and called the result a portfolio. In a crowded marketplace, your portfolio needs to be more than that—it must stand out. It must have *style*. Your style, as expressed through your portfolio, speaks volumes about you and your suitability for every creative position you apply for—all without you having the chance to utter a single word.

So, what is *style*? I consider it to be the way in which you integrate the building blocks of design—color, white space, contrast, rhythm, balance, and others—into your work and create a visual pattern that is uniquely yours. Think of it as your "creative fingerprint." For a select few, that fingerprint just seems to come naturally. There's probably a designer in your program right now (there was in mine) who is so creative and talented that they leave you and your classmates scratching your heads after every presentation. *How on earth do they turn out such incredible work so effort-lessly?* For the rest of us (and I mean *most* of us), our individual style evolves as we gain experience and our design skills mature and merge with the influences of our teachers and mentors.

I began my career in New Orleans working with a very influential mentor, L. Azeo ("Ace") Torre. Ace is a landscape architect well known for his rapid conceptualization skills and signature freehand drawing style. To this day, I've never met another designer so confident and fast with their hands. When I started working with him, though I felt I had good drawing skills, I was intimidated by his speed and effortless drawing ability. For years, I mimicked his style and worked hard to learn from him. As you might expect, over time, my style began to resemble his. Gradually, I developed greater confidence in my own abilities. Though I might have told you at the time I didn't think I had a distinctive style, I was nonetheless developing one. Initially, my rendering and design style looked much like Ace's, but as I added my own touches here and there, my work began to assume a character of its own. Today, though my style continues to evolve, Ace's early influence on my style is still quite visible in my work. Few of us are just born with style; we must learn it.

You don't have to look far to see this same assimilation of style occurring among much more celebrated designers than myself. Frank Lloyd Wright, for example, began his career as just another Victorian draftsman. He went on to work as an apprentice under architect Louis Sullivan, a mentor who deeply influenced his style and approach to design. It was while working with Sullivan that Wright began his quest to create a uniquely "American" style of architecture. Despite his obvious talents, it took Wright over a decade to develop the essence of his "Prairie School" style. When he finally got there, however, the result was something you wouldn't confuse with any other designer. Developing one's signature style can also take time.

What if I don't have a signature style yet? Don't let that trouble you too much. I'll go out on a limb here and say, without even seeing your work, that I am confident you do have a style of your own. I say that because I see elements of distinctive style in every student portfolio I review. If you somehow can't see it yourself, it may be because it's still in its initial stages of development. It could also be that you've been so focused on studying and assimilating the work of famous designers that you haven't focused inwardly enough to recognize it. The evolution of my own style was concealed a bit as I emulated the work of the famous designers that we studied in school. I was, like many students, trying to discover my own creative aesthetic through the work of others. For a time, I was heavily influenced by Lawrence Halprin (1916–2009), the San Francisco landscape architect whose work focused on recognizing human scale and designing for a dynamic user experience. The very next semester, while on a student field trip to Taliesin West in Arizona, I was captivated by the work of Frank Lloyd Wright and began incorporating the bold horizontal lines of his work into my own. A year later, after studying the design of Central Park (Figure 3.1) in New York City, I was adjusting my style again as I imitated the work of Frederick Law Olmsted.

Figure 3.1 Central Park.
Source: Adobe Stock/Andrew Kazmierski.

Over time, the fusion of these many influences and my work experience evolved into something I finally began to consider my own. Having the realization that my work was unique gave me a new confidence in my abilities; it was quite empowering. While your style may not yet be as distinctive as that of the legendary designers you are inspired by, it is there—you just have to look for it. Your style may manifest itself in diverse ways—some obvious, some not. Maybe it's that graceful curvilinear form you work into your designs (e.g., architect Santiago Calatrava derives inspiration for his work from living organisms)? Perhaps you integrate a signature color into every project (e.g., Frank Lloyd Wright used the color "Cherokee Red" in his work)? Or could it be the bold simplicity of your design (e.g., graphic designer Paul Rand's signature was his bold design—think of the IBM logo)? Whatever your style may be, embrace it and make it yours. This chapter is focused on helping you recognize your distinctive style and integrating it into the individual components of your portfolio.

STYLE: YOUR COVER LETTER

Let's look first at your cover letter. Certainly, *what* you say in your letter—your story—is important, but if it is to communicate anything about your style, it must also make a positive visual statement. It must create a favorable enough impression on recruiters to encourage them to keep reading. Aside from being concise, good graphic design and an understanding of business letter style are central to achieving this goal. Many applicants understand this and write excellent cover letters, others send lifeless

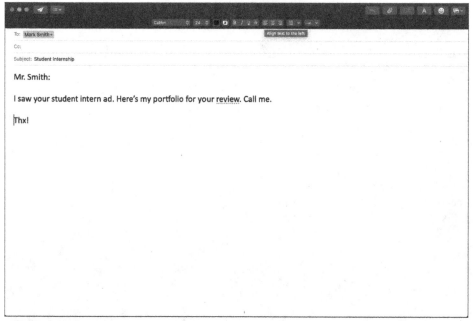

Figure 3.2 Lifeless email.
Source: Mark W. Smith.

emails that say something like, "I saw your ad. Here's my portfolio. Call me. Thx!" (Figure 3.2). Your goal is to look and sound like a candidate who communicates professionally, not someone texting their best friend. *Your letter should have the look and the voice of professional correspondence.*

Not everyone will agree with me on the importance of a cover letter. Writing a cover letter seems to be losing ground as we continue our transition into the digital age. On a recent flight to Phoenix, as I thumbed through *Southwest: The Magazine,* I came across an article about a recruiting survey[1] indicating that 74% of recruiters no longer consider a cover letter to be important to the hiring decision. The author took the position that this is because recruiters are handling more applicants than ever before, and the hiring process is accelerating. The conclusion? They don't have time to read letters anymore. Another recent survey[2] conducted by the Society for Human Resource Management found that 84% of organizations now use social media and mobile apps for talent acquisition—they don't require cover letters at all.

To be clear, I disagree with the view that a cover letter is unnecessary. In *my* book, a cover letter is an essential part of a job application. How else can you properly introduce yourself? Imagine dropping your car off at the shop for repair service, leaving

---

[1] "74% of recruiters don't consider cover letters important when hiring an applicant." *Southwest: The Magazine.* January 2018: p. 39. Print.

[2] "Using Social Media for Talent Acquisition." Society for Human Resource Management. 20 September 2017. p. 1. Web. 13 April 2018. http://www.shrm.org

only a note on the windshield that says, "Here's my car. Thx!" The mechanic wouldn't have any idea what you wanted him to do with it! You must explain what you want him to do with your car if you are to get the desired result. The same theory applies to job applications: you can't just "drop off" your portfolio and expect a recruiter to understand what you want. If you want a recruiter to consider you a serious candidate, you must provide an appropriate introduction and tell them what you seek. *Clearly state why you are writing and what you want in your cover letter.*

Our office believes so strongly in the need for a cover letter that we require one with *every* application. And we're not alone. I just did an informal survey of postings on the American Society of Landscape Architects *JobLink*[3] jobs board to see how many firms require cover letters with job applications. Of the ads I reviewed, roughly 65% required applicants to submit a cover letter. It seems clear that, at least in the A/E industry, the cover letter is not dead. Yes, we *are* working through the hiring process faster these days. But the idea that a cover letter is unnecessary is laughable. As recruiters review your submittal, they want to get to know you. Your cover letter provides the best way for you to share something unique about yourself and provide needed context for their review. You can't easily do that with a mobile app.

All right, you've made your point! How do I show my "style" in a cover letter? Let me start by saying that most recruiters will make a snap judgment about you—your skills, your character, your personality, your potential—with one brief glance at your cover letter. *How is that possible?* Psychologists report that it takes just one-tenth of a second for us to judge someone and make a first impression.[4] So, just as we make such impressions of others when we meet them in person, recruiters form an impression of a candidate within seconds of opening a submittal. Explaining how this happens in the article, "How Not to Write a Business Letter"[5] the author states, "Bad writing is like good art: you just know it when you see it." That impression springs from visual clues—organization, appearance, length—that you have complete control over. To help you make sure that your cover letter is more like "good art," here are some tips on making a good first impression with your cover letter:

- **Get organized:** Every recruiter appreciates an organized candidate. Good organization will make your letter easy to read and visually communicates that you're, well, organized. A well-organized letter also contains all the elements of an effective business letter (date, addressee, salutation, introduction, body, conclusion, signature) in predictable order and is concise. Fictional planner **Michelle Bayroot** submitted a cover letter that opens with references to the position and the office where she seeks work, demonstrates excellent networking

---

[3] "JobLink." American Society of Landscape Architects. Web. 22 June 2019. www.asla.org

[4] "First Impressions: Making Up Your Mind After a 100-Ms Exposure to a Face." Association for Psychological Science. Abstract. Web. 1 July 2006. https://journals.sagepub.com/doi/10.1111/j.1467-9280.2006.01750.x

[5] "How Not to Write a Business Letter." Examples.com. Web. 23 November 23, 2019. <https://www.examples.com/business/how-not-to-write-a-business-letter.html>

MICHELLE BAYROOT

123 CREATIVE DR., Denver, CO 12345 | 555-555-1212 | MBAYROOT@SU.EDU

CreativeCo

11 Main St., Suite 1A
Nashville, TN 37011

Subject: Student Internship

Dear Mr. Smith,

Please accept this letter and attached portfolio as my application for the **Student Intern** position you recently advertised for your Nashville office on the APA *Job Seekers* website.

After talking with my classmate, Ebby Howard (your 2018 Student Intern), I became very interested in working with you at CreativeCo because of your unique internship program and your thoughtful approach to planning. Our Department Head, Professor Jones, told me that he felt I would be a good fit in your office and suggested that I contact you right away. He added that he knew you personally and would provide a reference for me.

My qualifications for the position include:

- 4th-year Planning student (anticipated graduation; May 2021)
- Large-scale planning experience
- Advanced AutoCAD, Land F/X, and GIS skills
- Internship at DesignCo Planning/Nashville (Jan-Aug 2018)
- Director: 2019 State University "Planning Week" Student/Professional Charrette

I am very interested in working with your firm in Nashville, getting involved with the community, and designing memorable places. I hope that you'll give my application serious consideration. If you have questions, I can be reached at 555-555-1212 or email at mbayroot@su.edu.

I appreciate your consideration and hope to hear from you soon!

Michelle Bayroot
Sincerely,

Michelle Bayroot

Figure 3.3 Well-organized cover letter.
Source: Mark W. Smith.

skills, incorporates all the key components of an effective business letter, and closes by clearly stating that she wants the job (Figure 3.3). *Your letter must be well organized.*

- **Demonstrate your graphic design skills:** A professional-looking letter can make a significant difference to a recruiter (who is probably also a designer). I realize we aren't all graphic designers, but most of us have graphic design skills that we can use to effectively communicate our creativity. If you are uncomfortable with this, find someone who can help you or use an online template. The main thing is that you develop a graphic theme that establishes a clear information hierarchy, incorporates generous margins and white space, and uses industry-appropriate fonts and colors. *Show off your graphic design skills.*

- **Coordinate your letter with your résumé and portfolio:** You fashionistas out there wake up every morning and coordinate your wardrobe for the day. Your belt matches your shoes, your shirt harmonizes with your pants, and so forth.

Likewise, your cover letter should be coordinated with your résumé and portfolio. Every element should work together to create an ensemble of documents. Employing the "Yellow Highlighter" theme she used in her résumé and portfolio, **Emily Bell** (Clemson University: Bachelor of Landscape Architecture, 2019) uses a simple graphic tool to highlight the header, date, and signature of her cover letter (Figure 3.4). Her letter has an instantly recognizable relationship to her

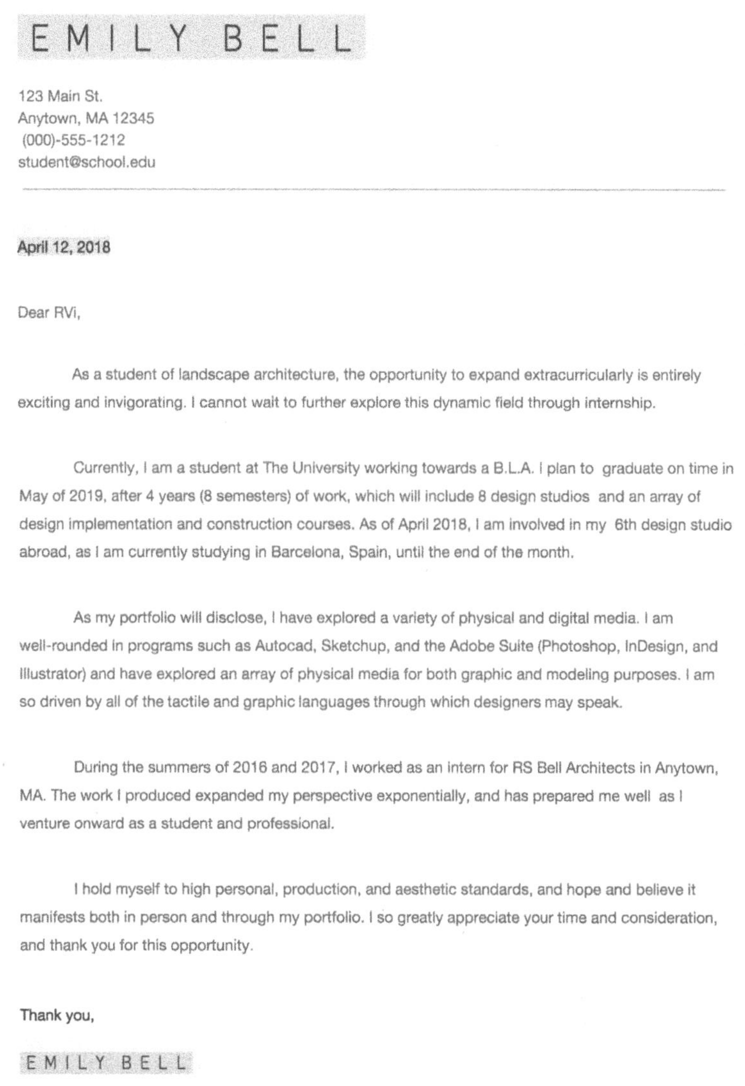

E M I L Y B E L L

123 Main St.
Anytown, MA 12345
(000)-555-1212
student@school.edu

April 12, 2018

Dear RVi,

As a student of landscape architecture, the opportunity to expand extracurricularly is entirely exciting and invigorating. I cannot wait to further explore this dynamic field through internship.

Currently, I am a student at The University working towards a B.L.A. I plan to graduate on time in May of 2019, after 4 years (8 semesters) of work, which will include 8 design studios and an array of design implementation and construction courses. As of April 2018, I am involved in my 6th design studio abroad, as I am currently studying in Barcelona, Spain, until the end of the month.

As my portfolio will disclose, I have explored a variety of physical and digital media. I am well-rounded in programs such as Autocad, Sketchup, and the Adobe Suite (Photoshop, InDesign, and Illustrator) and have explored an array of physical media for both graphic and modeling purposes. I am so driven by all of the tactile and graphic languages through which designers may speak.

During the summers of 2016 and 2017, I worked as an intern for RS Bell Architects in Anytown, MA. The work I produced expanded my perspective exponentially, and has prepared me well as I venture onward as a student and professional.

I hold myself to high personal, production, and aesthetic standards, and hope and believe it manifests both in person and through my portfolio. I so greatly appreciate your time and consideration, and thank you for this opportunity.

Thank you,

E M I L Y B E L L

Figure 3.4 Emily Bell letter with visual relationship to portfolio.
Source: Emily Bell.

résumé and portfolio (where she also uses the highlighter for titles) and communicates that she is a creative, thoughtful, and organized designer. *Your letter must complement the design of your résumé and portfolio.*

- **Keep it simple:** As a rule, recruiters scan cover letters very quickly. If it's extraordinarily long, most recruiters will scan the first few lines and move on to your résumé and portfolio. If you want them to read your entire letter, communicate as concisely as possible. Keep your letter visually simple, avoid crowding too much information onto the page, bulletize lists so they can be scanned quickly, and be succinct. Remember KISS: *Keep it simple, stupid.*

The Cover Letter: Sidebar Checklist

- ☐ Your letter should have the look and the voice of professional correspondence.
- ☐ Clearly state why you are writing and what you want in your cover letter.
- ☐ Your letter must be well organized.
- ☐ Show off your graphic design skills.
- ☐ Your letter must complement the design of your résumé and portfolio.
- ☐ Keep it simple.

STYLE: YOUR RÉSUMÉ

Résumé content is important; but so is its design. A well-designed résumé can help your submittal stand out from the rest of the pack. You see, the average applicant designs their résumé for just one purpose: to present their credentials. This approach is fine if you are applying for a position that requires little or no creativity, say, an insurance salesman. But you're not selling insurance. You are applying to be an entry-level creative professional and design industry recruiters expect more than just academic credentials from you; they expect creativity. *Your résumé serves two purposes: to present your credentials AND to display your creativity.*

Many candidates just don't get that. Applicants routinely submit garden-variety résumés that might be appropriate for a receptionist position but say little about their qualifications as a professional designer. Frankly, I am surprised at how many design graduates are so unconcerned about the design of a document that is so crucial to their job search. Oh, well... You can use this situation to *your* advantage by creating a unique résumé that visually proclaims, "I'm a designer!" Those of you trained in graphic design will, of course, have a field day with this assignment. The rest of you will just have to work a little harder. But I promise, it's definitely worth your effort.

I recently received a résumé that looked like it just came out of a typewriter—literally. Written in the *Typewriter* font, there was no hierarchy of information, no section spacing, no graphic enhancement of any kind—it was pure data. Visually, it was one of the weakest résumés I've seen in years. Just finding the candidate's basic credentials—degree, experience, skill set—was challenging. Though unimpressed, I moved on to review the portfolio. Much to my surprise, I found a great-looking portfolio. These documents looked as if they were done by two entirely different students. *Why the disconnect?* The candidate had the graphic skills needed to create a résumé that would complement his portfolio but chose not to. When viewed alongside applicants who had submitted excellent portfolios *and* who took the time to create well-coordinated submittals, this candidate was eliminated from consideration.

But you said the portfolio looked great! I did, but we're looking to hire the *best* candidate, not just a *good* candidate. While the best candidates are typically easy to spot, it's not unusual for us to narrow the field (make a "shortlist") to several good candidates for further evaluation. Once the review gets to that level of scrutiny, it may be a minor thing—poor grammar, weak graphics, or failure to coordinate the presentation—that differentiates a *good* candidate from the *best* candidate. All other credentials and experience being similar, you could be eliminated from consideration for a small deficiency. Don't let that happen to you.

What's the best way to design my résumé? Being a designer, I would hope your answer to this question would be, "I'd design my own résumé template." Designing your own custom résumé is the best way to ensure that it is unique. Before you start, however, I would recommend that you review a variety of online templates to get a feel for what is standard for our industry these days. It's important that you understand the acceptable range of design and there *are* a few important traditions that should be respected.

Remember that *Blueprint* portfolio cover of mine? I was determined to carry that style through my entire submittal package. Using that cover as my design template, I created a *Blueprint* cover letter and a *Blueprint* résumé that were closely coordinated with my portfolio (Figure 3.5). I used the same deep "Blueprint Blue" background to mimic an old blueprint and lend an "architectural" feel to the document. Recognizing that most résumés of the day were typed on real typewriters, I hand-lettered mine to personalize it even further. Looking back at it now, it's obvious I broke a few rules ... my name is too small, the job descriptions are too detailed, some of my personal data isn't relevant, and my hand lettering wasn't as legible as it might have been. But, hey, as a whole, my cover letter, résumé, and portfolio were original and well-coordinated, and they stood out in a crowd.

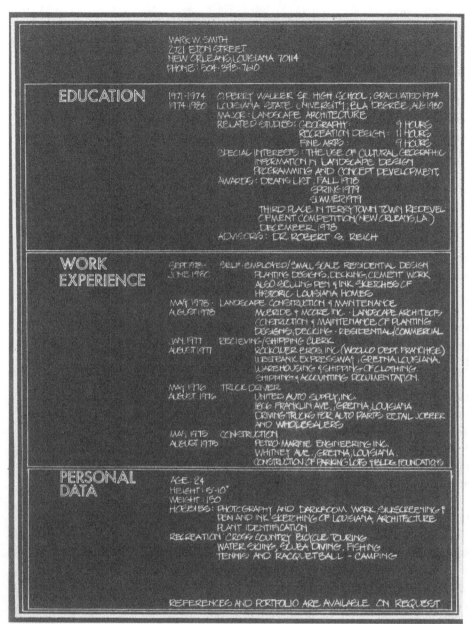

Figure 3.5 Mark W. Smith student resume.

Source: Mark W. Smith.

What if I'm weak at graphic design? If you just don't have confidence in your graphic skills, consider using a résumé template. Good templates are available everywhere. You use *Microsoft Word*, don't you? Word offers several basic templates that make creating your first résumé easy. If you need more options, *Adobe Stock* offers a subscription service that contains dozens of templates. And there are endless other options. I just paid $39.95 for a 90-day subscription to an online "résumé builder" website on which I created the Doug Designer's fictitious résumé. I found the site extremely easy to use. I created fictional designer Doug Designer's résumé from

Detail-oriented architectural designer with multiple student internships and well-developed conceptualization skills. Experienced project team leader and effective collaborator.

Experience

May 2017 -
Aug 2017
Student Intern
Acme Architecture, LLC
Responsibilities:
- Prepared AutoCAD and Revit construction documents under supervision of Project Manager (PM);
- Visited construction site with PM weekly to observe contractor progress;
- Participated in State AIA Design Competition. Entry received 1st place award;

May 2018 -
Sep 2018
Senior Student Intern
Big Dog Design
Responsibilities:
- Managed photorealistic rendering production for firm;
- Developed and documented firm CAD standards;
- Assisted Principal-in-Charge with re-design of office interiors;

Jun 2015 -
Jun 2016
Volunteer
Peace Corps
Served as volunteer in Central African Republic. Mission to provide social and economic development through technical assistance. Specific expertise in irrigation design and site planning for village improvements.

Education

Sep 2012 -
May 2017
Louisiana State University (LSU)
Bachelor of Architecture (BA): 2019

May 2017 -
May 2019
Louisiana State University (LSU)
Master of Architecture (MA)

Certificates

Jun 2013 Eagle Scout: Boy Scouts of America

Jun 2018 Dean's List

Interests

Urban Sketching (pen and ink)

Foreign and Domestic Travel: 47 countries and counting

Digital Photorealistic Rendering

Personal Info

Address
123 Main Street, No. 123
Anytown, TX 11111

Phone
555-555-5555

E-mail
ddesigner@creativenet.org

Skills

Advanced knowledge of AutoCAD and REVIT
●●●●●
advanced

Well-developed freehand drawing skills
●●●●
very good

Excellent Lumion photorealistic rendering skills
●●●●
very good

Advanced conceptualization abilities
●●●●●

Software

Adobe Creative Suite
●●●●●

AutoCAD: V. 14
●●●●

Revit
●●●●

Microsoft Office Suite
●●●●●

Lumion
●●●●

Figure 3.6 Online Resume Template.
Source: Mark W. Smith.

scratch in 15 minutes (Figure 3.6). Once I inserted my content, it was a simple task to preview it in each of the many templates offered. Doug's résumé isn't perfect, but it does illustrate how you can quickly use an online template to generate a professional-looking résumé.

There's another good résumé resource right in your own backyard that you may not be aware of: your university's Career Services department. Most universities offer this type of service for students. LSU's (my alma mater) Olinde Career Center, for example, offers a free *Student Career Guide*[6] that offers many useful resources. In addition to résumé templates, the career services department can help with cover letters, portfolio design, and preparation for interviews. Visit your university's website to locate your Career Services department. If you *still* need options, online recruiters like Indeed[7] and Monster[8] offer plenty of free job-hunting resources on their websites as well.

I'd like to close with a word of caution about using an online template: be sure to tweak it to make it your own—other students use these templates, too. You'd be embarrassed to find that another candidate submitted the *exact* same template you did, wouldn't you? I recently interviewed a talented designer who had a stunning résumé—white text on black background, beautiful graphs, all the latest graphic bells and whistles. Later that week, I was researching résumé templates for this book and found an online template identical to his. He had downloaded the template and simply dropped in his data without making a single graphic modification. While I am sure that millions of résumés are created this way, the discovery left me feeling that this candidate was just not as creative as I had imagined. Résumés for designers and artists are held to a higher standard; we must apply our creative touch to *everything* we do. *Personalize any résumé template you download.*

Now, let's look at layout options for your résumé:

- **Layout:** Your résumé must be organized and easy to read. Why? Most recruiters don't *read* résumés—they *scan* them. In many cases, their computers do the scanning for them. Organize your résumé so that it can be scanned easily and, for the benefit of computers, accurately. From the perspective of *style* (as opposed to *substance*, which we'll look at more closely in Chapter 4), you can be as creative with your résumé as you like, if the result is organized, legible, and professional. From my perspective, there are two basic résumé layout options that can help you achieve this goal: single-column or multi-column.

- **Single-Column:** A single-column résumé is a traditional layout and the easiest to create. Because of its simplicity, this style does not rely on complicated graphic style and is a good choice for candidates with average graphic design skills. On the receiving end, recruiters like this style because they can review its content quickly and computer applicant tracking systems (ATS) will reliably import the data. The fictitious architect **Frank Wrighte** used subtle design enhancements (unique font, select use of bold fonts, generous white space, use of "Cherokee Red") to personalize his layout (Figure 3.7).

---

[6] "2018–2019 Student Career Guide." LSU Olinde Career Center. Web 4 December 4, 2018. <https://www.lsu.edu/careercenter/files/2018-2019studentcareerguide.pdf>

[7] "Indeed, Career Guide." Indeed.com. Web. 4 December 2018. https://www.indeed.com/career-advice/resumes-cover-letters/how-to-write-a-resume-employers-will-notice?from=careeradvice-US

[8] "Resume Examples by Industry." Monster.com. Web. 4 December 2018. https://www.monster.com/career-advice/article/resumes

FRANK**WRIGHTE**

12621 Prairie Home Blvd, Scottsdale, Arizona 85259 | frankwrighte@mywebsite.com | (555) 555-1212

Summary

Architectural designer with multiple student internships. Excellent drafting skills and well-developed conceptualization abilities.

Education

Honorary Doctorate of Fine Arts: University of Wisconsin/Madison; 1955

Work Experience

Joseph Lyman Silsbee: Student Intern | 2016

Responsible for general drafting, construction site visits, running blueprints, and making coffee

Beers, Clay, and Dutton: Student Intern | 2017

Responsible for architectural concepts, technical drawing, construction observation

Adler & Sullivan: Student Intern | 2018

Responsible for architectural design, project management, and drafting

Selected Projects:

Fallingwater | Mill Run, PA
Capstone Project: Designed single-family residence spanning a waterfall

Taliesin West | Scottsdale, AZ
Collaborative studio project. Designed design studio for architectural fellowship

Proficient Skills:

Drafting
Architectural Design
Furniture Design

References:

Joseph Silsbee | Joseph Lymon Silsbee | (555) 555-1212 | joe@adlerandsullivan.com
Louis Sullivan | Adler & Sullivan | (555) 555-1212 | louis@adlerandsullivan.com
Dankmar Adler | Adler & Sullivan | (555) 555-1212 | dankmar@adlerandsullivan.com

Figure 3.7 A single-column résumé.
Source: Mark W. Smith.

- **Multi-Column:** A multi-column résumé, such as the one seen here from fictitious architectural designer **Lay Corbooseay**, has a more contemporary look than a single column layout (Figure 3.8). This is the layout preferred by most students and professionals. Multiple columns, often in the form of sidebars, offer greater flexibility when using infographics or other special graphics such as photos or project imagery. This format also permits the insertion of more information than a single-column format. I've used a two-column layout for years and found it most adaptable to my evolving needs.

I should note here that many firms (including my own) now use ATS software. While ATS is an efficient way to download and organize many résumés quickly,

123 GRANDE RUE DU DESIGN, PARIS, FRANCE 75000
+00 123 4567890 | CORBU@EXAMPLE.COM

LAY
CORBOOSEAY

■ ARCHITECTURE STUDENT

ABOUT

French-born American architecture and urban
planning student with mulitple student internships
and well developed construction documentation
skills. Multilingual (English, French, Catalon).
Experienced project team leader.

SKILLS

Architecture	Concept Development
Rendering	Technical Writing
GIS	CAD

EDUCATION

2017- 2021 (anticipated graduation)
BACHELOR OF ARCHITECTURE
THE STATE UNIVERSITY/GOTHAM CITY

EXPERIENCE

2017-2018
JEANNERET PARTNERSHIP
STUDENT INTERN
CAD drafting and GIS for multi-discipline design firm
on the French Riviera. Also served as firm project
photographer and drone pilot.

2018
CORBU
STUDENT INTERN
Construction Observation and specifications trainee
in London office. Learned Revit and became LEED
certified.

2018 - 2019
THAT FRENCH COMPANY
STUDENT INTERN
Provided Catalon-language translation services for
construction documents for public-sector project in
Barcelona.

REFERENCES

GUSTAV KLIMT	PIERRE JEANNERET
PAINTER	ARCHITECT
PHONE	PHONE
+00 123 4567890	+00 123 4567890
EMAIL	EMAIL
gus@example.com	pierre@example.com

Figure 3.8 A double-column résumé.
Source: Mark W. Smith.

it frequently misreads unusual fonts, infographics, linework, and shaded backgrounds. A simple layout with limited graphics is easiest for ATS to accurately
read and improves its accuracy. In my experience, having to manually type in

information because a résumé was too "busy" for the ATS to read really slows things down.

- **Formatting:** A recruiter may spend just a few seconds reviewing your headings, scanning content, and checking for errors before deciding whether to spend more time on your résumé. Because of this, it is essential that you format your content with the goal of leading recruiters directly to what they need to see: your credentials and your strengths. I just received a dense two-page résumé that got everything wrong—microscopic font, no section spacing, narrow margins, no white space, no organization. The credentials were there (somewhere), but the viewing experience was more like reading a municipal ordinance than a résumé. Reviewing a résumé should not be painful for a recruiter—it should be a pleasant experience. Though I found that candidate to be technically qualified, she did not measure up creatively and was passed over in favor of more creative applicants. In a creative industry like ours, recruiters often make hiring decisions based as much on their perception of your creativity as on your actual qualifications; you've got to address both. *Incorporate professional graphic design into your résumé.*

Let's look at the individual elements of your résumé:

- **Header:** Your header is THE most vital information on your résumé. Without it, you're nobody. Don't laugh too hard, I do occasionally receive résumés without names and/or contact info. Your name must be at the top of the page where it will be seen immediately. Just how visible should it be? It depends on what kind of designer you are; a graphic designer might want to make a bolder statement than an architect. I recommend at least a 24pt font, but I've seen them as large as 60pt. Your contact information (address, phone, email) should be subordinate to your name. If you have social media or website links to share, this is the place for those as well.

- **Subheadings:** The information in your résumé should be divided into sections (e.g., Experience, Education, Skill Set) to increase legibility and facilitate quick review. They should be bold enough to be easily seen above your body text. The use of accent color for subheadings and graphics is a clever way to brighten things up. Coordinate any color with your cover letter and portfolio and be consistent with your industry (e.g., a graphic designer might use bold colors while a landscape architect might select something "earthy"). Be sure to leave generous space between sections to maintain a good white space balance. *Use a bold header and subheadings.*

- **Text:** Except for infographics, your résumé is entirely text. Because of this, you should use a font that is easy to read on all media; computer monitors, mobile devices, hardcopy. To ensure legibility, I recommend a font size between 10 and 13 points for body text. Regarding font selection, ask yourself what you want your résumé to feel like. If you lean toward a traditional look, a Serif font (e.g., Times Roman, Georgia, Bookman Old Style) might be a good choice. A Sans

Serif font (e.g., Arial, Calibri, Helvetica) will lend a more contemporary look to your work. While many recruiting experts suggest that a San Serif font is the best choice for creative professionals, I wouldn't let that advice stifle your creativity too much. Legibility is by far the most important selection criterion. I would also be careful about mixing multiple fonts. *Limit the number of different fonts and font sizes you use.*

- **Line spacing:** Relax your line spacing; a crowded résumé is hard to review. I recommend single-spaced text with a line height multiple (spacing) of 1.2 to 1.5 for body text. That should be tight enough to allow you to say everything necessary without wasting precious space.

- **Margins:** The look and feel of your résumé rely, in large part, on finding an agreeable balance of text and white space. The size of your margins impacts that balance significantly. Narrow margins and too much text make a page feel cramped. Use margins too wide and you'll run out of space for your credentials. What's the right balance? I suggest generous 1-inch margins on all sides.

- **Bullets:** Rather than writing long paragraphs, bulletize your data for quick scanning. Bullets help you organize your data, they look great, and they're easy for recruiters to scan. Good applications for the use of bullets on a résumé include lists of academic achievements, software skills, language skills, and work experience.

- **Color:** If you step out of the relative safety of black-and-white (B&W), do so with care. Color is a wonderful tool when used with purpose, but it can also work against you. It should be used for visual emphasis and to reflect the graphic trends of your profession. If you use color, be sure it has enough contrast to print as well in B&W as it does in color. Yellow, for example, prints poorly in B&W. Also be sure to coordinate your color choices among all your documents. To give the recruiter subtle clues about his background (hint: he grew up in Southwest Louisiana) and profession (Landscape Architecture), **Wes Gentry** (Louisiana State University: Bachelor of Landscape Architecture, 2015) set his résumé in clean white san serif type set over a rich blue-green map of coastal Louisiana (Figure 3.9). The result is colorful and distinctive without distracting from his résumé content. *Use font and background colors carefully.*

- **Infographics:** Increasingly, students are using infographics to list software skills, language skills, and special interests. Done well, infographics are easy to understand and add visual style to a résumé. Take care, however, to avoid relying on them too heavily—too many infographics make a résumé look busy. Also note that ATS often fail to recognize infographic content. Our ATS routinely misreads them, requiring that I go back and manually enter (grudgingly) any missed information. *Use infographics judiciously.*

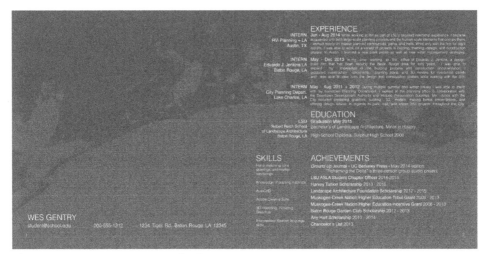

Figure 3.9 Wes Gentry use of color.
Source: Wes Gentry.

I'd like to close this section with a note on résumé placement. I've heard faculty advise students that a résumé should not be placed in the portfolio; they recommend attaching it to an email separately. I don't totally agree with this. I feel it should be in your portfolio—both hardcopy and digital—so that it can be reviewed as an integral part of your portfolio package. Because I store every portfolio on our server, I find it easier to review a submittal when it's all one document, as opposed to opening two separate documents. I also suggest that you place it in the front of your portfolio where I can see it right away; I want to know if you're qualified before I spend more time reviewing your work. Placing it in your portfolio also keeps it from being accidentally misplaced. Don't worry, placing it in your portfolio won't prevent you from attaching a separate copy to an email if required; having two copies is a redundancy that shouldn't bother any recruiter. *Place your résumé in your portfolio.*

The Résumé: Sidebar Checklist

☐ Your résumé serves two purposes: to present your credentials AND to display your creativity.

☐ Personalize any résumé template you download.

☐ Incorporate professional graphic design into your résumé.

☐ Use a bold header and subheadings.

☐ Limit the number of different fonts and font sizes you use.

☐ Use font and background color carefully.

☐ Use infographics judiciously.

☐ Place your résumé in your portfolio.

STYLE: YOUR PORTFOLIO

As I stepped off the elevator and walked into the conference room, my heart was pounding. *What if they don't like my portfolio?* I had just flown 900 miles, clutching my portfolio on the plane as if it were a vintage Stradivarius, to interview with a firm I knew little about. Now, as I took in the opulence of their office, I realized I might be out of my league. "Now, let's have a look at that portfolio," the interviewer said as he reached across the polished granite conference table. He was referring to the leather-bound portfolio binder I had been piecing together since I was a student. Each page contained a carefully assembled blend of original drawings and photos. A professional scrapbook, everything in my binder was hand-crafted. It was, in every way, uniquely mine. Despite my nervousness, the interview went well. As it ended, the interviewer told me he was looking for a creative designer—like me. *Great, when do I start?* He added that he hadn't seen a portfolio like mine in a while. *Groovy! Whoa...is that good or bad?* Finally, he concluded with, "We'd like to hire you." *Yes!* My portfolio played a key role in securing that job. It supported my assertions that I was a good candidate for that position, it demonstrated that I did quality work, and it confirmed that I had a robust design aesthetic—a style—that was unique, yet consistent with the target firm.

That meeting took place in a day and time when a successful interview relied entirely on a high-quality presentation portfolio and the candidate's ability to present it professionally. Digital portfolios didn't exist, so we couldn't send our portfolios in advance of an interview. The typical job application included only a cover letter and a résumé. Whatever impression we were going to make on a recruiter started the moment we walked into the interview—not before. Today, with the recruiting process being primarily digital, the presentation binder seems a little dated, doesn't it? Recruiters advertise online, you submit your portfolio digitally, and, until an interview is scheduled, everything is done by email or video conference.

If everyone's going online, why do I need a presentation portfolio? You need a presentation portfolio because you may be invited to an in-person interview. Despite the advancements in digital technologies, I am confident that in-person interviews will never completely go away. Hey, recruiters are humans, too; we like to physically meet the people we're considering for a position. There is, however, a caveat; as I write (2022), we have been in the midst of a global pandemic for two years. The COVID-19 pandemic has forced us to rethink how we interact with others. For now, working remotely is the "new normal" and most recruiting is being done entirely online. Initially, videoconferencing made recruiting more difficult, but after working remotely for months, most of us have found it to be safe, convenient, and effective. Regardless of what happens with this virus, videoconferencing is here to stay. Yes, we'll all return to in-person interviews at some point and your presentation portfolio will once again see some action. Until then, get comfortable with sharing your portfolio online.

When we do return to in-person interviewing, I still don't feel that we're ready to make the leap to making interview presentations on portable digital devices. I've seen enough failed presentations on tablets and laptops to conclude that the technology is not yet foolproof enough for such an important presentation. I recall a recent interview in which the student brought in a laptop for his presentation. As he opened his first project file, it looked like he was off to a good start. Things unfortunately went south when he was unable to pull up his next project. As he fumbled with the laptop, he lost his composure and never really recovered. The presentation was a flop. While we felt he had talent, his presentation kept him off the shortlist. I can foresee a time when portable digital devices will replace the physical portfolio in the interview; I just don't think we're there yet.

Regardless of the format and venue in which it's presented, your portfolio presentation must communicate your style professionally. As an attachment to an email, it must speak on your behalf without any help from you. In an online interview, the focus shifts from the portfolio to you, the candidate, and your ability to make a professional digital presentation. In an in-person interview, where your portfolio must be physically shared with the recruiter, its content, craftsmanship, and presentability are all important presentation considerations. Some students present beautifully crafted presentation portfolios, others show up with unprofessional plain-paper copies stapled in the corner. Choose wisely; the impression you make with your portfolio is completely within your control.

The Cover

We've already addressed the role that your portfolio cover plays in telling your *story*. What about the way it expresses your *style*? Cover design is highly personal and meaningful for some candidates and flat out superficial for others. Regardless of how you feel about it, one thing is certain; your cover establishes an immediate and lasting first impression of what kind of designer you are. Can you judge a book by its cover? Perhaps not, but the cover should at least provide clues regarding its content. I feel the same holds true for a design portfolio. *Design your portfolio cover to convey professionalism, creativity, and something about yourself—all at a glance.*

A review of how our office evaluates job candidates might help you see why I consider this first impression so important. Like most offices, we initiate a search to fill an open position using an online ad. As applications come into the office, each is automatically downloaded into our applicant tracking system, and a candidate profile is created. I then evaluate each candidate's suitability for the position and shortlist those who are qualified. As the ad expires (usually in 30 days), I print the shortlisted portfolios and schedule a review meeting with my partners. During that meeting, as everyone thumbs through the hardcopy portfolios, I summarize the highlights of each candidate. Finally, with all those portfolios lying on the conference room table, we debate the merits of each candidate and decide who we'll call in for an interview. At that moment, a memorable and well-designed cover that shouts, "Hey, I'm a talented designer!" has the potential to influence that decision, a poorly designed cover does not.

What makes a portfolio cover memorable? To answer that, let's look at a few portfolio covers that have impressed me during that first glance. One approach to creating a memorable portfolio cover involves *bold* design. Graphic designer **Dakota Baños**

(Louisiana State University: Bachelor of Fine Arts in Graphic Design, 2020) incorporated bold color, sweeping lines, and a unique font into her cover design. When asked what inspired the design, Dakota explained that she was after something aligned with her minimalist design style. Then she had a thought: "My personality and the things I really enjoy are usually bright and colorful and evoke more of a cheerful feeling." She changed course and created a new brand, *Tilde Design Co.* The name, *Tilde*, is derived from the tilde ("ñ") in her last name, a gesture she now incorporates into all her work. And, yes, that tilde also inspired the flowing patterns on her cover. Dakota studied Cuban-inspired graphics and found a tropical color palette that happily coincided with her desire to create something bright and fun. To carry this theme into her portfolio, Dakota incorporated a variation of the cover into her *Get to Know Me* page. Then, to tone it down and make the transition to the minimalist style of her projects, her *Table of Contents* employs a cooler color palette and more generous use of white space. As Dakota sums it up, "I wanted it to be eye-catching and bold, but it also had to have a special underlying significance to me." As you can see, the boldness in Dakota's design isn't just being bold, it represents something important to her (Figures 3.10 and 3.11) . She blended her *story* with meaningful *style* to create a unique and memorable portfolio cover.

Figure 3.10 Dakota Baños portfolio cover.
Source: Dakota Baños.

Figure 3.11 Dakota Baños get to know me.
Source: Dakota Baños.

Also using brilliant color to make an opening statement, landscape designer **Dylan Schmer** (Colorado State University: Bachelor of Science in Landscape Architecture, 2010) designed his portfolio cover for one purpose: immediate impact. Dylan set his name in large san serif letters positioned across the full width of a brilliant red background. Dylan chose red to represent passion; a striking color that he felt would reflect the hard work and energy that he puts into his projects. He has always been drawn to landscapes with bold colors and dramatic contrasts and wanted to bring that into his portfolio as well. To carry his signature color theme into the portfolio, Dylan inserted red divider pages between projects, then added red "Project Title" bars and page number tabs to every project. He concluded the document with a solid red back cover. Dylan's cover design is one of the simplest, and yet most impactful, I've seen in quite some time (Figure 3.12). If you're feeling bold, color can be a highly effective way to stand out in the crowd.

Figure 3.12 Dylan Schmer bold portfolio cover.
Source: Dylan Schmer.

While we're on this subject of using color boldly, I'd like to share another portfolio cover on which color is the dominant element. The result is striking, but for different reasons than the previous example. Landscape architect **Brittany Geist** (Louisiana State University: Bachelor of Landscape Architecture, 2009) created a minimalist cover design containing only a green rectangle. Only the document's title, *Portfolio,* and her name break up the serenity of this big green "lawn." Initially, it was the restraint of this cover that caught my eye; then the "mystery" of the green rectangle piqued my curiosity (Figure 3.13). On further inspection, I discovered a small caption in the bottom corner explaining that this color is *Greenery*, Pantone's *2017 Color of the Year.* I thought, *how fitting for a landscape architect!* As I flipped through her portfolio, it was obvious that Brittany was a talented designer with exceptional graphic design skills. In addition to incorporating color effectively into her cover, she used *Greenery* throughout her portfolio for headings and titles to visually tie the document together (Figure 3.14), then wraps it up with a conclusion saying simply, "Thank you" (Figure 3.15). Brittany used a distinctive style and color palette to create a cover that does what every portfolio cover should do—reveal something intriguing about your creative capabilities and invite the recruiter in.

On a quieter note, **Brynn Macinnis** (Colorado State University: Bachelor of Science in Interior Architecture and Design, 2016) used only text and white space to communicate her style. Brynn divided her title, *portfolio*, into three letter groups stacked vertically along the centerline (Figure 3.16). She added a thin orange horizontal bar for accent and separation, then printed her name below. The entire composition is positioned over a white background. That's it. Brynn's confident use of white space and a unique font choice creates a cover design that shows restraint and sophistication.

Figure 3.13 Brittany Geist portfolio cover.
Source: Brittany Geist.

CONTENTS

Brittany Geist 5

Figure 3.14 Brittany Geist TOC relationship to portfolio cover.
Source: Brittany Geist.

Figure 3.15 Brittany Geist conclusion.
Source: Brittany Geist.

Brynn continues this crisp graphic style on each of her project cutsheets and uses the orange accent for captions and project titles throughout. Brynn's style is clearly communicated and is competently integrated into a portfolio that is visually cohesive.

Another approach to cover design is *contextual*; a design that makes a clear visual reference to the work inside. **Haley Wagoner** (University of Texas: Master of Landscape Architecture, 2018; Portland State University: GIS Certificate, 2012; University of Arizona: Bachelor of Science, Urban and Regional Development, 2008) designed her cover to provide clues about her passion for large-scale planning. This background is textural and abstract. Upon closer inspection, however, it becomes clear that it is an infrared aerial photo of a mountainous region (as we review her project experience, we find it is an infrared aerial photo of one of her projects). Titled simply, *Haley Wagoner*, Haley set her name in an outline san serif font (red to coordinate with the infrared trees) over a floating transparent band (Figure 3.17). Haley carried this font into her *Table of Contents* where she coordinated the font and color with each of her project cutsheets. Haley's portfolio cover gives us a clue about her work, is visually interesting, and provides a fitting introduction to the high-quality work in her portfolio. *Use graphic design to tie your cover and content together.*

pOr
tfO
lio

brynn lee macinnis

Figure 3.16 Brynn Macinnis portfolio cover.
Source: Brynn Macinnis.

Figure 3.17 Haley Wagoner portfolio cover.
Source: Haley Wagoner.

Some portfolio covers are designed to reveal something *personal* about the individual. **Elliot Williams** (Texas A&M University: Bachelor of Landscape Architecture, 2016) designed a cover that speaks to his passion for the artful side of his profession. Its title, *Elliot Williams, Artist and Landscape Designer*, is positioned in a highlighted box above a nicely composed photo of a technical pencil with additional analog drawing tools in soft focus beyond (Figure 3.18). It suggests an appreciation for vintage design tools, and it establishes the impression that Elliot is a creative and artful individual. A quick review of his portfolio reveals that he is, in addition to being a talented designer, an accomplished artist with an impressive range of drawing, painting, and digital arts skills.

One glance at this next portfolio cover suggests that **Emily Bell** (Clemson University: Bachelor of Landscape Architecture, 2019) has graphic design talent and enjoys photography. Focused on a dark atmospheric photo of the wooden framing inside an old building, Emily positioned her name and portfolio title, *Emily Bell/Recorded*, right in the center of the cover (Figure 3.19). She draws immediate attention to her name by accentuating it with a bright "yellow highlighter" and contrasting it against the dark background. While Emily's cover design does not make a direct reference to her profession, it does provide clues about her creativity, skill set, and personal interests. A logical question, then, might be, "What does this candidate do?" Emily quickly put that to rest on the next page by announcing, on a bold yellow background, that this is a *Landscape Architecture Portfolio* (Figure 3.20). For visual continuity, the balance of Emily's portfolio is held together by the continued use of the "yellow highlighter" for project titles and backgrounds and by the extensive use of personal photographs.

Being an urban designer, **Roger Montelongo** (University College London: MSc Urban Design + City Planning, 2018; Texas State University: Bachelor of Science: Community and Regional Planning, 2016) wanted his cover to share his passion for urban culture and history and give the recruiter a taste of his advanced graphic skills. Having gone to school in London, he was fond of St. Paul's Cathedral and decided to create a "posterized" image of that historic building to provide a background for his cover. His name and portfolio title, *Roger Montelongo—Urban Design Portfolio*, are prominently displayed at the top of the page, yet without dominating it (Figure 3.21). His personal logo further communicates a creative touch. To carry the graphic theme through his portfolio, Roger repeated the title font and horizontal bar on each project cutsheet (Figure 3.22). At a glance, Roger's cover communicates that he's an urban designer with an appreciation for historic architecture, he has well-developed graphic design skills, and he has a great sense of style.

Some students design portfolio covers that are *entirely* style. The student portfolio of **Kaitlin Craig** (Texas Tech University: Bachelor of Landscape Architecture, 2017) contains one of the most artful covers I've seen in years. Completely hand-drawn and colored, this cover shows off the fanciful linework and bold use of color that are

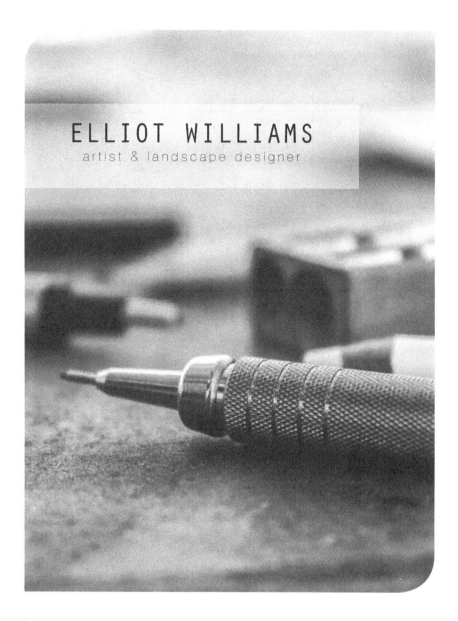

Figure 3.18 Elliot Williams portfolio cover.
Source: Elliot Williams.

Figure 3.19 Emily Bell portfolio cover.
Source: Emily Bell.

LANDSCAPE ARCHITECTURE PORTFOLIO

Figure 3.20 Emily Bell portfolio sleeve.
Source: Emily Bell.

Figure 3.21 Roger Montelongo portfolio cover.
Source: Roger Montelongo.

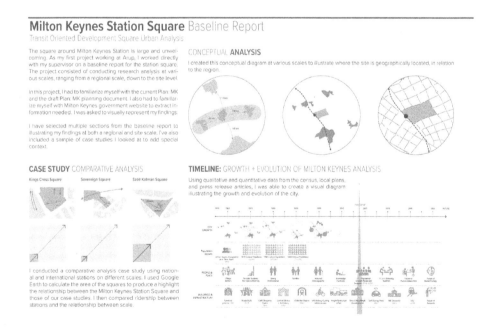

Figure 3.22 Roger Montelongo cutsheet organization.
Source: Roger Montelongo.

Figure 3.23 Kaitlin Craig creative portfolio cover.
Source: Kaitlin Craig.

hallmarks of Kaitlin's unique personal style (Figure 3.23). And it's not just for show; Kaitlin confidently integrates this playful use of color and pattern into every corner of her work. After personally reviewing Kaitlin's spirited presentation of her portfolio at a student portfolio review, I found an authenticity about Kaitlin and her work that was honestly portrayed in her portfolio. Let your passions and style shine through on to your portfolio cover!

Sometimes, a good photograph says it all. Whenever I see a cover containing a photograph during portfolio reviews, I ask the student why they chose that image. Some chose photos that have deep personal meaning, others chose a certain photo simply because they like it. Still others use photography to create a particular ambience for their portfolio and communicate their photographic talents. If you choose to use a photograph on your cover, use one that you actually took yourself, that is attractive and well composed, says something about you, and is meaningful enough to you to speak about in an interview.

However you decide to approach the design of your portfolio cover, remember that it should communicate your *style* in some way. *Be original; your cover should say something unique about you.*

Table of Contents

Whether you're trying to find "Changing a tire" in your vehicle's Owner's Manual or navigating a website on the internet, having a roadmap to guide the way is helpful. For a design portfolio, a *Table of Contents* (TOC) is essential to provide an overview of your portfolio content and set the tone for the document. A TOC can also provide several other benefits for your portfolio. Let's look at a few:

- **Managing expectations:** It tells a recruiter as they open your portfolio what to expect—overall organization, categories of work, number of sections, page count. Rather than coming off as a random collection of material, your TOC communicates that you and your portfolio are organized.

- **Orientation:** It provides a reference that helps recruiters quickly find the specific information they want to see.

- **Professionalism:** It creates a professional appearance. It conveys the impression that you are professional and that you've given thought to your portfolio's layout and content; it's much more than just a "bunch of drawings."

Now that we've established the TOC's value to your organization, let's look at some ways you can organize your portfolio. There are three types of organization I commonly see in student portfolios: *Reverse Chronology*, *Project Type*, and *Experience Type*. Each type achieves the desired goal of organizing your work; the approach you select depends on your personal preferences, your level of experience, and your portfolio content.

- **Reverse chronology:** Recruiters aren't concerned with the order in which you present your work, they just want to see your best work presented in a logical and professional way. I would imagine that, in most cases, your best work might also be your most recent work. If that's the case, reverse chronology will allow you to open your presentation with your best project, then follow with secondary work, and close with another of your best projects. The projects that you open and close with during an interview are the most impactful of all your projects and can establish the tone of the meeting. Most student portfolios I receive are organized using reverse chronology.

    In one of the more interesting TOC's I've seen recently, **Christine Johnson** (Ball State University: Bachelor of Landscape Architecture, 2016) introduces herself with a freehand self-portrait at the top of the page. She added a brief *Designer Profile* to describe her education, then arranged her projects—each with its own graphic icon—in reverse chronology across the bottom of the page (Figure 3.24). In keeping with the creative graphic style that runs through all her work, this TOC provides a highly personalized introduction and gives us a sense of what to expect next.

Designer Profile
······················

Ball State
University

BLA '16 candidate
Minor in Asian
Studies

Projects
······················

Songdo River Redesign	USS Indianapolis War Memorial	The Downtown Muncie Hub	Faces of the Cheonggyecheon

Figure 3.24 Christine Johnson personalized.
Source: Christine Johnson.

Dylan Schmer (Colorado State University: Bachelor of Science in Landscape Architecture, 2010), also using reverse chronology, carried the bold color he used on his portfolio cover into his TOC. By reversing the color scheme and using red and white letters on a gray background, the design maintains a strong relationship to his cover and to each of the individual project cutsheets that follow (Figure 3.25).

- **Project type:** This approach organizes experience by project type (e.g., Parks, Urban Design, Transportation, Signage). This is particularly effective for students with internships and a wider range of academic project experience. This organization makes targeting a portfolio to a particular firm easier by spotlighting projects relevant to the recruiter (e.g., highlight "Academic" projects when targeting a firm that specializes in campus planning). Most professional portfolios I receive are organized in this fashion.

With the aim of visually linking his TOC directly to his project cutsheets, **Wes Gentry** (Louisiana State University: Bachelor of Landscape Architecture, 2015) developed a unique design that provides just a glimpse of each project. To achieve this, he cropped a thin strip from the primary graphic of each project in his portfolio, then grouped them in a vertical stack on his TOC page.

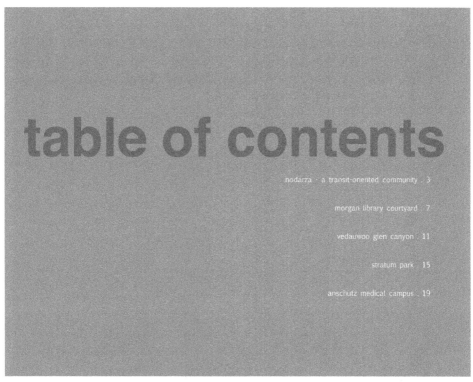

Figure 3.25 Dylan Schmer bold TOC.
Source: Dylan Schmer.

Each project is identified by *project type* along the left edge of the page and by *project name* and *page* on the right (Figure 3.26). The result is professional and colorful and quickly orients the recruiter to the content of his portfolio.

Figure 3.26 Wes Gentry TOC graphics.
Source: Wes Gentry.

Also using *Project Type* organization, **Eric Garrison** (Texas Tech University: Bachelor of Landscape Architecture, 2002) designed his TOC to show us the full range of his experience. Using a bar with page numbers and a series of thumbnail images, Eric gives us a visual "hint" of each project and leads us to its location (Figure 3.27). This design is bright, immediately orients the viewer to the portfolio content, and is graphically coordinated with the rest of the portfolio.

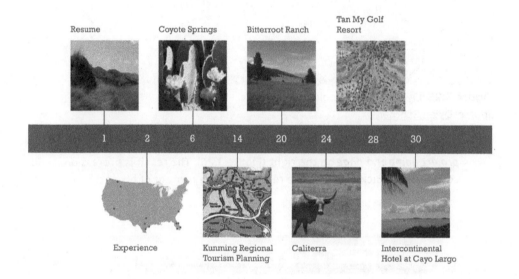

Table of Contents

Resume   Coyote Springs   Bitterroot Ranch   Tan My Golf Resort

1   2   6   14   20   24   28   30

Experience   Kunming Regional Tourism Planning   Caliterra   Intercontinental Hotel at Cayo Largo

ericgarrison

Figure 3.27 Eric Garrison TOC graphics.
Source: Eric Garrison.

- **Experience type:** Many portfolios are, as noted earlier, little more than random collections of project experience. If *Chronological* or *Project Type* don't work well with your material, try grouping it by your *Experience*. For students, this usually divides work into two groups: *Academic Work* and *Professional Experience*. Using *Experience* organization, **Haley Wagoner** (University of Texas: Master of Landscape Architecture, 2018; Portland State University: GIS Certificate, 2012; University of Arizona: Bachelor of Science, Urban and Regional Development, 2008) organized her work into two categories: *Academic Work* and *Professional Work*. Aside from creating a clear structure for her portfolio, her TOC also places emphasis on something every recruiter is looking for—internship experience. Printed on a white background, Haley's TOC incorporates the outline font she used on her cover for the title, *Selected Works*. To maintain a visual connection to her cutsheets, she numbered and assigned a unique color to each project (Figure 3.28). Each section, such as in the *Advanced Drawing* section shown here, incorporates that unique number and color into its heading (Figure 3.29). The result communicates that Haley is organized and quickly leads the recruiter to what they want to see.

SELECTED WORK

The University of Texas at Austin.

01 **OPEN SOURCE SALTILLO** .... p 2-7
Saltillo, Coahuila, Mexico

02 **TESTING OURSELVES IN THE UNIVERSE** .... p 8-13
McDonald Observatory, Fort Davis, Texas

03 **THE STRETCH OF WALLER CREEK** .... p 14-19
UT Austin, Texas

04 **SAVE THE BAY** .... p 20-25
Houston Ship Channel, Texas

05 **POINT OF OBSERVATION** .... p 26-29
Bastrop State Park, Texas

06 **ADVANCED DRAWING** .... p 30-31
UT Austin, Texas

Professional Work.

07 **WETLAND TRAJECTORY SKETCHES** .... p 32-33
PC Trask & Associates | Lower Columbia River, OR & WA

08 **LANDSCAPE PLANNING FRAMEWORK** .... p 34-35
PC Trask & Associates | Lower Columbia River, OR & WA

09 **ASSORTED SUMMER INTERN WORK** .... p 36-37
Design Workshop | Stateline, Nevada

Figure 3.28 Haley Wagoner TOC organization.
Source: Haley Wagoner.

ADVANCED DRAWING
UT Austin

Time Period: Spring 2018
Instructor: John Blood

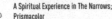

A Spiritual Experience in The Narrows;
Prismacolor

A Spiritual Experience in The Narrows, Abstracted;
Prismacolor

30

Figure 3.29 Haley Wagoner advanced drawing section.
Source: Haley Wagoner.

While a *Table of Contents* is not necessarily an *expected* component of a student portfolio, you should keep in mind that your goal is to exceed expectations and prompt a recruiter to pick up the phone or email and invite you for an interview. Anything you can do that makes your portfolio easier to understand and communicates that you are an organized candidate is worth including. Bottom line: there is no right way to organize your portfolio; it's simply the act of organizing your material that counts. *Use a Table of Contents to create a logical organization for your portfolio.*

Section Dividers

Another organizational enhancement that adds a professional touch to a student portfolio is *Section Dividers.* In similar fashion to the chapters in a book, breaking your portfolio into sections lends organization to your document. Dividers signal a transition from one project to the next and give the recruiter "resting places" as they review your work. From the perspective of style, they also provide an excellent way for you to carry your graphic theme through your portfolio.

Rather than buying pre-packaged index dividers (which would, of course, be better than nothing at all) at the office supply store, think about how you could address this creatively. A custom-designed divider coordinated with your portfolio's graphic theme is the best solution. Before you get started, let's look at a few examples that I feel are particularly well designed.

To keep her portfolio organized, architectural designer **Jessica King** (University of Texas at Austin: Master of Architecture, 2017; University of Tennessee/Knoxville: Bachelor of Science in Interior Design, 2012) created a divider system that skillfully introduces each project and keeps the viewer oriented. Each divider includes a screened-back index of projects from her TOC, with only the current project in bold type. Jessica provides the title, date, project type, and team information, then adds a "teaser" image of the project. The project description and a full range of project images are provided on the pages that follow (Figure 3.30). This system keeps the viewer oriented to their location in the portfolio, provides a smooth transition from project to project, and emphasizes Jessica's exceptional organizational skills.

04 .... an oblique intermission

date/ fall 2013
instructor/ matt fajkus
institution/ university of texas at austin
course/ arc 394-395

Figure 3.30 Jessica King section divider system.
Source: Jessica King.

Graphic designer **Dakota Baños** (Louisiana State University: Bachelor of Fine Arts in Graphic Design, 2020) developed section divider templates that integrate the graphic theme she designed for her TOC and introduce each project. Each divider includes the bold project number and color-coordinated bar from her TOC and an *About this Project* description (Figure 3.31). Here, she provides a brief description of the project, identifies the client and any awards received, and lists software

05

Amite, Louisiana Poster
2019

Software Used

Adobe Illustrator

About this project

This project was prompted as a paying homage to various locations throughout Louisiana mimicking the Works Progress Administration (WPA) Style of posters seen in the United States in the early to mid-1900s. The final project would be displayed in Louisiana Courthouses.

When first approached, I chose to design the poster as something that reflected my home town's own heritage: a corner with a famous building that developed alongside a railroad track. The color palette is limited and muted to give the poster a vintage look, as though the poster itself is from the 1940s.

Figure 3.31 Dakota Baños section divider template.
Source: Dakota Baños.

used for the project. This design reduces portfolio thickness by requiring only one divider/introduction page per project and frees up the remaining pages to focus on project imagery. This layout conveys the project information in a crisp and professional fashion.

Being a landscape designer and a passionate photographer, **Emily Bell** (Clemson University: Bachelor of Landscape Architecture, 2019) used her section dividers to introduce each project and to display her photographic skills. Each divider contains an image representative of the project—typically a black and white photo—and its title. To spotlight each title, she employed her signature "yellow highlighter" tool (Figures 3.32 and 3.33). To minimize visual clutter, Emily placed project descriptions on the second page of each project section. The result is artful and suggestive of a photo on display in an art gallery. The strategic placement of photos throughout the portfolio also weaves the document together visually. And to be sure we get the "message," Emily dedicated the last section of her portfolio exclusively to her photography.

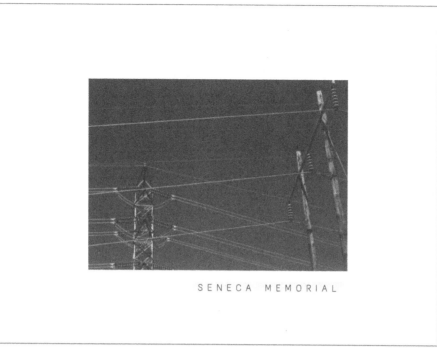

SENECA MEMORIAL

Figure 3.32 Emily Bell project section divider.
Source: Emily Bell.

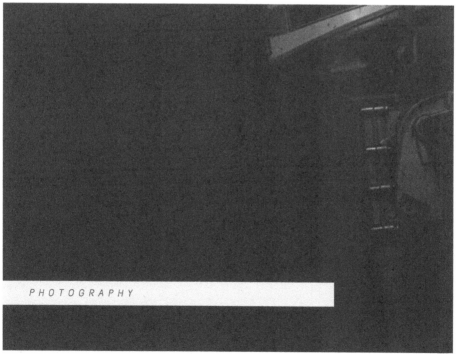

PHOTOGRAPHY

Figure 3.33 Emily Bell photography section divider.
Source: Emily Bell.

Project Cutsheets

Project cutsheets are the heart of every design portfolio and say more about a designer's style than any other portfolio component. I'm not referring only to the project design itself; I'm talking about the look and feel of your cutsheets and what they say about your personal design aesthetic. Upon receiving a job application package, most recruiters will scan your introductory materials (cover letter and résumé) to confirm that you're qualified, then move quickly to your project cutsheets. They know that's where they are going to find tangible evidence of what kind of designer you are. Consider your cutsheets as "snapshots" of your problem-solving skills *and* presentation style that tell recruiters—at a glance—whether you are a candidate in whom they should invest more time.

To provide what a recruiter is looking for in that review and keep them interested long enough to shortlist you for an interview, your project cutsheets must professionally present the following:

- **Graphic design:** Sometimes, as artists, we get so caught up in painting the picture that we forget how important the frame is. Your project cutsheet template is your frame. The elements you choose to place in that frame and how you arrange them are part of your *style*. What is your graphic design style: clean and minimalist, retro, organic and natural? Be creative and share your true colors: how you express yourself here has the potential to set you apart from your classmates.

- **Project data:** Designers generate a lot of data. Just because you have a lot of data, however, doesn't mean that you must share it all. A cutsheet should communicate your ability to get to the point. A summary of the assignment and solution, skills used, the date, and team members (if any) are all that's needed. Don't let project data overwhelm the page. Restraint and white space are quite stylish these days!

- **Problem-solving skills:** Rather than focusing entirely on the finished design, share your design process and conceptualization skills, too. Show how you develop your ideas. Recruiters want to know how you work and your cutsheets are the right place to highlight that.

- **Project graphics:** The content and quality of the exhibits you select have more impact stylistically than any other element. Present only your highest quality imagery and demonstrate the full range of your graphic skills. Every image you include should reveal a different facet of your style. If necessary, reformat your graphics to ensure clarity and legibility. Consider including freehand sketches, digital graphics, site photos, physical and digital models, and photorealistic visualization. And please, limit the number of AutoCAD plans you place in your portfolio. A few AutoCAD plans go a long way!

Your cutsheets must visually support what your cover letter and résumé convey. They must be well-designed, professional in appearance, and present a unified image; collectively, that's *style*. I've been thinking about what this "unified image" really means and would like to offer a couple of examples. One example I particularly like in the music world is that of the *concept album*; an album whose songs have greater meaning collectively than they do individually. In the 1960s, The Beatles released an album still considered to be one of the greatest albums of all time. That album, Sgt. Pepper's Lonely Hearts Club Band, is also one of the most recognizable "concept albums" ever released. The album was conceived and recorded as a collection of individual songs, all unified by a single idea; a live recording by a fictitious Edwardian-era military band. With that in mind, imagine that your projects are songs and that your portfolio is the album. *Is your portfolio designed around a theme that unifies your work?*

Another more contemporary example might be the Apple.com website (it's their portfolio, right?). There are many distinct products presented—computers, phones, pads—but as you flip through the website, you can easily see how seamlessly every element of Apple branding and product design contributes to the company's overall image. Again, this illustrates the use of a strong unifying element to tie their website together visually. *Your individual project cutsheets should work together to present a unified image.*

Architectural designer **Jessica King** (University of Texas at Austin: Master of Architecture, 2017; University of Tennessee/Knoxville: Bachelor of Science in Interior Design, 2012) has designed cutsheets that display a remarkable range of skills, yet all contribute to the continuity of her overall portfolio. Just one project, *Ridge House Addition*, shows off a great diversity of skills: graphic design (cutsheet layout), writing (project description), freehand drawing and conceptualization (concept sketches and renderings), site planning (grading and site planning), architectural design (CAD plans and sections), and photorealistic visualization (digital rendering skills) (Figures 3.34–3.38). Each project in Jessica's portfolio highlights additional skills, such as large-scale planning, digital and physical model-building, and photography. If I was considering Jessica as a candidate for a position in our firm, her portfolio would make it easy for me to visualize what kind of skills and talents Jessica would bring to the firm on day one. From a recruiter's perspective, that is exactly the kind of message your project cutsheets should convey.

date/ spring 2013
instructor/ michael benedikt
institution/ university of texas at austin
course/ arc 384-395

Figure 3.34 Jessica King section divider link to TOC.
Source: Jessica King.

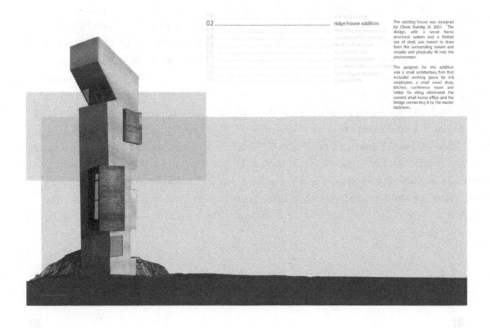

The existing house was designed by Olson Kundig in 2001. The design, with a wood frame structural system and a limited use of steel, was meant to draw from the surrounding nature and visually and physically fit into the environment.

The program for the addition was a small architecture firm that included working space for 6-8 employees, a small wood shop, kitchen, conference room and lobby. Its siting eliminated the current small home office and the bridge connecting it to the master bedroom.

Figure 3.35 Jessica King cutsheet A.
Source: Jessica King.

One of the main motivations behind the existing structure's design was its desire to be as true to the surrounding environment as possible. While doing research, it was discovered that the final product seemed to be designed to fit the existing landscape, when in fact, it was the other way around (i.e. the gully that the bridge extends over was man-made). This spurred the idea of creating opposition with a tower: an object completely honest and obvious to its insertion into the landscape.

Figure 3.36 Jessica King cutsheet B.
Source: Jessica King.

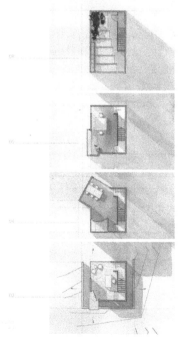

The proposed addition took ideas of materiality and spatial moments from the existing structure and filtered them throughout. This offered the new space with experiences that had subtle, familiar hints of similar moments possible within the house next door. These moves included maximizing the amount of built-in furniture, providing wide views of the landscape (also meant to cast similar shadows), and employing the same angles to pieces that broke away from the original geometry.

The experience within the tower was meant to be analogous to the experience of working in an architecture school studio with both the potential for collaboration and isolation. The vertical circulation is stacked and as contained as possible, but forces an ascent through every adjacent space, maintaining and encouraging office relationships and teamwork.

Figure 3.37 Jessica King cutsheet C.
Source: Jessica King.

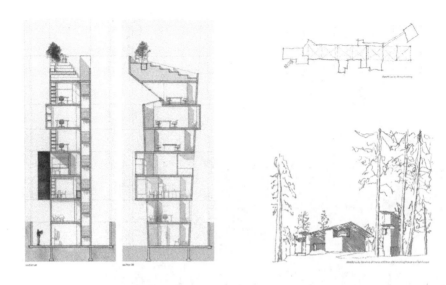

Figure 3.38 Jessica King cutsheet D.
Source: Jessica King.

Each of your projects will have different layout needs. Recognizing this, it is good practice to design a cutsheet template versatile enough to accommodate the widest variety of content possible while unifying your portfolio. As you begin placing project data and imagery on your cutsheet, your template should allow a unique layout for every project. I know some of you are thinking, "*I'm a designer! I don't want a cookie-cutter look for my cutsheets.*" And I would agree with you. Years ago, I worked for a company that employed a very rigid cutsheet template. Titles were fixed, the text had to be precisely 50 words, images were a prescribed size in locked locations; the result was boring and static. This might have been an acceptable outcome in the twentieth century, but it is not today. Contrary to widespread belief, using a flexible template does not limit your creativity—it enhances it. A well-designed template gives you a predictable starting point that expedites production, improves quality control, and enhances overall visual continuity. *Create a cutsheet template that allows flexibility and keeps your content interesting.*

Graphic designer **Dakota Baños** (Louisiana State University: Bachelor of Fine Arts in Graphic Design, 2020) developed a cutsheet template that illustrates the benefits of designing for flexibility. Let's take another look at Dakota's "Amite City" cutsheet and compare it with another from her portfolio (Figures 3.39 and 3.40). While each responds to a unique project and has its own character, it is easy to see that both are from the same portfolio. *Why?* Because Dakota created a framework of consistent graphic elements to ensure visual continuity among each of her cutsheets. If we compare these two, we can see that both contain generous white space, the same font family, project number, and colored underbar, and consistent use of the *Software Used* and *About This Project* text sections. To make sure each has its own personality, however, she changed the background colors, flipped the title and project data locations, and varied the exhibit formatting—all within the limits of her template. Dakota's template is crisp and professional and nicely unifies her portfolio.

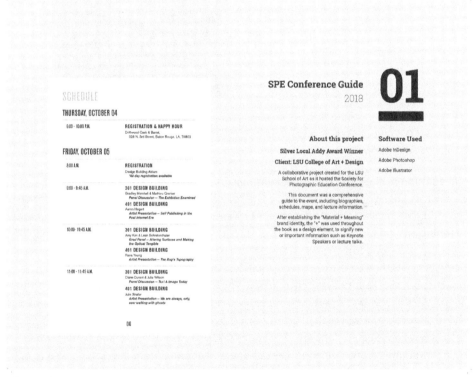

Figure 3.39 Dakota Baños cutsheet template.
Source: Dakota Baños.

05

Amite, Louisiana Poster
2019

Software Used

Adobe Illustrator

About this project

This project was prompted as a paying homage to various locations throughout Louisiana mimicking the Works Progress Administration (WPA) Style of posters seen in the United States in the early to mid-1900s. The final project would be displayed in Louisiana Courthouses.

When first approached, I chose to design the poster as something that reflected my home town's own heritage: a corner with a famous building that developed alongside a railroad track. The color palette is limited and muted to give the poster a vintage look, as though the poster itself is from the 1940s.

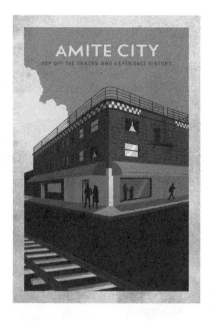

Figure 3.40 Dakota Baños alternate cutsheet layout.
Source: Dakota Baños.

In addition to the need for visual continuity, your cutsheets *must* be legible. To achieve this goal, your projects need to be formatted for use on a portfolio cutsheet. A common mistake among students and professionals alike is the reduction of massive presentation graphics down to an 8½" x 11" format without consideration for legibility. Of course, it looks good on your monitor; you have 1080p resolution! Unfortunately, after it is printed on an office copier, it will lose much of that resolution. I see single project cutsheets that contain microscopic 2pt fonts and dozens of miniature thumbnail graphics every day. If reading your project information requires the use of a magnifying glass, no one will read it! Scale *everything*—graphics, photos, text, title blocks, north arrows and scales, captions—to your portfolio format for legibility. Reformat any information that will be important to a recruiter and delete everything else (e.g., survey data, lengthy notes, legends). When you're done, print a draft and confirm that you can easily read everything on the page.

Planner **Paul Yoder** (University of Cincinnati: Bachelor of Community Planning, 2021; University of Cincinnati: Bachelor of Urban Planning, 2020) designed his cutsheets for legibility. Every cutsheet incorporates text, graphics, and captions scaled for his 8½" x 11" format. For his *Uber Mobility Competition* cutsheet, Paul provided just

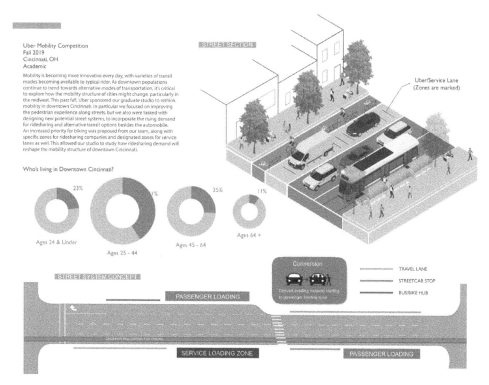

Figure 3.41 Paul Yoder cutsheet layout.
Source: Paul Yoder.

enough project data (title, date, location, project description) and graphics for us to understand how he approached the project without crowding the page (Figure 3.41). The resulting presentation is bright and easy to read. *Format your cutsheets so that ALL text and imagery is legible.*

That brings us to another important formatting consideration. Your cutsheet should have a clear hierarchy of information; it must visually guide a recruiter to the important stuff. Ask yourself what's most important about each project. *Did it win an award? Are my leadership skills notable? Does it illustrate my incredible graphic capabilities?* Identify elements you feel are important, then lead the recruiter there. It should be amazingly easy to flip through your portfolio and see what your strengths are. Placing too much text, inserting scores of tiny graphics, or using inferior quality imagery muddy up a cutsheet and make it hard to identify your strengths. *Establish a clear hierarchy of information.*

Including too many pages can also challenge your cutsheet hierarchy. While most professional and corporate design portfolios limit cutsheet length to one page per project, students usually have fewer projects to share and, for that reason, typically include additional pages for each project to fill out a portfolio. Recruiters understand that, but you still need to limit the numbers of pages you use for each project. *Limit each project cutsheet to five pages.*

In line with this recommendation, architectural designer **Alex Yen-Jung Wu** (University of Texas at Austin: Bachelor of Architecture, 2017) uses four to five pages for each cutsheet. He starts each project with an introductory page, such as this one for his *Vertical Monastery* project, that includes a single graphic and a project description (name, location, date, class, and skills used) (Figures 3.42–3.46). Alex then employs three to four pages per project to illustrate the range of his skill set: digital and hand-built modeling, conceptualization, architectural design, and photorealistic rendering skills. Notice there's no crowding; his layouts incorporate generous white space, the graphics are nicely distributed, and he includes a descriptive caption for every illustration. In each case, the graphics are interesting, the layout is professional, and the work is a pleasure to review. *Use only enough pages and exhibits to communicate your style— nothing more.*

Figure 3.42 Alex Yen-Jung Wu cutsheet A.
Source: Alex Yen-Jung Wu.

Figure 3.43 Alex Yen-Jung Wu cutsheet B.
Source: Alex Yen-Jung Wu.

Figure 3.44 Alex Yen-Jung Wu cutsheet C.
Source: Alex Yen-Jung Wu.

Figure 3.45 Alex Yen-Jung Wu cutsheet D.
Source: Alex Yen-Jung Wu.

Figure 3.46 Alex Yen-Jung Wu cutsheet E.
Source: Alex Yen-Jung Wu.

For her *USS Indianapolis* War Memorial cutsheet, **Christine Johnson** (Ball State University: Bachelor of Landscape Architecture, 2016) opens with a rendering overlaid with a "Project Snapshot" that provides project data (name, awards, scope of work, client, role, date, tools used) (Figure 3.47), then follows with a modified layout showing a plan view and rendering vignettes on the second page (Figure 3.48). Each project in her portfolio follows this template.

In each case, her template makes quick work of creating a new cutsheet and presenting the project data clearly. Christine typically uses additional graphics on the pages that follow her title page. In just a few well-organized pages, she demonstrates that she has brilliant design conceptualization skills, has well-developed graphic design and rendering skills, is an organized Project Manager, and understands the importance of professional presentation.

Figure 3.47 Christine Johnson cutsheet template.
Source: Christine Johnson.

Figure 3.48 Christine Johnson alternate cutsheet layout.
Source: Christine Johnson.

Portfolio Conclusion

I happen to be a recruiter who feels that a portfolio also needs a proper ending; a *Conclusion*. Just as movies often conclude with "The End," your portfolio should contain a page that communicates friendly closure. Your conclusion should say, in so many words, "Thanks for visiting." Many students do an excellent job of leading a recruiter through their portfolio only to end without any notice. A portfolio that ends this way feels a little like having a door shut in your face; it leaves you standing there wondering what happened to the conversation.

Like a *Table of Contents* or a *Design Philosophy*, a *Conclusion* adds a nice finishing touch to a portfolio. Because so few students take the time to place a *Conclusion* in their portfolio, when I see one, it always stands out. In my eyes, it's another indicator that you are a student who is serious about creating a complete document and making a good first impression. I've been collecting examples of nicely designed portfolio conclusions I've received. Let's look at a few.

Looking for a unique way to bring closure to her portfolio, landscape designer **Charlotte Paganini** (University of Florida: Master of Landscape Architecture, 2008) chose to wrap it up with one of her own landscape photographs. With the view trailing off down the beach, *Seaside, Florida* also provides a scenic backdrop for a floating box where Charlotte provided her references (Figure 3.49). While not everyone will want to provide references in their portfolio, I like Charlotte's decision to place hers in this location. If a recruiter is interested in learning more after reviewing her work, a call or email to request references would be the next logical move. This layout simply eliminates the need for that call. This composition also nicely bookends her portfolio cover (containing a wonderful photo; *Jardin du Luxembourg*; Figure 3.50), reiterates her photographic skills, and brings closure to her portfolio without coming right out and saying, "The End."

Figure 3.49 Charlotte Paganini conclusion.
Source: Charlotte Paganini.

Also using a photograph to conclude his portfolio, **Zheng Lu** (Texas A&M University: Master of Landscape Architecture, 2011) organized his last page around a selfie taken on a train, the blurred background suggesting that he is going somewhere quickly. The caption reads, "Be a Traveler in Life…" (Figure 3.51).This is a fitting counterpoint to his résumé/introduction page. There, he provided a photo of himself in an urban environment, the world busily speeding by, with the caption reading, "In the crowds, you can always see me" (Figure 3.52). It's obvious that Zheng travels and has a keen interest in photography, something he confirmed later in his *Other Works: Photography* section. To keep the recruiter oriented while online, Zheng included navigation tools from the preceding pages. To be sure an interested recruiter could easily find him, Zheng added his contact information and a "Contact Me" button for online connectivity. As I close Zheng's portfolio, I am left with the impression that he communicates well, that he is thorough and detail-oriented, and that he is a clever designer who enjoys experiencing everything the world has to offer.

Figure 3.50 Charlotte Paganini relation to portfolio cover.
Source: Charlotte Paganini.

Figure 3.51 Zheng Lu conclusion.
Source: Zheng Lu.

LANDSCAPE
PORTFOLIO

Navigation

ABOUT ME

DESIGN PROJECTS

OTHER WORKS

CONTACT ME

RESUME

EDUCATION BACKGROUND
MLA candidate LAUP, Texas A&M University, USA, Expected Graduation: 05/2011
B.A., School of Architecture, Tianjin University, China, 2005-2009

WORK EXPERIENCE
Sep. 2009-present Art teacher in TAMU Chinese school in USA
Aug.2008-Oct.2008 Internship,landscape designer, Cityscapes Associates in Beijing, China
Mar.2008-Apr. 2008 Internship, landscape designer, Rainstorm landscape Architecture Institute, China
Apr. 2008-June.2008 Assistant, Tianjin University Architectural Academic Research Center, China

COMPUTATIONAL SKILLS
Mastered in Auto CAD, Adobe Photoshop, Adobe Illustrator, Adobe InDesign, Google SketchUp
Autodesk 3ds Max

AWARDS RECEIVED
2009   LAUP scholarship, Texas A&M University
2008   XuZhong Scholarship, Tianjin University
2008   2nd Prize of Sino-Japanese Landscape Design Competition, *LANDSCAPE DESIGN* Magazine
2007   Nanbo Scholarship, Tianjin University
2006,2005   Excellent Student, Tianjin University

EXTRACURRICULAR ACTIVITIES
Sep. 2009-Dec.2009   Mentor of International Student Mentor Association, TAMU
Sep. 2009-Dec.2009   Student Leader of Chinese American Association, TAMU
Sep. 2006-Sep.2007   Minister of Secretary Department in School of Architecture, Tianjin University

◀ ALL PROJECTS ▶   ABOUT ME

In the crowds,
you can always see me

Figure 3.52 Zheng Lu relationship to introduction/resume.
Source: Zheng Lu.

Simply repeating design elements from one's portfolio cover is another way of signaling the end of your document and reinforcing your style. Graphic designer **Brandi Reed** (Louisiana State University: Bachelor of Interior Design, 2021) subtly modified the background design of her portfolio cover and, using the same font, added "Contact Me" (Figures 3.53 and 3.54). This is a little more direct than saying, "Thank You," but is a remarkably effective way of communicating that you want to start a dialogue with the recruiter. That is the point of sending your portfolio, isn't it?

Sometimes, simple solutions work best. Graphic designer **Dakota Baños** (Louisiana State University: Bachelor of Fine Arts in Graphic Design, 2020) designed her *Conclusion* to boldly say just one thing: *Thank you.* If you remember our review of Dakota's portfolio cover, you'll recall her use of brilliant color and pattern in a nod to her personal style. Here, she brought that bright color to the back of her portfolio and simply added a spirited, "Gracias!" (Figure 3.55). This one grabs your attention, doesn't it? This conclusion feels like a firm handshake at the end of an enjoyable conversation and does an excellent job of reinforcing Dakota's vibrant personality and optimistic attitude.

Eric Garrison (Texas Tech University: Bachelor of Landscape Architecture, 2002) kept the design of his last page simple. Using his familiar "signature blue" accent color (Eric also used the color for his cover, titles, captions, dividers) as a full-page

Figure 3.53 Brandi Reed conclusion.
Source: Brandi Reed.

Figure 3.54 Brandi Reed relation to portfolio cover.
Source: Brandi Reed.

Figure 3.55 Dakota Baños conclusion.
Source: Dakota Baños.

background, he simply centered his personal logo, name, and contact information in a white font at the bottom of the page (Figure 3.56). Without saying, "Goodbye," Eric cleverly reminds the recruiter that he is a talented designer, signals the end of his portfolio, and reminds the recruiter how to get in touch with him. This is a very professional closing.

I'll close here with an example of a *Conclusion* that beautifully illustrates the "Less is more" philosophy we discussed earlier. Landscape designer **Christine Johnson** (Ball State University: Bachelor of Landscape Architecture, 2016) simply centered her elegant and playful signature (also used on her cover) on the page and added the year (Figure 3.57). No background, no color; just *Christine Johnson 2016*. It just doesn't get any simpler than that. And yet, it closes her portfolio with a distinctive touch and says so much about Christine's creativity and professionalism.

Each example of a *Conclusion* shown here used a different approach. Some are delicate, others are bold, but they have all signaled, "You've reached the end of my portfolio." I sure that some of you—the more pragmatic designers in the group—might feel that the fact that there are no more pages after a certain point would be enough to indicate "The End." From a purely functional perspective, you may be right. Remember, though, that this discussion is about *Style,* not *Substance*. I am suggesting that you

Figure 3.56 Eric Garrison conclusion.
Source: Eric Garrison.

must find ways to communicate your style through your portfolio. The absence of a *Conclusion* to your portfolio surely will not harm your chances of being shortlisted for an interview, but it won't help either. Just as you say, "Goodbye," to a friend when you hang up the phone, a thoughtful ending to your portfolio can make a favorable impression on a recruiter who is looking for a candidate willing to go the extra mile.

The Digital Portfolio

For the sake of style and brand continuity, your digital portfolio should be formatted to look as much like your hardcopy presentation portfolio as possible. Once you've started an online dialogue and familiarized a recruiter with your digital portfolio content, it's good practice to design your in-person interview presentation to be as closely

Figure 3.57 Christine Johnson conclusion.
Source: Christine Johnson.

aligned with your online presence as you can make it. Properly coordinating this is another way of communicating that you understand the importance of a professional presentation.

Unlike an interview, where you lead a recruiter through your portfolio, your digital portfolio is usually reviewed by a recruiter without any input from you; your portfolio stands entirely on its own. It must be easy to open and navigate, it must present a seamless viewing experience, and it must motivate a recruiter to call you—all without saying a word. Today's students—you—are a digitally savvy group; if anyone understands how to create this experience, it should be you. Unfortunately, we still see problems in student portfolios when it comes to managing the digital experience.

Over the years, I've kept a running list of things that I feel keep a digital submittal from looking its best or functioning smoothly. Let's look at each:

- **Too many attachments:** In lieu of attaching a single portfolio document, some candidates attach separate pdfs for each project. Most job ads request a copy of your portfolio, not a random collection of projects. And for good reason, recruiters want to confirm that you can present yourself properly and they expect an orderly viewing experience. Requiring a recruiter to open multiple project files (which, by the way, many will simply not do) creates a fragmented viewing experience. *Attach a single pdf or an online portfolio link to your email.*

- **Files cannot be opened or downloaded:** The portfolio cannot be accessed: the attachment doesn't open, the portfolio link has an incorrect or broken URL, the recruiter is led to a 404-error page or "Coming Soon" landing page, or the document can't be opened or downloaded because access is locked by the author. Do not let this happen to your portfolio! *Confirm that every file attached can be opened by the recruiter before you send it.*

- **Website registration required:** The website requires a recruiter to create an account before the portfolio can be viewed. Because of the abundance of "digital evil" lurking around the internet these days, many recruiters are understandably reluctant to open links they don't recognize or create new accounts just to open a portfolio. *Use a well-known online portfolio service.*

- **Erroneous links:** The link provided takes the recruiter to the wrong website. This is a rare occurrence but one that communicates carelessness. We sometimes are in such a rush to make a submittal that we fail to confirm that the links work properly. *Confirm that the link you provide goes to your correct portfolio.*

- **Too much information:** Project information is not prioritized, is unfocused, or is in such enormous quantities, it's difficult to review quickly. Recruiters want to see a focused, well-assembled package from every candidate. *Design your portfolio for ease of review.*

- **Inconsistent formatting:** The page size is inconsistent, formatting requires the reviewer to rotate between portrait and landscape layouts, or inconsistent layout makes it hard to find information. Every well-formatted portfolio starts with an orderly template. *Use consistent formatting throughout your portfolio.*

- **Distracting websites:** The host website or online portfolio incorporates distracting banners, transitions, and flash graphics. Like a PowerPoint presentation, the best online portfolio is the simplest. Avoid the temptation to use all the digital bells and whistles at your disposal. *Focus on your content, not the website.*

As you can see, your portfolio content is not the only thing you should be paying attention to as you prepare to make a job application submittal. Your portfolio's performance is also important. Before you forward your portfolio to anyone, take the time to be certain that it performs as intended and provides a professional viewing experience that will elicit an invitation to an interview.

Recognizing the possibility that you may need to present by video interview, I recommend that you get acquainted with the "sharing" tools on the commonly used video software, namely Zoom and Microsoft Teams. I recently did an interview using Microsoft Teams in which the student was unable to share his portfolio with me. After 5 minutes of waiting while he fiddled around with it, I finally suggested that he email the portfolio to me so I could share it with him. Thankfully, for him, that worked. Though I'm sure most of you are pros with videoconferencing by now, you need to practice so you can do it seamlessly. I suggest that you practice sharing your portfolio presentation with a professor or mentor and get comfortable with the process. You don't want the digital tools to get in the way of making a good impression.

The Presentation Portfolio

If your digital submittal hits the mark and a recruiter feels you might be a good fit for their office, there's a possibility you'll be shortlisted and invited to visit for an interview. Congratulations! Now, unless it's a video interview, you'll need a hardcopy presentation portfolio. While its content is the same as that of your digital portfolio, the look and feel of your presentation portfolio must bring something new—some added value—to the interview. Once you sit down for an interview, your success relies on two things: the quality of your portfolio and your ability to present it. No amount of showmanship during an interview will cover for a poorly assembled portfolio with weak content. Just as there are pitfalls to avoid in digital portfolio design, there are mistakes you should avoid in your presentation portfolio as well. Let's look at my hit list:

- **Poor packaging:** Portfolios without any packaging or that are amateurishly designed make a weak first impression. Recruiters expect you to make a presentation befitting a designer. Examples of this weakness include lack of a cover or binding, absence of introductory materials (table of contents, personal bio, etc.), and printing on mediocre quality paper. *Produce a professional looking portfolio package.*

- **Organization:** Disorganized portfolio content results in weak presentations. The organization of your portfolio, whether in digital or presentation form, must flow smoothly page-by-page from beginning to end. A well-organized portfolio supports a well-organized presentation. *Organize your portfolio to facilitate an orderly presentation.*

- **Too much material:** A presentation portfolio should contain only enough material to highlight your skill set and strengths—15–25 pages. Anything longer will be difficult to present during an interview without rushing. The average interview entry-level interview lasts 30 minutes. Half of that will be reserved for portfolio review, the other half for discussion. If you don't complete your presentation within that schedule, your interviewer may cut you short. My first interview was cut short because I hadn't practiced my timing and I was thoroughly embarrassed by the situation. *Size your portfolio to allow for a focused presentation and time for follow-up discussion.*

- **Low-quality content:** A portfolio containing weak design, inferior graphics, or poor resolution imagery reflects poorly on your abilities and judgment. Improve the quality of any weak graphics or purge them from your portfolio. *Show only your best work.*

- **Presentability:** Your portfolio presentation should be seamless, and your packaging should make it easy to present. Is it easily oriented to the recruiter? Will it lay flat without holding it down? Are your graphics and text large enough to understand? Is it too reflective (such as on many portable tablets) to see? Make sure that your packaging does not inhibit the presentation. *Design your portfolio to ensure a smooth interview presentation.*

Portfolio Cover

We've talked about your portfolio cover from the perspective of graphic design and content. Now, I'd like to address its physical presence. What does your portfolio *look* and *feel* like as you place it on the conference table and start an interview? Your design portfolio is a professional document and the experience of handling it should be like that of a high-quality professional report. As a recruiter opens your portfolio, that first impression is an important part of every hiring decision.

As you sit down for an interview, your portfolio cover is the first thing a recruiter sees; whether you create a good impression or not is in your hands. You do want to make a great first impression, don't you? Great! Here's my first tip: You need a professional portfolio cover. A portfolio with a plain paper 24 lb. bond cover will not impress a recruiter. To do it right, you have three basic options: (1) print on high-quality cardstock; (2) create a custom cover from unique materials; or (3) or buy a professional binder.

- **Cardstock:** At a minimum, your cover should be printed on high-quality cardstock. Aside from making your portfolio durable and protective, a heavy cover and backing gives your work a professional feel. Some students laminate their cover to give it a glossy finish and protect it, others bind clear or frosted plastic sleeves over their cover. Any stock heavier than 32 lb. is considered cardstock and is suitable for this purpose.

- **Custom:** The most creative binding is one you make yourself. Over the years, I've seen all sorts of plastic, cardstock, and metal materials bound with rivets, wire, or bolts used as portfolio covers. Some are downright bizarre, others quite professional. A few years ago, we received a portfolio from a graphic design student that was packaged in a custom hand-made envelope constructed of colored illustration board. The portfolio binding was saddle-stitched and subtly embossed with the candidate's name. Each page was printed on very high-quality paper. And it contained an equally beautiful résumé and cover letter, both coordinated with the portfolio. The presentation was breathtaking and, to this day, makes a big impression on anyone I show it to (I still use it as an example of professional packaging during portfolio reviews). If you're willing to put in the time, a well-designed custom portfolio package makes quite a statement.

- **Binder:** If you choose to purchase a binder, there are plenty of options available. The *multi-ring artist portfolio* is durable binder offered in a range of materials (typically vinyl and leather), sizes, and colors. Because each project is in a separate plastic sleeve, a *multi-ring* binder allows you to easily modify content as needed. They are affordable and widely available. This binder has a professional appearance and lays flat for presentation. A *vinyl* art portfolio is a less expensive presentation option. Available in a variety of sizes and colors, this portfolio has a lightweight polypropylene cover and is pre-packaged with clear pocket pages and black acid-free mounting paper inserts. Be sure it has a center-mounted spine that will lay flat during presentations.

Section Dividers

Section dividers help a recruiter locate individual projects or portfolio sections more easily and they communicate that you are an organized candidate. If your portfolio only contains a few projects, I recommend using the same weight paper you use on your cutsheets and using the divider as an introduction or title page for each project. For thicker portfolios, consider using a heavier stock. Some students use section tabs that protrude from the edge of the portfolio, then coordinate them with the *Table of Contents* numerically or by color. However you choose to approach it, dividers will add a professional aesthetic touch to your portfolio.

Binding

The last step as you prepare for an interview is binding your portfolio. I know it's hard to get excited about binding, but your binding choice has a significant impact on the look and feel of your portfolio and its presentability. Unfortunately, many students don't consider this to be important and simply staple their project cutsheets together. Though this approach might be appropriate for an informal or informational review, it is not an acceptable way to bind a presentation portfolio. As you review binding options, here are a few considerations to ponder:

- **Availability:** Can it be purchased and assembled on short notice?
- **Appearance:** Does it look professional?
- **Presentability:** Does it facilitate a smooth presentation?
- **Size:** Will it accommodate your materials comfortably?
- **Cost:** Is it cost-effective?
- **Durability:** Will it hold up well over multiple interviews?
- **Flexibility:** Can the content be modified later?

Commonly available binding options include double wire, spiral coil, comb, VeloBind, saddle-stitching, and perfect binding. Let's look at each type.

- **Double wire binding:** Double wire binding is a pre-formed wire spine that is inserted into slots punched along the edge of the document, then compressed to lock the pages in (Figure 3.58). This durable low-profile binding comes in a range of colors (black or silver are the most commonly used), is widely available in print shops, and lays flat for presentation. It comes in a variety of sizes (up to 1" thickness) and can accommodate all but the heaviest portfolio. Its only negative feature is that, once bound, the content is not easily modified. This is the most professional binding option out there. I *highly* recommend this one.

Figure 3.58 Double wire binding.
Source: Adobe Stock/Kednert.

- **Spiral coil binding:** Spiral coil binder is a plastic or metal coil that is inserted into place in holes punched along the edge of the document (Figure 3.59). Widely available in print shops, it is durable, inexpensive, and available in a

Figure 3.59 Spiral coil binding.
Source: Adobe Stock/Jayannpro.

variety of colors and sizes (up to 2" thickness). Like the double wire, it lays flat for presentation and has a professional look.

- **Comb binding:** Comb binding is a pre-formed plastic spine that is inserted with a machine into rectangular slots punched along the edge of the document (Figure 3.60). Though widely available and inexpensive, it has a less professional appearance than a double-wire or spiral binding and it doesn't easily lay flat for presentation. It has a bulky appearance and pages tend to bind as they are turned; I don't recommend it for an interview.

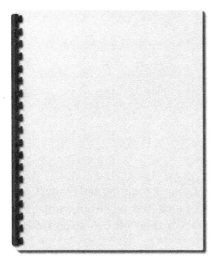

Figure 3.60 Comb binding.
Source: Adobe Stock/JMG.

- **VeloBind:** VeloBind is a durable plastic binder strip with pins that are inserted into holes punched along the edge of the document, then heat-sealed to bind it together. Also, a low-profile binder, VeloBind comes in a range of colors and is available at most print shops. It can bind a portfolio up to 3" thick. Unfortunately, VeloBind cannot be separated after binding to allow for a change in portfolio content. And worse, it is difficult to present in an interview; it will not lie flat.
- **Saddle-stitch binding:** Saddle-stitching is a binding system that is used for thin (max. 64 pages) leave-behind portfolios (Figure 3.61). It is an inexpensive binder that produces a professional-looking document. It is available in most

Figure 3.61 Saddle-stitch binding.
Source: Adobe Stock/Threedy Artist.

print shops. While attractive, it does have limitations; ordering and production require lead time and, once bound, it cannot be modified. While not a smart choice for your presentation portfolio, a saddle-stitched left-behind portfolio leaves a great impression.

- **Perfect binding:** With this binding method, the pages and cover are all glued together at the spine with flexible thermal glue. Once glued, the other three sides are trimmed to give them clean "perfect" edges (Figure 3.62). Perfect bound books look professional, are inexpensive to produce, and can be printed using On-Demand Printing. For those of you good with your hands, this can be done DIY (Google it for instructions). Despite its clean appearance, a perfect binding doesn't lay flat on its own and may require a little manhandling during an interview.

Whatever your binding choice, just be certain that it has a professional appearance, that it is stylistically consistent with your industry and your personal style, and that it will allow you to make a smooth presentation in the interview. *Bind your presentation portfolio with a professional quality binder.*

Figure 3.62 Perfect binding.
Source: Adobe Stock/Shabeeq.

Paper

The quality of the paper that you print your portfolio on communicates style, too. To make a good impression, print on the best quality paper stock you can find. Fortunately, the range of quality paper products available for this purpose is extensive. Let's look at some of the options:

- **Weight:** Printer paper weight ranges from 20 lb. paper to 70 lb. paper. On the lower end of this spectrum, 20 lb. and 24 lb. papers are used for everyday copies. On the higher end, 70 lb. paper is considered light cardstock and is used to print postcards and covers. If you're printing portfolio drafts for review, a **20–24 lb. bond** is fine. It is not, however, good for a presentation portfolio; it feels like it just came out of the office copier. For a professional appearance that will impress a recruiter, print on heavier high-quality stock, such as a **32 lb. bond** 100% cotton paper. The extra weight gives your work a crisp professional feel, your graphics will print beautifully, and you can print on both sides without any image bleed-through. Anything heavier than 32 lb. is more appropriate for your cover.

- **Texture:** A quick review of paper available at my favorite big-box office supply reveals four basic options for 32 lb. bond paper: laser or inkjet (smooth), granite (smooth to lightly textured), premium gloss (smooth), and linen (crisp linen texture). Whatever your preference, select stock that matches your personal style. For example, I used a "recycled" stock for many years to communicate my commitment to environmental conservation. Today, I use a bright white smooth texture to be sure my graphics print cleanly and pop off the page.

- **Color:** Though your favorite stock may be available in a wide range of colors, white and ivory are the safest choices for a portfolio. Remember that its primary purpose is to provide background for your content; it should not compete with your work.

Once you've shortlisted a few products, get samples and run a test to determine how they look *and* feel. *Print your portfolio on the highest quality paper you can afford.*

The Portfolio: Sidebar Checklist

COVER

- ☐ Design your portfolio cover to convey professionalism, creativity, and something about yourself—all at a glance.
- ☐ Use graphic design to tie your cover and content together.
- ☐ Be original; your cover should say something unique about you.

TABLE OF CONTENTS

- ☐ Use a Table of Contents to create a logical organization for your portfolio.

PROJECT CUTSHEETS

- ☐ Your individual project cutsheets should work together to present a unified image.
- ☐ Create a cutsheet template that allows flexibility and keeps your content interesting.

FORMATTING

- ☐ Format your cutsheets so that ALL text and imagery are legible.
- ☐ Establish a clear hierarchy of information.
- ☐ Limit each project cutsheet to five pages.
- ☐ Use only enough pages and exhibits to communicate your style— nothing more.

- ☐ Attach a single pdf or an online portfolio link to your email.
- ☐ Confirm that every file attached can be opened by the recruiter before you send it.
- ☐ Use a well-known online portfolio service.
- ☐ Confirm that the link you provide goes to your correct portfolio.
- ☐ Design your portfolio for ease of review.
- ☐ Use consistent formatting throughout your portfolio.
- ☐ Focus on your content, not the website.
- ☐ Produce a professional-looking package.
- ☐ Organize your portfolio to facilitate a logical and orderly presentation.
- ☐ Size your portfolio to allow for a focused presentation and time for follow-up discussion.
- ☐ Show only your best work.
- ☐ Design your portfolio to ensure a smooth interview presentation.

PACKAGING

- ☐ Bind your presentation portfolio with a professional quality binder.
- ☐ Print your portfolio on the highest quality paper you can afford.

Like it or not, *style* is an important criterion by which you and your portfolio will be judged. Unfortunately, judging style is not as black-and-white as evaluating grade point averages. As an applicant, you should know that most recruiters work hard to do their jobs without letting personal bias affect their hiring decisions. Accordingly, they evaluate candidates using *objective* selection criteria, such as education, skill set, and work experience. Such objective criteria are great for evaluating a candidate being considered for a non-creative position, such as a drone pilot or a stockbroker, but they don't provide the full picture when it comes to hiring a designer. Recruiters must, of course, confirm that you have the required education, skill set, and work experience, but much of what you will do as a designer is also *subjective*. You've got to provide something *extra* that will help a recruiter see your full creative potential.

You can fill your cover letter with self-praise about your design aesthetic and claims that you're a fabulous designer and that you've got the best grades in your class, but the only way you can *really* communicate your style is to provide solid visual evidence throughout your portfolio. If you're looking for a way to assert your superiority over candidates who have submitted only enough to prove they're minimally qualified, here is your golden opportunity.

Chapter 4
Give It Substance

Let's see ... are you qualified for this position?

Picture this. You're the recruiter for a growing design firm. You've posted an ad for a "Creative entry-level architect with a bachelor's degree in Architecture, with excellent communication skills and expertise with BIM. Please forward résumé and portfolio for consideration." By the end of the week, your inbox is filled with eager applicants. You scan each portfolio, truly hoping you'll find the talented individual you pictured as you wrote the ad. Some candidates won't graduate until next year, others didn't bother to attach a portfolio. Then there are draftspeople looking for a career change and a host of other applicants without the required AutoCAD or BIM skills. Didn't anybody read the ad? All you want is to hear from a qualified candidate who has the education and skill set you're looking for.

This story plays out in design firms across the country every day. Of course, there are *many* qualified candidates who *do* submit outstanding submittals. But for every qualified candidate, there are many more who send untargeted submittals for every position they see advertised, whether they are qualified for it or not. This "shotgun" approach to applying for work might secure a job as a car wash attendant or a fast-food cashier, but it is rarely successful in the search for a professional position. In the scenario I described above, we aren't looking for someone who can wash cars or push buttons on a cash register, we're looking for someone with a specific college degree and a well-developed set of professional design skills.

Given this high volume of untargeted submittals, it's not difficult to see why a high percentage of job applicants are eliminated from consideration during the initial résumé screening. In fact, according to recent research from *Workopolis*, only 2% of candidates are ever invited in for an interview.[1] These odds don't sound particularly

---

[1] "Why Only 2% of Applicants Actually Get Interviews." Workopolis.com. 10 November 2016. Web. 21 April 2018. https://careers.workopolis.com/advice/only-2-of-applicants-actually-get-interviews-heres-how-to-be-one-of-them/

good, do they? *What can you do to improve your chances of being one of "The 2 percent"?* You can read the ad carefully, research the firm, and submit a targeted application that provides everything the ad requested. As I screen new submittals for an open position, my first step is to quickly verify two basic questions about each application:

- Did the candidate submit a complete application (cover letter, résumé, and portfolio)?
- Is the candidate qualified for the position?

If you've provided the required materials and you qualify for the position, your submittal will move on to a second, more thorough review of your materials; if not, your candidacy ends right there. This chapter is focused on the materials—the **Substance**—that your submittal must contain to get through that initial review.

SUBSTANCE: YOUR COVER LETTER

We've already discussed the need for your cover letter to share something about you (to tell your *Story*) and the need for it to be visually persuasive (to define your *Style*). Here, we'll be looking at the *Substance* your cover letter must contain if it is to capture the attention of a recruiter and move you on to that second crucial step in the recruiting process.

What's in your submittal—just enough to meet the minimum requirements of the job ad or something that will exceed a recruiter's expectations? Because many candidates do not write a cover letter, whether one is required or not, they miss an outstanding opportunity to highlight their strengths and succinctly state why they stand out from other candidates. Without providing this to a recruiter, you force them to "weed" through your résumé and portfolio searching to determine your strengths. Leading them directly to this information is much more effective and gives you an edge over your classmates. You do want that advantage, don't you? *Write a cover letter, whether one is required or not.*

Here are a few things to consider as you draft your cover letter:

- **Write a complete letter:** If you really want to stand out, take the time to write a professional letter. A well-written business letter includes contact information, an introduction (explain why you are writing and identify the position you seek), a body (highlight strengths and qualifications that make you a good applicant), and a conclusion (say, "Thank you," and request an interview). Keep it simple; most recruiters aren't interested in the granular details of your views on "Recent Advances in Global Design Optimization." Your goal should be to answer the recruiter's central question: *Why should I hire you?* You can talk shop later. *Write a complete letter.*
- **Choose your words carefully:** Using industry buzzwords and business clichés clutters up a cover letter and distracts from your letter's core purpose. Journalist Una Dabiero calls that kind of filler language "cringeworthy." In a recent

article on the subject, Ms. Dabiero identified seven cringeworthy phrases "(my editorial notes in parentheses)" that job applicants should avoid:[2]

1. "I think …" (use confident language).

2. "As you can see on my résumé …" (of course I can see. Just present your strengths.)

3. "I'm writing to apply …" (we already know that).

4. "Think outside the box" (cliché alert).

5. "Excellent communication skills" (your letter *should* have already revealed this).

6. "My name is …" (yes, it's in the header. Get to the point).

7. "Perfect fit" (Are you *really* a perfect fit?).

- **Target the position and the firm:** Do your research and understand the firm's work and culture before you write. Read the job ad carefully and identify key words describing the personal qualities and professional skills they seek. For example, we once posted a job ad for an opening in our Houston, Texas, office. The position required the following: experience in Houston, professional registration in Texas, and experience designing master planned communities. That afternoon, an interested candidate called my office. During the call, I learned that the candidate had never been to Houston, was not a registered Landscape Architect, and had no experience with master planned communities. Realizing this, I asked, "These requirements were all listed in our ad … why are you applying for this position in Houston?" Her response was, "Houston? Oh, I thought this was for a position in Austin." There was not faintest hint of targeting in that call! *Carefully read the job ad and target the firm.*

- **Emphasize your strengths:** The purpose of a cover letter is to introduce yourself, highlight your strengths, and summarize why you are a viable candidate for the position you seek. Resist the urge to restate what's already in your résumé. It's all there on the next page, right? Repeating yourself wastes valuable cover letter space and misses the whole point of the letter—to emphasize your unique qualifications for the position. *Emphasize your strengths and qualifications that align with the position and the firm.*

- **Connect the dots:** Use personal connections you have with the target firm. Perhaps one of your professors knows the recruiter? Maybe a classmate works at the firm and can make an introduction? Any connection you can make will improve your chances of getting an interview. Not long after graduation,

---

[2] Dabiero, Una. "7 Cringeworthy Phrases That Are Ruining Your Cover Letter." Theladder.com. 11 December 2019. Web. 14 December 2019. https://www.theladders.com/career-advice/7-cringeworthy-phrases-that-are-ruining-your-cover-letter

I moved to Austin about the same time one of my college roommates moved to Atlanta. A few years later, during one of our routine check-in phone calls, I told him I was concerned about the faltering Texas economy (the late 1980s Saving and Loan crisis was in full swing). Nervously, I said, "Firms are laying people off. I may have to move." He told me I should consider moving to Atlanta—the economy was booming there! Later that week, his boss just happened to ask him if he knew any landscape architects looking for work. He said he did, and he referred me for the position. I was in Atlanta interviewing with that firm within a week and got an offer shortly thereafter. Though I might have discovered the opening and applied on my own, my odds of ever getting to that interview without my friend's referral would have been much lower. Networking is a much more effective way of finding a job than just responding to ads. *Use personal connections to your advantage.*

The Cover Letter: Sidebar Checklist

- ☐ Write a cover letter, whether one is required or not.
- ☐ Write a complete letter.
- ☐ Carefully read the job ad and target the firm.
- ☐ Emphasize your strengths and qualifications that align with position and the firm.
- ☐ Use personal connections to your advantage.

SUBSTANCE: YOUR RÉSUMÉ

When it comes to designing a résumé, most students view this document as being little more than a synopsis of their quantifiable *hard skills*: education, credentials, awards, technical skills, and experience. While there's no question that the focus of your résumé should include this kind of information, to be most impactful, your résumé should also clearly demonstrate your *soft skills* and achievements.

I just finished reading an article that reveals a three-part formula recruiters at Google say applicants should employ if they wish to improve their chances of being noticed.[3] Like recruiters in any industry, Google's recruiters want to understand a candidate's strengths and credentials, but they also want to know what kind of person you are and what you have achieved. They are looking for *achievement-based* résumés. This is important to them because your achievements are a reliable indicator of your future potential. To communicate this kind of information, your résumé should include the measurable results of your actions.

---

[3] Murphy, Jr., Bill. "Here's Why Google Wants to See the 'XYZ Formula' on Every Résumé." Understandably.com. 5 October 2019. Web. 9 February 2020. https://www.understandably.com

The average student's résumé does a good job of providing basic credentials but usually falls short of providing details about what the candidate achieved. Did you achieve anything notable during your student internship or did you just keep the seat warm? The entries in a typical headline-oriented résumé might look something like this:

• **Degree**	BA (2019)
• **Employment**	Student Intern: Design Firm International (2018)
• **Activities**	College of Design DesignWeek Coordinator (2019)

OK, so you have the required degree, had an internship, and coordinated something but it doesn't help me understand your potential. To give a recruiter a better sense of what you did, you could take these entries a step further and provide additional detail about your responsibilities while in those positions. Though more descriptive than a headline-oriented résumé, this format still falls short on achievements. The entries in a responsibility-oriented résumé might look like this:

• **Degree**	Bachelor of Architecture (BA, 2019): Minor: Regional Planning, Course Work: Advanced GIS, Urban and Physical Geography
• **Employment**	Student Intern: Design Firm International (Rome; Spring/Summer 2018): Prepared construction documents, managed in-house reprographics, managed drone activities.
• **Activities**	College of Design DesignWeek Coordinator (2019): Responsible for contacting and recruiting visiting professionals for DesignWeek lectures.

As you can see, the added detail helps, but to create the kind of achievements-oriented résumé that the folks at Google are advocating, you will need to include notable accomplishments along with your credentials. The author of that article on Google recruiting goes on to explain that Google's "X-Y-Z Formula," a résumé format that details *what a candidate accomplished* (X), *as measured by* (Y), *by doing* (Z), is the best way to achieve this. A résumé entry employing this formula might read, "**(accomplished)** Won first place, out of 8 teams, in ULI Hines Student Competition **(by)** working with a multi-disciplinary team to design a mixed-use plan **(as measured by)** that increased residential lot yield by 27%." Craft each entry to provide a clear picture of your role, your responsibilities, and any notable achievements associated with your role. An achievement-based résumé is more likely to be noticed and read by a recruiter. *Be specific about your achievements and provide measurable results.*

Let's look at a few examples of achievements-based résumé bullets:

- **Degree**   *Bachelor of Architecture (BA; 2019): Graduated with 3.75 GPA*
  - Outstanding Graduate with Expertise in Architectural Graphics
  - Dean's List (2017 and 2018)
  - Course Work: Minor in Regional Planning. Also Advanced GIS, Urban and Physical Geography

- **Employment** *Student Intern: Design Firm International (Rome office; Summer 2018)*
  - Worked directly with Principal-in-Charge preparing construction documents for Italia Flag Factory (Bergamo, Italy). Managed drone activities and Site Scan for ArcGIS
  - Maintained 97% utilization rate during internship
  - Researched AutoCAD standards and updated office AutoCAD standards
  - Managed in-house reprographics
  - Received offer for Entry-Level Designer position in May 2021
- **Activities** *College of Design 2019 DesignWeek Coordinator*
  - Responsible for contacting and recruiting visiting professionals for Design-Week lectures
  - Coordinated program with department faculty and contacted alumni
  - Secured seven nationally recognized speakers for the program
  - Obtained nine sponsorships totaling $13,000 each. Exceeded prior work-shop sponsorship goal by $5,000

At the end of the day, recruiters really want to know that you are a motivated candidate. Personally, I don't feel that you need to go overboard quoting numbers and percentages to make your point. What's more important is that you communicate that you have the ability and desire to achieve tangible results wherever you work.

Regardless of how you present your achievements, your résumé must still answer those fundamental questions about your education, credentials, awards, skill set, and work experience. At a minimum, your résumé should provide the following information:

- **Contact information:** Your *full* contact information is important to recruiters. I tell you this because I routinely receive résumés providing only a name and an email address; they provide no clues as to where the candidate is. I understand that some of you may have concerns about identity theft or personal safety, but you should know that, at some point in the hiring process, a recruiter *will* need your address. This could be for any number of reasons; the position requires experience in a particular region, they need to do a background check, or they want to know if you will need to relocate. To a recruiter, there's a significant difference between living in the same city as the job opening and starting work next week versus needing eight weeks to pack up and move across the country. I recommend that you share your name, address, phone number, email address, and any relevant social media links. *Provide full contact information at the top of your résumé.*
- **Summary headline:** You really don't need to have an *Objective Statement* on your résumé; recruiters already know that you "want a good job in a creative office environment." A résumé is not so much about what *you* want as it is about

confirming you have what a *recruiter* wants. Because of this, it is more effective to summarize your strengths and spell out what you have to offer in a *Summary Headline*; consider this your "elevator pitch." Keep it short and to the point. Be sure to use Key Words from the job posting and avoid using worn-out business clichés like "Design rock star" or "Results-driven synergistic team player." Here are a few examples of summary headlines that will help you get started:

- Award-winning Graphic Designer with one year of intern experience in product prototyping.

- Bilingual Planning graduate specializing in GIS and Remote Sensing. Planning Student Organization (PSO) Student Representative (2018–2019).

- Versatile Architecture graduate with three professional student internships. Professional level AutoCAD and BIM skill set. Excellent writing skills with ability to provide communications support.

- Landscape Architecture graduate (MLA) with BS in Civil Engineering. Extensive experience with AutoCAD, Land F/X, and Civil 3D. Well-developed photographic skills.

My own summary headline looks like this:

Registered Landscape Architect with extensive design, project management, business development, and administrative/HR experience. Over thirty years of design practice focused on landscape architecture design throughout the US. Project experience ranging in construction value to $25 million. I am currently licensed to practice in twenty states.

Obviously, my headline is longer than those I shared above. That's only because my level of experience is significantly greater than that of a recent graduate. Regardless of its length, a well-written summary headline explains—at a glance—why you would be a valuable addition to a firm. *Write a summary headline that concisely describes your strengths and what you have to offer.*

- **Education:** Since you are just now graduating, your education is of great importance. Here are examples of the academic information you should include in your résumé:

- *Institution:* Provide full university name and location, followed by graduation month and year. If you are still in school and seeking an internship, state when you anticipate graduating.

- *Degree:* Provide full degree name; avoid abbreviations. If you have multiple degrees, list them in reverse chronology, with your most current degree first. Omit institutions you attended but did not receive a degree or certificate from. If there are significant gaps in your academic history, explain why they exist in your cover letter; a brief explanation will avoid leaving it to the recruiter's imagination (Recruiter: *Did you skip a year to work for tuition money or were you hanging out on the beach?*) to determine why you dropped out for a year.

- *Grades, coursework, special training:* Include your GPA and any courses, certifications, and special training relevant to the position you are applying for. Unless you're seeking an academic position (in which case, submit a CV), exclude research and publications unrelated to the position.

- *Key skills:* In addition to confirming that you have the required credentials, recruiters need to verify you have the key skills required for the position. Key skills are those you already possess and can apply without significant training on your first day of work. Your new employer may like that you have conceptualization or marketing skills, but those are not the skills you will use on your first day. Most firms will, on day one, need you for the key skills they described in the job posting. *Place your key skills and credentials at the top of the résumé.*

- *Software skills:* Most design graduates know how to use all sorts of software. Rather than listing all the software you know, however, align your software strengths with the firm and the position. Look at the firm's website and identify any software they might use. In my office, for example, we use Lumion—something you'd quickly notice if you visit our website. While virtually every new hire is an AutoCAD expert, not all understand Lumion as well as we'd like. If you apply for a job in my office, having Lumion strengths would be a plus. If you're good with specialty software that your classmates may not know, make that known, too. In addition to Lumion, software I rarely see on student résumés, but are heavily used in our office, include Adobe InDesign, Microsoft Project, M-Color, and Land F/X. Be sure to leave off any software that is outdated and no longer relevant (Anybody out there still using MiniCAD?). If you plan on using infographics to show your software strengths, keep them visually simple and recognize that applicant tracking systems (ATS) may not read that information during a scan.

- **Internships and work experience:** Student internships are valuable experiences—*really* valuable. Intern experience communicates to a recruiter that you understand the office environment and won't need extensive orientation on your first day at work. I recently reviewed a résumé in which the candidate had summer internships with three nationally known design firms. Oddly, they were listed in small text at the bottom of the résumé—as if it was an afterthought. This was a great candidate, I just had to look harder to understand why.

  - *Internship experience:* Place your internship experience near the top of your résumé where recruiters can easily find it and provide a description of your responsibilities as an intern. Don't make the recruiter search for reasons to call you! *Highlight your internship experience.*

- *Other work experience:* If you don't have internship experience, don't fret; non-intern work experience can be valuable if presented properly. A summer job with the local art supply, for example, might be valuable experience if you are applying for a Graphic Designer position. You got to know the tools of your trade better, didn't you? A job as a counselor at a Youth Summer Camp would certainly reveal that you have leadership abilities. I used my role as Teaching Assistant while in school as leadership experience that I felt was valuable.

Consider your work history in light of the position you seek and try to package it in ways that will make it valuable to that employer. My first résumé listed *Landscape Contractor, Warehouse Manager, Auto Parts Delivery Driver, and Construction Worker*; all jobs I held as a student. Unfortunately, I had no design internship experience. During my first college portfolio review, my reviewer recommended that I leave out the *Warehouse Manager* and *Truck Driver* positions because they were unrelated to my profession. Without any internships to show, though, I felt I needed to list *something*. During my first interview, I explained that my auto parts delivery experience "enhanced my time management skills" and my warehouse job had "enhanced my organizational abilities." Luck would have it, time management and good organization skills turned out to be qualities that my first employer valued. Not at all by coincidence, I was appointed to develop a new drawing filing system to organize the office's abundant project files. *Re-package non-intern work experience to show any valuable skills obtained.*

- **Achievements:** Academic and personal achievements are also valuable. If you have notable achievements, such as serving in a leadership role in your student professional society or you've received student awards, be sure recruiters can easily see them, too. These types of activities are valuable because they communicate that you are a motivated individual. A few years ago, we interviewed a talented intern candidate with a fabulous portfolio. What really caught my eye, however, was his résumé. It indicated that he oversaw organizing his department's annual Design Workshop. The position required good organization, communication, and leadership skills; just the soft skills we value in a candidate. Compared with other candidates with equal academic achievements, this made him the best candidate and we invited him in for an interview. And, yes, we hired him.

  - *Awards:* Awards you might list in this section could include scholarships, Dean's List certificates, Outstanding Graduate with Expertise in Graphics, or a Merit Award from your student chapter. If you were a Boy Scout or a Girl Scout, the Eagle Scout rank, and the Gold Award, respectively, are significant indicators of your personal achievement.

  - *Competitions:* If you've entered any competitions, include them. Examples might include entries in a professional student awards program or a local design competition. I joined a team of students during my senior year to design a new town center for a nearby town. We won Second Place and I proudly placed that certificate in my portfolio and noted it on my résumé.

- *Certifications:* Certifications, such as Certified Arborist (ISA) or a Charrette System Certificate (NCI), can be achieved by anyone with the motivation to learn. If you have certifications relevant to your industry, they are important and should be listed.

- *Organizations:* Many of you have been involved with educational and extra-curricular organizations. By all means, add them to your résumé if they are relevant. A few good examples I often see include membership in honors fraternities or sororities or a membership in the student chapter of your professional organization (e.g., AIA, ASLA, APA). Perhaps you volunteered with the Peace Corps and traveled around the world, as one of our former employees did.

- *Publications:* One last area of achievement that I like to see in a résumé is publications. For those of you with a master's degree, your thesis might be one obvious candidate. If you worked with a student newsletter or managed your own blog, you might consider listing these as achievements as well. This kind of involvement shows off your writing or organizational skills.

- **Personal interests and soft skills:** Though personal information does help a recruiter get to know you better, I recommend that you share only interests that are relevant to the position you seek.

  - *Languages:* I often see résumés listing valuable language skills. While my firm does not regularly work outside of the US, many firms do and would value those skills. I recently read an article on Brainscape.com that claimed that multilingual people also perform better on tasks that require high-level thought, multitasking, and sustained attention.[4] Even without the need to work bilingually, I think any firm would want to have employees who perform at that level! Again, remember how important targeting is. If you are applying to an international firm, your language skills might be more impor-tant to emphasize than would be the case if you were applying to the city planning department in Des Moines, Iowa.

  - *Hobbies:* List hobbies that can transfer skills to your target firm. Urban sketching, hobbyist drone piloting, and street photography would be inter-ests that transfer well to an Architectural Designer position and show a recruiter that your personal and professional interests are aligned. Hanging out with friends and playing Minecraft (yes, I do see entries like this) may be important to you, but are not relevant to the job (except, perhaps, for an online game designer position). Other possibilities might include furniture

---

[4] "The Cognitive Benefits of Being Multilingual." Brainscape.com. Web. 4 February 2021. https://brainscape.com

design, watercolor painting, website design, VR technology, or an extensive travel history.

- **Information not to include:** Some personal information is not relevant to the recruiting process at this early stage. In some cases, it may not even be legal for an employer to request it. You may be asked for detailed personal information if offered a position; until then, avoid sharing the following information in your résumé:

  - *Personal data:* You are not required to share your age, date of birth, religion, race, gender, weight, height, Social Security Number, driver's license number, marital status, citizenship, or nationality.

  - *Personal details:* While some personal details, such as your travels or relevant hobbies, may contribute to your value as a candidate, others (e.g., your love of Corgi dogs) do not. Unless such details relate to the position or will help you make a personal connection with a recruiter (perhaps you know the recruiter enters his Corgis in dog shows?), you might want to leave them out.

  - *Profile photo:* Whether you insert a profile photo in your résumé or not is a personal decision. Most candidates do not—I estimate that only 5% of the résumés we receive contain one. Most recruiters, myself included, advise against using photos because they can unintentionally lead to discrimination in hiring. As with infographics, ATS will not read photos either. If you decide to use a photo, I recommend the following guidelines:

    - Use only a recent photo and update as needed to keep it current.

    - Make it personable and approachable.

    - Keep it strictly professional.

  - *Salary history:* Do not provide your salary history. Federal law prohibits employers from requesting it. It *is* allowable for an interviewer to ask about your wage expectations. If you are asked this question, the worst answer is, "I don't know." I hate to admit it, but that's how I answered the question during my first interview. I had no idea what the salary range for an entry-level position might be. I received an offer during that interview, but my lack of knowledge limited my negotiating abilities. I accepted the offer, only to discover later that my wage was lower than what some of my classmates had negotiated. Do your research; websites like www.glassdoor.com and www.salary.com can provide salary data. Faculty and professionals you know may also help you understand fair salary ranges. Be sure to consider adjustment for location; San Francisco, California, for example, has a much higher cost of living than Amarillo, Texas. *Research salaries for the position and be prepared to offer, if asked, a salary range you could accept.*

  - *References:* Don't waste résumé space providing references or saying, "References available upon request," on your résumé. Most recruiters won't contact references until after you've been shortlisted for a position. When that happens, you'll receive a request for references (three references are typical). You'll need to provide them quickly (like, the same day), so be sure that you've talked with your references, let them know they may be contacted by an employer, and have their letters prepared and ready to send. *Contact your references before you share them with a recruiter and let them know they may receive a call.*

- *Curriculum Vitae (CV):* A CV is a document submitted for academic and research positions. This document is credential-based and provides a comprehensive (often lengthy) listing of a candidate's education, certifications, research experience, and professional affiliations and memberships. I occasionally receive CVs in submittals for private sector design practice. While recruiters in the academic environment are accustomed to receiving 10-page documents, private sector recruiters are not. Send a CV for an academic or research position (or when requested in the job posting), send a résumé for private sector positions.

To recap, your résumé must contain all the objective data and credentials that prove your *Substance* to a recruiter. But it must also provide insight into soft skills and your motivations and achievements that make you a unique candidate. Work toward a balance and I'm confident that you'll create a highly effective résumé.

The Résumé: Sidebar Checklist

- ☐ Be specific about your achievements and provide measurable results.
- ☐ Provide contact information at the top of the résumé.
- ☐ Write a summary headline that concisely describes your strengths and what you have to offer.
- ☐ Place your key skills and credentials at the top of the résumé.
- ☐ Highlight your internship experiences.
- ☐ Re-package non-intern work experience to show any valuable skills obtained.
- ☐ Research salaries for the position and be prepared to offer a salary range you can accept.
- ☐ Contact your references before you share them with a recruiter and let them know they may receive a call.

SUBSTANCE: YOUR PORTFOLIO

The Cover

In addition to the important roles of revealing something about yourself (*Story*) and establishing the aesthetic of your portfolio (*Style*), your portfolio cover should demonstrate what kind of designer you are the instant a recruiter looks at it. To accomplish this, you should create a portfolio cover with an appropriate balance of information (*Substance*) and aesthetics.

Some students go overboard and put way too much information on their cover; images, title, name, address, email, university, date, graduating class, and so on. All good information, but this tends to create an overly technical and visually cluttered cover that may cause a recruiter to question your creative sensibilities. Other students provide almost nothing on their cover, leaving the recruiter to wonder just who they are.

I just received a portfolio, appropriately titled *Portfolio*, but with no personal identification provided at all; nothing on the cover, nothing inside. If it weren't for the email it was attached to, I wouldn't have known who the candidate was. Trying to be a thoughtful recruiter, I emailed the candidate to suggest that it might be beneficial to identify himself on the portfolio. His defensive reply: It was intentional—he didn't like the way "all that stuff" messed up his design. For the record, a portfolio without any identification is worthless. If it gets separated from your email, a recruiter won't know who you are and won't bother trying to find you. *Identify yourself on the cover.*

Students at every portfolio review I host ask the question, "*What's the best title for my portfolio?*" At a minimum, your title should identify it as a "design portfolio" and contain your name. You don't need to reinvent the wheel here. Just as in the case of naming a good book, a succinct title is usually the best title. To show you what "the competition" is doing, I've assembled a list of some of the better student portfolio titles I've received lately (I've used my name in lieu of the student's to respect their privacy). Some of these titles, such as *The Design Portfolio of Mark Smith*, have been popular for decades; others, like *Mark Smith/Recorded*, have a decidedly contemporary feel. As you can see, each title here is brief and clearly identifies its owner.

- Mark Smith/Portfolio
- Mark Smith/Recorded
- Mark Smith: Architecture Portfolio
- Mark Smith—LSU Graphic Design
- Mark Smith: Collected Works
- Mark Smith: Artist and Architect
- Mark Smith: Master of Interior Design/University of Florida
- Portfolio of Design/Mark Smith
- Portfolio/Mark Smith/2019
- The Design Portfolio of Mark Smith
- DesignPortfolio/Mark Smith
- Works/Mark Smith
- Student Work: Mark Smith
- Design Work: Mark Smith
- Selected Works: Mark Smith

Any one of these titles would be perfectly acceptable for your portfolio. As for imagery, give your cover *Substance*. Use imagery that shows off your talents or identifies your personal passions. I have assembled a few examples to share that may inspire you.

Landscape designer **Wes Gentry** (Louisiana State University: Bachelor of Landscape Architecture, 2015) chose to keep his portfolio name simple; *Wes Gentry: Portfolio*. For his cover, Wes used a screened map of coastal Louisiana (a subtle hint about his upbringing in southwest Louisiana) overlaid with thin white horizontal lines (Figure 4.1). The graphic treatment is contemporary, suggesting that Wes has well-developed graphic design talent, and is nicely balanced with his title printed in the bottom right corner. He skillfully used the same graphic theme on his résumé and on the rear cover (where he subtly repeats his contact information) (Figure 4.2). Overall, the design is tasteful, professional, and makes a positive statement about Wes's design abilities.

Figure 4.1 Wes Gentry portfolio cover background.
Source: Wes Gentry.

Wes Gentry   student@school.edu   000.555.1212

Figure 4.2 Wes Gentry rear cover background.
Source: Wes Gentry.

Landscape designer **Joshua Black** (Louisiana State University: Master of Landscape Architecture, 2019; McGill University: Masters of Science, 2013; York University/Glendon College: Bachelor of Arts, 2010) is deeply inspired by the natural landscape—particularly water—and wanted to convey that passion on his portfolio cover. Also, a nature photographer, Joshua, while canoeing on Lake Pontchartrain in Louisiana, photographed a rainstorm trailing off into the fog that he felt represented the absolute vastness of the landscape (Figure 4.3). To create visual structure for his cover, Joshua placed a white grid over the photo. The top left square in the grid was intentionally left white to represent the endless opportunity we have, as designers, to explore the unknown. He titled his work, *Portfolio of Design: Joshua Black*; simple yet effective.

Figure 4.3 Joshua Black portfolio cover.
Source: Joshua Black.

Landscape designer **Konner Pendland** (Kansas State University: Master of Landscape Architecture, 2020) placed a freehand sketch of a tree on her cover (Figure 4.4). The sketch itself suggests that she's a landscape designer and gives us a playful hint of her creative skill set. Her title, *Konner Pendland, Landscape Architecture Portfolio, 2018*, is clear and to the point. Konner also inserted a light blue bar to emphasize her portfolio title. She carried this simple design through her portfolio by integrating the blue bar into her Table of Contents (Figure 4.5) and into all of her cutsheets; simple yet effective.

The common theme among these examples is brevity. They aren't trying to say *everything* about themselves on the cover; they provide just enough to identify what the document is and who the candidate is. Just like a good book, the real nitty gritty is best provided inside the portfolio. *Give your portfolio a title.*

Project List

A *Project List* is simply a list of projects that you've worked on as a student and/or as a student intern. For many of you, a *Table of Contents* may suffice as a project list, and you won't need the additional page. For those of you who have deeper project experience, as a student intern or because you have multiple degrees, a project list will allow you to show off the full range of projects you've worked on without having to place *every* project in your portfolio. An acceptable graphic alternative to a project list might be a *Project Experience Map*, such as those we reviewed in Chapter 2. Either way, as you

Konner Pendland
Landscape Architecture Portfolio 2018

Figure 4.4 Konner Pendland portfolio cover.
Source: Konner Pendland.

Table of Contents
Selected Works

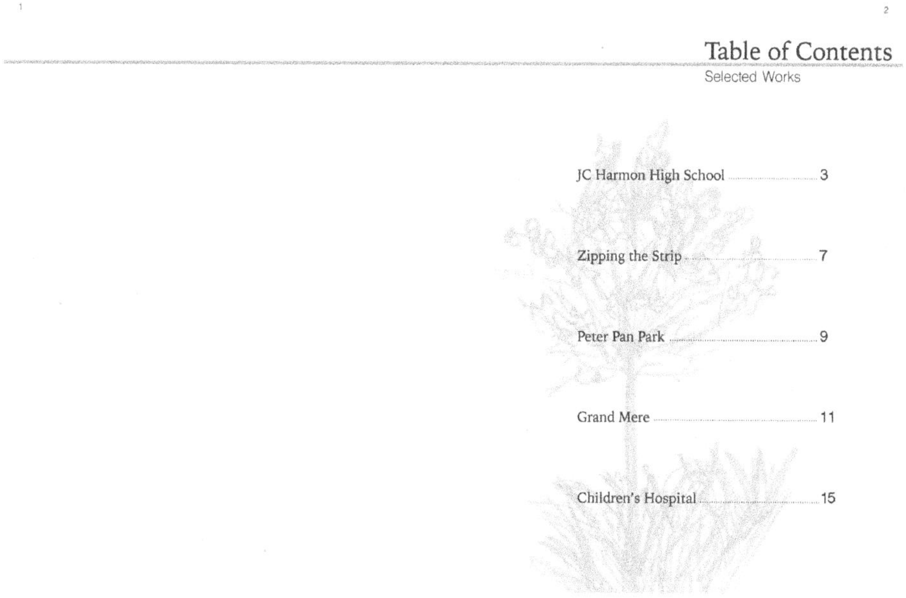

Figure 4.5 Konner Pendland TOC.
Source: Konner Pendland.

gain professional experience, you'll find keeping an inventory of your project history to be quite useful.

To give you an idea of what a project list might look like, I've provided my own as an example (Figure 4.6). My full project list has multiple pages, so I've abbreviated it here just to show how I categorize projects by project type. You can list your projects alphabetically or group them by type, date, client, or location.

MARK W. SMITH, ASLA

PROJECT EXPERIENCE

ACADEMIC
- Arkansas State University (Mountain Home, AR)
- Emory University Physics Bldg. (Atlanta, GA)
- Georgia Tech G-89 Dormitory (Atlanta, GA)
- Mercer University-Jesse Mercer Plaza (Macon, GA)

CEMETERY
- Dallas Fort Worth National Cemetery/Phase Two (Dallas, TX)
- Houston National Cemetery/Phase Four (Houston, TX)
- National Cemetery of the Alleghenies (Pittsburgh, PA)
- South Florida National Cemetery (Lake Worth, FL)

CIVIC
- Carter Presidential Library (Atlanta, GA)
- Cedar Park Justice Center (Cedar Park, TX)
- Douglas County Courthouse (Douglasville, GA)

COMMUNITY
- Banning Lewis Ranch (Colorado Springs, CO)
- Loma Colorado (Albuquerque, NM)
- Ole Miss Golf Course Residential Master Plan (Oxford, MS)
- Solera at Apple Valley (Apple Valley, CA)

CORPORATE HEADQUARTERS
- Adtran Corporation (Huntsville, AL)
- Federated Systems Group (Atlanta. GA)
- Scientific Atlanta (Atlanta, GA)
- Sun-Sentinel Newspaper (Ft. Lauderdale, FL)

HOSPITALITY
- Embassy Suites-Centennial Park (Atlanta, GA)
- Emory Inn (Atlanta, GA)
- Norfolk Marriott (Norfolk, VA)

PARKS
- 1984 Louisiana World's Fair (New Orleans, LA)
- Audubon Zoological Gardens: Louisiana Swamp Exhibit (New Orleans, LA)
- Bayou Segnette State Park (New Orleans, LA)
- Smithgall Woods Conservation Area Master Plan (Helen, GA)
- Southbank Riverwalk (Jacksonville, FL)

TRANSPORTATION and STREETSCAPES
- IH-35 Urban Design Study - Concept Development (Austin, TX)
- Kelly Parkway Corridor Study (San Antonio, TX)
- Lancaster Avenue Redevelopment (Fort Worth, TX)
- St. Charles Avenue Streetscape Improvements (New Orleans, LA)

Figure 4.6 Mark W. Smith professional resume.
Source: Mark W. Smith

Project Cutsheets

Project cutsheets (i.e., project summaries) are the heart of your portfolio. They provide visual confirmation of the substance that recruiters are looking for when they review your portfolio. Each cutsheet should illustrate the range of your skill set and provide evidence of project experience that is transferable to a job in the real world. For a cutsheet to do this successfully, it must concisely summarize and illustrate your work. A typical cutsheet should include project data and project graphics, as follows:

- **Project data:** Your project data should include a summary of the most important aspects of your project. The aim is to make it easy for the recruiter to quickly understand the project and your involvement with it. I know from my own experience that designers tend to generate a lot of data and imagery for every project we work on. Just because you create a lot of data, however, does not mean that you must share it all; an effective project cutsheet must be concise. A typical cutsheet should include the following project data:

  - *Project data:* Bullets for the project name, location, date, scope of work, size, budget, project team, and awards.

  - *Project description:* 50–100-word description providing information concerning the design objective, design process, and problem-solving skills and tools employed. Focus on what *you did*, rather than on describing the project.

  Here's the project summary I wrote for one of my first professional projects (while working at Cashio Cochran Torre/Design Consortium, LTD), the *Louisiana Swamp Exhibit* at the Audubon Zoological Gardens in New Orleans, LA:

  > The Louisiana Swamp Exhibit was designed to increase public awareness of Louisiana's distinctive swamp environment and its inhabitants. Guided by an "animal-as-client" concept, the design focused on each animal's environmental needs, with regional cultural artifacts and architecture added to enhance the human experience. The exhibit includes a trapper's cabin (bookstore) and local cuisine at the Cypress Knee Cafe. My role as Junior Project Manager included site analysis, project graphics, consultant coordination, construction documentation, and construction observation. The project has won numerous design awards and was selected by Landscape Architecture Magazine as a "Landmark Project of the 1980s" for its "Timeline of American Landscape Architecture" series.

  Note that this was a complex project with a $2.5 million construction budget that our project team worked on for over two years. Though we generated a massive amount of research, data, graphics, and photos for the project, this description boils it all down to just 105 words.

- **Graphics:** Project imagery is a critically important part of your cutsheet. Like it or not, your imagery may be the only part of your cutsheet that some recruiters study. Knowing this, select only your highest-quality graphics and photos to illustrate your abilities. This can include freehand concepts, finished sketches, digital presentation graphics, physical and digital models, photorealistic visualization, and photos of completed work. It is worth noting that the quality of your imagery is important here. Good composition, high resolution, lack of clutter, and clear organization are all hallmarks of a good project cutsheet.

Here are a few additional tips on selecting content for your cutsheets:

- **Prioritize:** Please don't try to include every drawing you've ever done; limit your content to the most important project data and your best imagery. Be honest with yourself about whether an image is good enough for this use or not. If it doesn't measure up, don't use it. Throughout my career, I've maintained an archive of images and data from *every* project I've ever worked on, regardless of its quality. There's a lot of material in there that I've never used in my portfolio. If necessary, I revisit old cutsheets and work on improving their quality with updated graphics and text.

  I saw a portfolio at a recent student portfolio review that contained just three projects. The student did excellent work but, unfortunately, decided to include everything he'd ever prepared—roughly 25 sheets of photos, charts, drawings, and design solutions for each project. Because it was so thick, it was difficult to identify the student's strengths and even harder to get through it all in a 15-minute interview. I recommended that he reduce the content of each project to 4 to 5 pages using only his best work, then focus on communicating the skills he used and how he solved the problem. A student portfolio with two or three well-presented projects and 15–25 pages *total* is vastly superior to a portfolio filled with weak imagery and too much information. *Show only your best work; quality wins interviews and job offers—not quantity.*

- **Personalize:** Find ways to go beyond the *what* of your project and give the recruiter a sense of your unique personal experiences and skill set.[5] Perhaps your background as a Boy Scout or Girl Scout has helped you develop a unique approach to park design or your interest in ergonomics has led you to a unique site furnishing design. The CBS television show *60 Minutes* recently did an interesting story about an architect who went blind mid-way through his career.[6] Instead of letting the disability end his career, architect Chris Downey found ways to use his impairment to create a new business: architectural design for the blind. Mr. Downey's case is an inspiring example of using one's individual experiences to enhance one's creative abilities.

  What personal skills or experiences give you a unique perspective on this project? Personalization will help you stand out from other applicants.

---

[5] "5 Ways to Make Your Student Design Portfolio Stand Out to Employers." blog.prototypr. io. 23 April 2017. Web. 30 October 2018. https//blog.prototypr.io/5-ways-to-make-your student-design-portfolio-stand-out-employers-dcb27ba2961a

[6] *60 Minutes.* "Architect Goes Blind, Says He's Actually Gotten Better on the Job." CBS. 11 August 2019. Television.

Personalization is particularly important with your group projects because recruiters will want to know what *you* contributed to the project. When I visit universities, I often see the same group project graphics presented in every member's portfolio. While it may be a fabulous project, your work will look just like everyone else's if you don't re-format it and focus the attention on *your* contributions to the project. *Showcase work that personalizes you as a designer.*

- **Content:** Illustrate what makes your design approach different and show off your problem-solving abilities. You might do a case study that describes your design process, alternative solutions you worked through, what worked and what didn't; prove you have problem-solving skills. Include a variety of graphics that display your full range of abilities. One cutsheet might include a hand-rendered plan while another might show off your Lumion skills. Add a good site photo, use a striking site analysis layer (you don't need *every* layer), insert an attractive graph. Avoid using the same type of graphic on every cutsheet. While the images may be well executed, seeing the same type of graphic page after page gets boring. The materials you include in a cutsheet to achieve this might include any of the following items:

  - *Freehand graphics:* Provide examples of your graphic and concept development skills. You won't be tasked with concept development on your first day at work, but you should show you understand the basics. This might include program diagrams, doodles, sketches, concept plans—anything that will convey how you handle the design process. To illustrate his freehand sketching abilities, **Wes Gentry** (Louisiana State University: Bachelor of Landscape Architecture, 2015) prepared a nighttime axonometric view of his Railroad Park project to convey his initial concept (Figure 4.7). Then, to show how he advanced the idea, he added perspective views prepared in mixed media (Figure 4.8). These images, all quickly produced, effectively give the recruiter a real sense of what kind of designer Wes is.

Figure 4.7 Wes Gentry freehand graphics.
Source: Wes Gentry.

17 Graffiti Wall Perspective, Mixed Media   Sections, Mixed Media   18

Figure 4.8 Wes Gentry digital graphics.
Source: Wes Gentry.

To help recruiters understand the evolution of his design process for the *Nodarza Transit-oriented Community* project, **Dylan Schmer** (Colorado State University: Bachelor of Science in Landscape Architecture, 2010) developed a series of drawings that leads us from his initial freehand concept, through a sequence of progressively refined

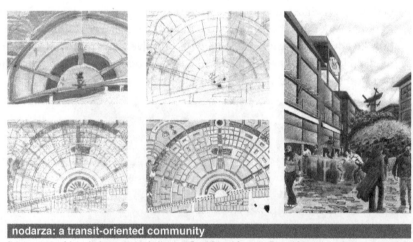

nodarza: a transit-oriented community

Above are a series of design development drawings for Nodarza: a Transit-Oriented Community. The top-left image is a preliminary concept with the intent of further refinement. The image at top-middle is the first pencil refinement that begins to express the form of the community. The bottom-left image is a further pencil refinement developed to begin to show a relationship between built entities and space as well as the character of the community. The images at bottom-middle and on the previous page are the color composite plan. The image at the far right is a rendering of one of the prominent courtyards within the community.

Nodarza is located at an under-utilized light rail stop in downtown Denver, CO. Through a series of figure ground and urban analysis studies of prominent foreign cities, a baseline for urban design was established. Research was then furthered with a focus on transit-oriented development. Through a series of additive and deductive processes, a concept was developed that was then refined to include the design of prominent areas in the community.

nodarza - design development and perspective - prismacolor and photoshop cs4 extracted from plan   5

Figure 4.9 Dylan Schmer design process.
Source: Dylan Schmer.

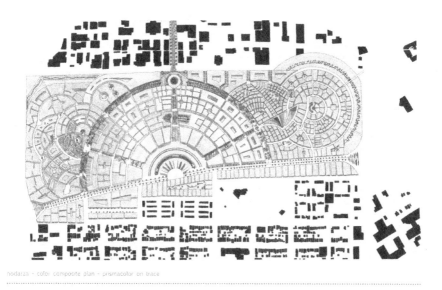

nodarza · color composite plan · prismacolor on trace

Figure 4.10 Dylan Schmer presentation drawing.
Source: Dylan Schmer.

sketches, and finally to the site plan (Figures 4.9 and 4.10). Showing how you use free-hand drawing skills to work through the conceptualization process is a winning formula with every recruiter. *Illustrate your knowledge of the problem-solving process.*

- *CAD drawings:* There's no doubt that CAD is central to project production these days, but it's important not to let your CAD work dominate your portfolio. Incorporate it judiciously—show just enough to prove you can do it well. While recruiters need to know you have well-developed drafting skills, most won't need to review sheet after sheet of working drawings to confirm them. In response to a Project Manager position we posted a few years ago, one candidate submitted a compact disc containing his "portfolio." The disc contained hundreds of raw DWG files; no organization, no descriptions, nothing but CAD files. While the candidate may have been an AutoCAD genius, I only had to open the first few files to realize that this candidate also had no idea how to package and present his work professionally.

Let's look at a more effective approach to showing CAD skills. For his *KMA 3.0 Interrelational Communities* project (Berlin, Germany), architectural designer **Alex Yen-Jung Wu** (University of Texas at Austin: Bachelor of Architecture, 2017), working with Connie Chang, used a blend of CAD diagrams, plans, axonometrics, and sections to show how he uses CAD as a design tool *and* to reveal the full range of his CAD abilities

(Figures 4.11–4.15). Rather than just dropping a CAD plan onto the page and calling it a day, Alex shows the recruiter how he used the software to study each component of the community and layer them into the urban fabric of Berlin. As a recruiter, these studies give me a keen sense that Alex would be well-prepared to do some serious CAD design on his first day in the office.

Figure 4.11 Alex Yen-Jung Wu design process A.
Source: Alex Yen-Jung Wu.

Landscape designer **Konner Pendland** (Kansas State University: Master of Landscape Architecture, 2020) created a single cutsheet for her *Grand Mere* project that includes a CAD-generated grading plan, site profiles, and a deck elevation (Figure 4.16). Collectively, they illustrate Konner's diversity of CAD skills without overstating them and without requiring multiple cutsheet pages. It should be noted that this is the only totally CAD drawing she included in her portfolio; the balance of her portfolio contains a range of sketches, digital renderings, and photos. Konner communicated just enough to prove she has CAD skills, then moved on to show the full range of her skills with other media. *Show how you use CAD and provide a variety of CAD skills throughout your portfolio.*

- *Digital graphics:* Digital rendering skills such as Lumion, SketchUp, and Photoshop are valuable to every design firm. To get a recruiter's attention, be sure to include examples of work that show the range of your digital skills and identify

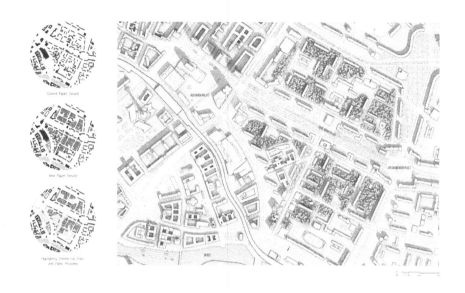

Figure 4.12 Alex Yen-Jung Wu design process B.
Source: Alex Yen-Jung Wu.

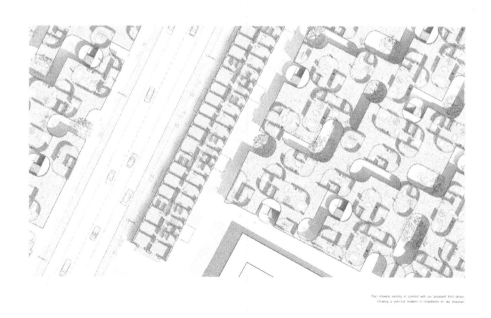

Figure 4.13 Alex Yen-Jung Wu design process C.
Source: Alex Yen-Jung Wu.

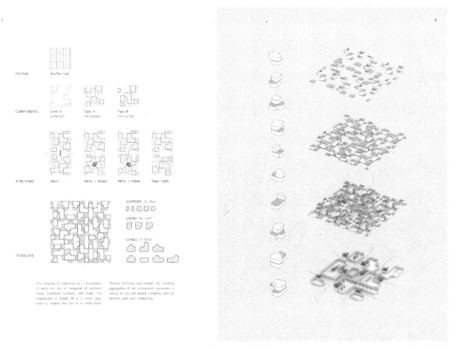

Figure 4.14 Alex Yen-Jung Wu design process D.
Source: Alex Yen-Jung Wu.

Figure 4.15 Alex Yen-Jung Wu design process E.
Source: Alex Yen-Jung Wu.

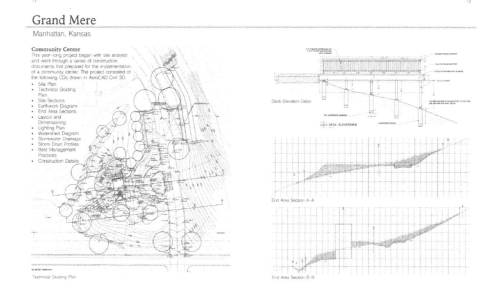

Figure 4.16 Konner Pendland CAD drawings.
Source: Konner Pendland.

your strengths. Include captions on each graphic explaining the software you used. Avoid inferior quality images or low-resolution graphics. If necessary, reformat your work specifically for your portfolio format to be sure that everything is legible. Cutsheets with dozens of miniature diagrams labelled with microscopic fonts are not effective. A primary graphic with two or three legible support images and a brief project description are all that's needed. For more complex projects, multiple pages are acceptable.

In a show of digital diversity, architectural designer **Alex Yen-Jung Wu** (University of Texas at Austin: Bachelor of Architecture, 2017), in collaboration with Rossina Ojeda and Dominic Sergeant, experimented with the translation of designed form from the digital realm to the physical. For his *Objects 1, 2, 3* project, Alex employed 3dsMAX, Rhino, Grasshopper, Illustrator, and V-Ray software to create digital models, then translate those forms into physical models of folded chipboard (*Object 1*), folded polypropylene (*Object 2*), and MDF (*Object 3*) using a laser cutter and router (Figures 4.17–4.19). The design and the variety of imagery presented here are interesting in themselves, but they are also much more than that; they reveal Alex's willingness to experiment with form and material and technology to achieve his design goals. To some recruiters, the *way* you approach your work is more important than *what* you produce. *Reformat your work to your portfolio format to ensure that all information is legible.*

For his *Manipulating the Archetype* project, architectural designer **Josh Lamden** (University of Texas at Austin: Master of Architecture, 2016; University of California/ Los Angeles: Bachelor of Arts, 2010) analyzed and manipulated the archetypal "gable

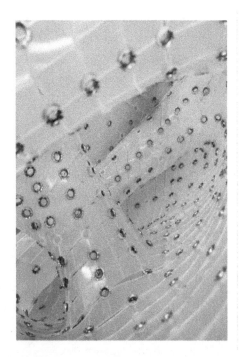

48

OBJECTS 1, 2, 3

Design V • Fall 2014
Critic: Kory Bieg
Object 3 in collaboration with Rossina Ojeda and Dominic Sargeant

With digital technologies playing an ever-
growing role in architectural design, the
purpose of Object was an experiment with
the significance of form from the digital realm
to the physical. Object 1 + 2 were created
individually, while Object 2 contributed in
response to the failures of Object 1.

Object 1 was constructed using a 3D-ed
displaced surface in which panel sizes set
its limits. The object failed to withstand its
own weight, leading to collapse of its form.
Object 2 was constructed with folded sheets
of polypropylene. Dimensioned in 30.6 Max,
the sheets were fastened with double-sided
wheel spring system. The system generated
an additional pattern on the surface

allowing the fused element to express the
limits in Object 1 to become a structural
object – instead of merely disruptive.

Object 3 was constructed as a collaboration
to explore the collective assembly of the
individualities of a larger scale, looking at
relationships of mass, volh, and envelope.
The object was massed initially with MDF
sheets, that created an undulating surface
pattern through the varied openings. Object 3
was approximately 3 by 3 ft with a height
of 3.6 ft.

Skills Used: 3dsMAX, Rhino, Grasshopper,
Laminate, CNC-Router, Bandsaw, V-Ray

left – Inside Object 1,
constructed from folded polypropylene and spikes

Figure 4.17 Alex Yen-Jung Wu modeling

Source: Alex Yen-Jung Wu.

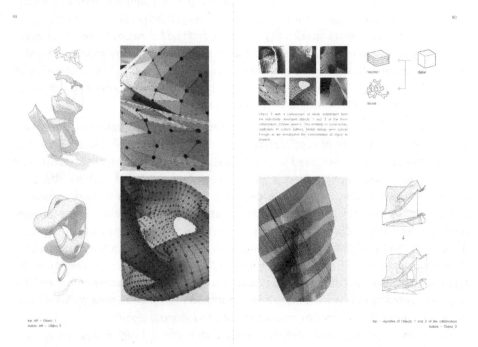

49

50

Object 1 was a continuation of ideas established from
the individually developed objects 1 and 2 at the their
collaboration (Object above). The emphasis on constructing
application of surface battens, forced design were carried
through as we investigated the transformation of digital to
physical.

top left – Object 1
bottom left – Object 3

top – vignettes of Objects 1 and 2 of the collaboration
bottom – Object 3

Figure 4.18 Alex Yen-Jung Wu modeling B.

Source: Alex Yen-Jung Wu.

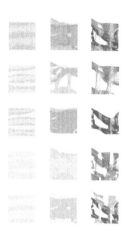

Figure 4.19 Alex Yen-Jung Wu modeling C.
Source: Alex Yen-Jung Wu.

house" to design an addition to a residence in Los Angeles. Using a combination of sketches, digital technology, and physical models, Josh explored the problem thoroughly and arrived at a solution he illustrated beautifully with photorealistic software (Figures 4.20–4.22). I found the study fascinating to review, but more importantly, Josh's cutsheets help a recruiter understand how he approaches design and how professionally he executes a solution.

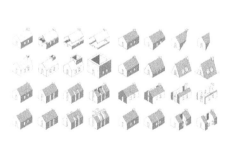

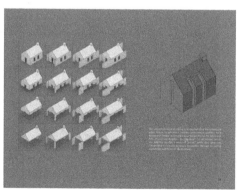

Figure 4.20 Josh Lamden modeling A.
Source: Josh Lamden.

Figure 4.21 Josh Lamden modeling B.
Source: Josh Lamden.

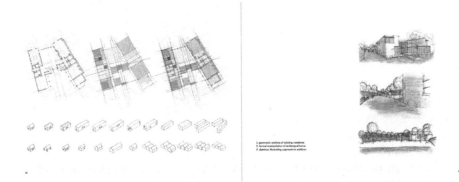

Figure 4.22 Josh Lamden diagramming.
Source: Josh Lamden.

For the *Loop in New Orleans* project, landscape designer **Jia Li** (Louisiana State University: Master of Landscape Architecture, 2012; Tongji University: Bachelor of Engineering in Landscape Architecture, 2010) was tasked with developing a planning concept that would address the need for transitional space between a sensitive coastal environment and human settlement. Jia developed a pair of digital photorealistic site sections that help the recruiter understand how her plan would affect the various land uses and coastal zones involved (Figure 4.23). Unlike many regional planning studies that rely on overly complex graphics and data to communicate their findings, Jia's imagery is refreshingly simple and easy to understand.

- *Prototyping and modeling*: Though most offices don't build study models as they used to, some firms still use them and look for candidates that possess well-developed handcraft skills. Personally, even if my office never built models, I see

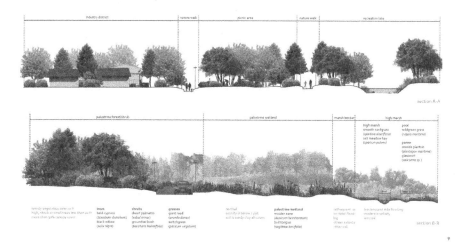

Figure 4.23 Jia Li digital sections.
Source: Jia Li.

such skills as another good indicator of your creative abilities. Placing examples of your handcraft talents in your portfolio is an effective way of showing that you are a well-rounded candidate.

To show off her impressive digital drafting and modeling skills, **Jia Li** (Louisiana State University: Master of Landscape Architecture, 2012; Tongji University: Bachelor of Engineering in Landscape Architecture, 2010) used a series of physical and digital studies she prepared for the *Nanhai Welcome Plaza*. During a student internship, Jia prepared CAD studies for an organic trellis design that served as the basis for development of numerous 3D digital models and laser-cut wood models (Figure 4.24). Presenting the progression from concept to physical models illustrates that Jia has model-making experience that might be valuable to any design office.

In another example of illustrating prototyping on a cutsheet, graphic designer **Dakota Baños** (Louisiana State University: Bachelor of Fine Arts in Graphic Design, 2020) shared concept sketches (right out of her sketch book) developed for the fictitious Modest Mans Brand Identity project, showed the final logo, then created clothing tags to illustrate the brand in context (Figure 4.25). Aside from creating a very classy logo, Dakota has done an excellent job of showing us her design process and helping us understand how she arrives at a solution.

- *Photography:* Every design firm needs good photographers—add some photos to your portfolio. Good photos of your work can reveal your photographic skills and at the same time they present valuable project experience and design abilities. Landscape designer **Christine Johnson** (Ball State University: Bachelor of Landscape Architecture, 2016) took a series of documentary photos of her

Figure 4.24 Jia Li modeling.
Source: Jia Li.

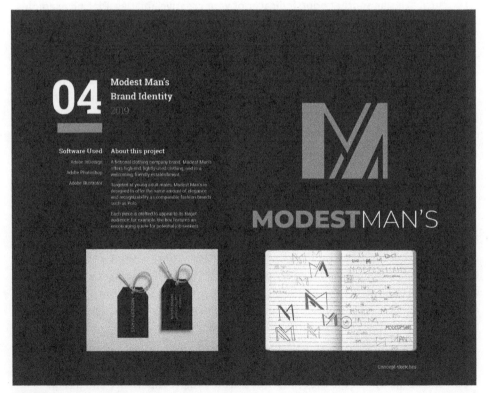

Figure 4.25 Dakota Baños prototyping.
Source: Dakota Baños.

project team engaged in a design charrette, interacting with local volunteers, and installing a memorial and a community garden at the *Downtown Muncie Hub* project (Figure 4.26). In addition to showing us that she's comfortable using a camera, Christine's before and after photos provide evidence of Christine's hands-on approach to her work and the dramatic transformation that resulted from her leadership on the project.

Figure 4.26 Christine Johnson photography.
Source: Christine Johnson.

- *Geographic Information Systems (GIS):* If you seek a planning position, GIS skills will be required for the job and you should provide examples of your work. Most recruiters, however, don't want to see endless volumes of GIS data—they want to know how you use this powerful tool to solve real planning problems. Show some of your GIS analysis capabilities, then focus on the outcome. For a design position, GIS is used less frequently. Many offices, like ours, use it only to develop base information for large-scale projects. In that instance, a single example of a project where you used GIS may be all you need to confirm you understand it.

  To fully understand the regional conditions that would influence decision-making on her *Save the Bay* environmental education center, **Haley Wagoner**

(University of Texas: Master of Landscape Architecture, 2018; Portland State University: GIS Certificate, 2012; University of Arizona: Bachelor of Science, Urban and Regional Development, 2008) initiated the project using GIS. This facilitated the study of existing conditions on this large site and the development of important data that would serve as the basis for her solution. Though her study produced volumes of data, Haley was able to neatly summarize her findings in a portfolio exhibit containing an interesting and informative series of sketches, sections, plans, and photorealistic models (Figures 4.27–4.30). Without showing *everything* she produced, Haley communicated important findings and concisely displayed her solutions. We can easily see that she knows how to effectively solve problems using GIS.

- *Competitions:* If you've ever participated in a student design competition, that experience can also make a valuable contribution to your portfolio. Competitions reveal many things about you, namely your willingness to take on a challenge, how you collaborate with others, and how you work under pressure. The design competition I entered to revitalize a small-town CBD that I mentioned earlier was featured in the local newspaper that week. In addition to showing my team's master plan, the certificate, and a photo of the team at the awards

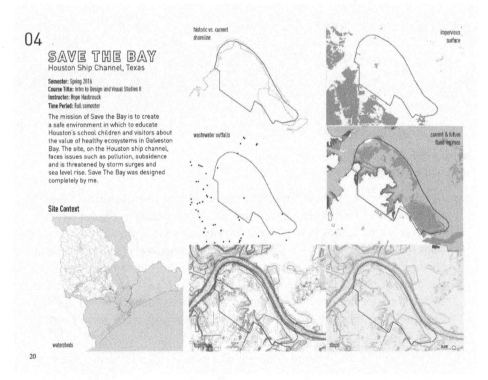

Figure 4.27 Haley Wagoner GIS data.
Source: Haley Wagoner.

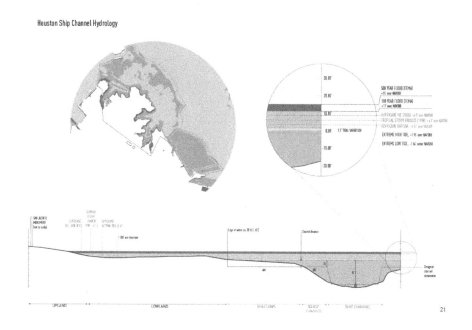

Figure 4.28 Haley Wagoner hydrology cutsheet.
Source: Haley Wagoner.

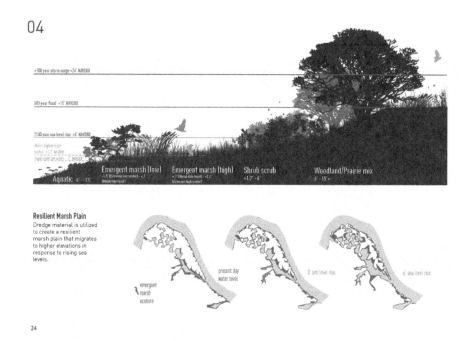

Figure 4.29 Haley Wagoner marsh section.
Source: Haley Wagoner.

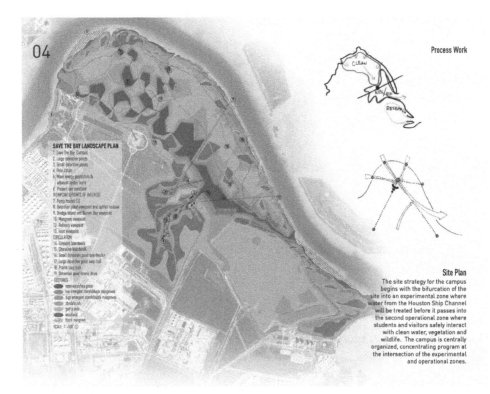

Figure 4.30 Haley Wagoner landscape plan.
Source: Haley Wagoner.

ceremony, my cutsheet emphasized my collaboration and design skills, presentation skills (I presented the design), and an understanding of real-world economics (we were required to prepare a cost estimate as well).

- *Writing:* Every design firm needs good writers. Most firms write newsletters, website articles, technical reports, and project descriptions and need employees with writing skills to produce them. Your cover letter, introduction, bio, design philosophy, and project descriptions all provide excellent opportunities to show off your writing skills. You should also consider incorporating any blogs or newsletters you contribute to, websites you manage, or reports that show off your creative and technical writing skills. Remember that *everything* you write in your portfolio reveals your attention to details. Be sure you review it carefully and avoid making any glaring tipos (oops, I mean, "typos") and grammatical mistakes. To display my own writing abilities, I created a *Writing* cutsheet to show off examples of blog posts, articles, and reports I've written. *Look for every opportunity to showcase your writing skills.*

- *Current trends:* Consider showcasing student projects related to current trends in your industry, particularly trends that your target firm might be engaged in. Green building, LEED, social justice and environmental campaigns, sustainability, and water harvesting are examples of trends that design offices everywhere are currently engaged in. Showing your expertise in any of these areas will improve your standing as a candidate.

The long-term sustainability of Southwest Louisiana's economy and agricultural industry was on the mind of **Wes Gentry** (Louisiana State University: Bachelor of Landscape Architecture, 2015) as he initiated his *Made in the Delta: A Film Landscape* project. Wes, working with Elizabeth Boudreaux-Gentry and Erin Percevault, established a principal goal of working to reduce regional unemployment and improve economic opportunity in the Mississippi Delta by integrating a new industry (film) to the area's existing agricultural infrastructure. His cutsheet provided a series of rural landscape interventions that would accommodate his proposed film initiative (Figure 4.31). I immediately found the idea fascinating but was also drawn in by its humanitarian foundation; this team wanted to make Southwest Louisiana a better place.

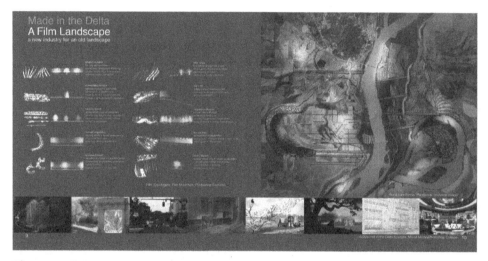

Figure 4.31 Wes Gentry current trends.
Source: Wes Gentry.

- *Internship experience:* Show your internship experience prominently; it is a VALUABLE part of your student experience. Given its value, I am surprised at how often students place their internship work in the back of their portfolios. Place it up front where it will be seen first! To make this task easier, secure copies of intern work and get permission to use it in your portfolio *while* you are in the internship to avoid any delays in obtaining exhibits later. *Showcase your internship experience right up front in your portfolio.*

- *Construction detailing:* I see AutoCAD construction details in almost every student portfolio. Most students place them onto a blank page, often with a jumble of other details, in the hope of showing off their detailing talents. The first question I ask when I see a page like this is, "Were these details developed for a particular project or are they just generic details downloaded from the internet?" Detailing is, of course, an important part of the design process and your educational experience, but simply showing a page of details doesn't tell a recruiter much about your understanding of detailing. Most recruiters would like to know how you create construction details to meet specific design challenges.

- *Built work:* Some candidates have built work they want to share. Built work is by far the best evidence that you understand how design translates into real-world projects. Your built work may be in the form of projects you worked on during an internship or a summer job. They might be personal projects such as custom furniture or building a treehouse, or they may be projects you did as a volunteer. Again, while some projects don't fall into the "traditional" internship model, I think anything you've designed and built that shows your creativity and ambition to get things built is fair game for discussion in an interview. *Showing examples of built work proves you get things done.*

Working closely with a local artist, architectural designer **Luca Smith Senise** (University of Texas: Bachelor of Architecture; 2016) developed detailed drawings for a unique sculptural canopy, known as "Rain or Shine" (by artist Iván Navarro), that was built in Seoul, South Korea. Using Rhino 6, Vray, Illustrator, and Photoshop, Luca refined the artist's concept and prepared the design drawings that fabricators used to build the sculpture. For his cutsheet, Luca shared a variety of images (courtesy of artist Iván Navarro) that showed the design process, the fabricators at work, and what the final product looks like in-place (Figures 4.32–4.34). A highly informative and convincing cutsheet!

Figure 4.32 Luca Smith-Senise built work.
Source: Luca Smith Senise.

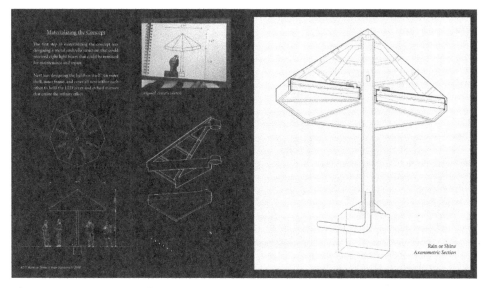

Figure 4.33 Luca Smith-Senise CAD details.
Source: Luca Smith Senise.

Figure 4.34 Luca Smith-Senise fabrication process.
Source: Luca Smith Senise.

In another project called *Three Wooden Chairs*, Luca shares photos of three proto-typical chairs that he built over the course of several years. All independent studies, the chairs show that Luca has a real taste for detail design resolution. Close-up photos show the precision with which the chairs were designed and built (Figures 4.35 and 4.36). It's clear, after looking at these projects, that Luca is a hands-on designer with a real taste for resolving design details and getting his work built!

Figure 4.35 Luca Smith-Senise prototyping.
Source: Luca Smith Senise.

Figure 4.36 Luca Smith-Senise prototype details.
Source: Luca Smith Senise.

Portfolio Organization

Maintaining orderly portfolio files is important, both now and later. After being in school for some time, you probably already have an overabundance of reports, presentation boards, images, certificates, awards, and other project records stored away. Soon, you will be a working professional and the rate at which you accumulate these materials will increase exponentially. Develop a system to organize your materials and preserve everything you produce now; you do not want to lose these materials. *Create a system to keep your materials preserved, organized, and ready for use.*

As a student, I stored my text documents in filing cabinets, drawings in cardboard tubes, and mounted presentation boards in the closet. I didn't have much choice; *everything* was analog. That approach had obvious shortcomings as some of those materials didn't survive storage in good condition. Like all designers, my filing system has evolved into a blend of analog and digital production, scanning, editing, and filing that keeps my materials safe, organized, and ready for use. Today, I archive project files using a system of four classifications, based on level of completion and quality: **Select Cutsheets**, **Secondary Cutsheets**, **In-Progress Cutsheets**, and **Project Images**. Let's look at each in detail:

- **Select cutsheets:** A *Select* cutsheet represents my absolute *best* work. These are the projects I present in interviews. They contain project descriptions with perfect spelling and grammar and the best quality photos and graphics I have. Every graphic is by my own hand (unless I'm trying to illustrate that I collaborate well) and of the highest resolution possible. Of the roughly 300 major projects I have completed during my career, about 50 of them have the distinction of being a *Select* project. Always looking to improve my portfolio, I routinely review these cutsheets and update them when I obtain better content.

- **Secondary cutsheets:** A *Secondary* cutsheet represents a project of *good* quality, but arguably not my best work. Though I typically don't pull these out in interviews, I might use a few to emphasize my depth of project experience with a particular project type. For example, when I was invited to interview for my current position, I knew that master planned communities and parks were the firm's core markets. I felt that I would need to show project experience in those areas. Unfortunately, my prior experience was focused on zoos, parks, transportation, and small-scale community design; I had never worked on a master planned community. For the interview, I assembled *every* community and park cutsheet I had (some were *Select*, others *Secondary*). Though some of those projects were not my best work, they did show depth of experience in the firm's core markets. I supplemented the presentation with *Select* work from other markets (to show diversity of experience) and work that illustrated design conceptualization and graphic skills (to show my strengths). During the interview, I focused on my *Select* work, all right up front in the portfolio, moved quickly through my *Secondary* work, and concluded with my best conceptualization and design process skills. I got the job.

The bulk of my secondary projects were all done earlier in my career, and many have since been superseded by projects of better quality. When I can obtain improved content (updated descriptions, new awards, better photos, or graphics), I upgrade these cutsheets and move them to my *Select* folder. There are currently about 150 projects in my *Secondary* folder patiently waiting to be improved.

- **In-Progress cutsheets:** *In-Progress* cutsheets are draft cutsheets. There are about 100 projects in this folder. They are placeholders and are incomplete due to lack of quality graphics or photos. I prepare these cutsheets in my InDesign template, then rough out the text and graphics. They stay in this folder until I can produce content that will improve them to *Secondary* or *Select* cutsheet status.

- **Project Images:** This folder is the location where all raw project content is stored. It contains a separate folder for every project I've ever worked on. Regardless of quality, I save *everything*—sketches, newspaper clippings, notes, doodles, awards, photos, websites, plans—related to a project in this folder. I constantly add to the folder as I find or generate new materials. You never know when you'll need something!

The Portfolio: Sidebar Checklist

- ☐ Identify yourself on the cover.
- ☐ Give your portfolio a title.
- ☐ Show only your best work. Quality wins interviews and job offers—not quantity.
- ☐ Showcase project work that personalizes you as a designer.
- ☐ Illustrate your knowledge of the problem-solving process.
- ☐ Show how you use CAD and provide a variety of CAD skills throughout your portfolio.
- ☐ Reformat your work to your portfolio format to ensure that all information is legible.
- ☐ Look for every opportunity to showcase your writing skills.
- ☐ Showcase your internship experience right up front in your portfolio.
- ☐ Share construction detailing in the context of your overall design.
- ☐ Showing examples of built work proves you get things done.
- ☐ Create a system to keep your materials preserved, organized, and ready for use.

We've reviewed in detail how **Story** provides the means for you to creatively differentiate yourself from your classmates by helping a recruiter get to know you; both as a candidate and as a person. We've looked closely at how you can use **Style** to visually communicate that you are more than just another problem-solver—you are a candidate with your own unique design aesthetic. And, as we close this chapter, it should now be clear that **Substance** is the material evidence you provide to a recruiter to support your claim that you have the education, skill set, and experience necessary to fill the position you are applying for.

Ideally, your submittal materials—cover letter, résumé, and portfolio—will all work together to portray a clear and compelling image of a competent, talented, and hard-working candidate: you. Think of your assembled package as your "Greatest Hits Album," a compilation of your absolute best material designed expressly for the purposes of quickly showing a recruiter exactly what a great designer you are.

Now, what good are a bunch of great tunes if you don't have an equally fantastic way of getting them to your intended audience? This is a good segue to our last 'S: **Sharing**. As you finalize your job submittal package and consider going after a particular position, you should already be working out the details of how you plan to share it with your intended target. You must share it in a way that will not only get it to the right person on time but will also leave a professional and memorable impression. In Chapter 5, we'll look closely at targeting firms, finding the right contact person, and packaging your submittal so that it gets results.

Chapter 5
Share Your Work

Let's have a look at your portfolio, shall we?

Cautiously, I placed my portfolio on the conference table and opened it to my first project. I began, "This first project is one that I…" Before I could complete the sentence, the interviewer grabbed my binder and began flipping through the pages. A few "hmmms" later, he looked up and asked, "When can you start?" Stunned, I asked, "You mean…you want to hire me?" He returned his attention to my portfolio, then glanced back at me and said, "Great, Monday will work fine. How much do you want?" Unfortunately, I didn't have a ready answer for that question either. Preoccupied, I was still debating the first question…*Oh no, I'm going to have to cancel next week's trip to the beach!* Before I could say a word, he said, "OK, you'll start at $5 an hour. We'll see you on Monday morning, 8:00 sharp." *Wait…is $5 enough? Let's see, I made $2.65 an hour pumping gas last summer. Monday? What?*

That interview lasted all of 15 minutes. I wish I could tell you that I was prepared, but it's obvious I wasn't. I requested an interview with that firm in early spring and had never heard back from them. The day after graduation, I decided to drop by unannounced; I was just passing by, right? Most recruiters will tell you not to just "drop by," that it's not professional (and, I agree, it's not), but I didn't have anything to lose. Luck would have it, I walked in during lunch and the President of the firm was the only person in the office. I hadn't practiced my presentation, I had no idea what a fair wage would be, I knew nothing about benefits; I was clueless. Yet, against the odds, I walked out with my first professional job at the best firm in New Orleans. *How did that happen?*

It happened because my portfolio was ready to share right when it counted. I had just spent the whole summer semester working on it and had the benefit of weekly portfolio reviews with my professor, Seishiro Tomioka. Each week, he would repeat his mantra, "Show only your best work." And so, the work I presented that day represented my best work—conceptualization, drafting, and rendering. In retrospect, it's clear that good timing also played a role in getting that offer. I walked into the right office on the right day. I was good with my hands, and they just happened to need someone, on that day, who was good with their hands. It's unlikely, however, that even the best of timing would have helped had my portfolio not been ready at that moment. Regardless of whether you're networking, requesting an informational interview, or applying for a job, be certain your portfolio is ready to present. You just don't know when a recruiter will call and ask to see it. When you do get that call, odds are they will want to see your work today, not two weeks from now; such a "window of opportunity" rarely stays open for long.

That first interview was not the only point in my career where being ready played a significant role in getting an offer. I would not have my current job had my portfolio not been ready to share at precisely the right time. During a reception at a business luncheon, I happened to bump into the CEO of the largest design firm in town (whom I already knew socially). As we were talking, he leaned forward and asked, "Would you be interested in working with us?" Caught slightly off guard, I said, "Well,…yes, I would like to learn more. When could we discuss it?" His answer left me little time for preparation. "How about tomorrow morning? Can you get a copy of your portfolio to my office today?" Whoa! I hurried home to print my portfolio, then raced to the print shop for binding, and finally, left a bound copy with their receptionist later that afternoon. During the interview the next morning, the CEO complimented me on my work and added that he was astonished at how quickly I had delivered a bound port-folio. Because I was prepared, I walked out with a job offer that day. I learned later that a senior designer had resigned the day before and they needed an immediate replacement. *How long do you think the position would have stayed open for me?*

American civil rights activist Whitney Young obviously understood this need to always be ready when he said, "It is better to be prepared for an opportunity and not have one than to have an opportunity and not be prepared."[1] I couldn't agree more. Still, many students don't seem to understand how important this is. Believe to or not, I've had students, with whom I've just scheduled an interview, email later to ask if they can reschedule because their portfolio "isn't ready yet." Please…DON'T DO THAT! If you aren't ready, someone else will surely be invited to interview in your place. Your portfolio will never be *finished* (trust me, it won't) but it must ALWAYS be *ready*. *Your portfolio must always be ready to share.*

SHARING: YOUR COVER LETTER

The first rule of thumb for sharing your work is to do so professionally. Regardless of what phase of the recruiting process you are in—sending your portfolio, responding

---

[1] "Whitney M. Young Quotes." *AZ Quotes*. Web. 20 December 2019. https://www.azquotes.com/author/16103-Whitney_M_Young

to an email, or doing an interview—recruiters will expect you to communicate professionally. Your cover letter is a crucial part of those communications. Even if you have a mind-blowing skill set and stellar academic credentials, failure to communicate professionally could keep you from getting to an interview. Get things off to a good start by taking the time to write a professional cover letter (see Chapter 2). *Communicate professionally throughout the entire recruiting process.*

Beyond the potential for communicating your professionalism, a well-written cover letter can also help you establish a personal connection with a recruiter. At the end of the day, a person, not a computer, will decide whether you will be invited to an interview or not. The better the connection you make with the person who receives your submittal, the better your prospects of being selected. Before you can do that, however, you'll need to identify a target firm and determine who the recruiter is.

As a student, the best way for you to connect with a target firm is to ask your faculty for help. Most teachers know plenty of working professionals and will be delighted to help you. As a student, I hadn't even considered this valuable resource until I was confronted about it by one of my professors. Just before graduation, our department head, Dr. Robert Reich ("Doc"), asked me if I had scheduled any interviews. "No," I said, "I don't know who to call." He couldn't believe his ears! Determined to nudge me into action, he shared the name of an LSU alum working at a firm in Colorado that was hiring and told me to write immediately. "He'll hire you," Doc stressed. *Well, that was easy!* I hurriedly prepared a letter and dropped it in the mail. Later that week, Doc asked to see a copy of my letter. After reviewing it, he looked up at me and exclaimed, "You misspelled his name, you'll never get a job there now!"

You know…that firm never did write back; maybe Doc was right. He had provided me with a contact with a great firm and I blew it. It took me a while to shake the feeling that I had squandered the opportunity simply because I misspelled the recruiter's name. Out of embarrassment, I never even called the firm to ask if they had received my letter. If I had just taken the time to follow up, I might have made a connection and improved my chances of being considered. Then again, perhaps the firm was one that just didn't write back to applicants they don't hire? Though I didn't get that job, I learned three valuable lessons from that experience that I want to share with you here:

1. Faculty members are your most valuable networking and job lead resource.

2. Every single detail of your job application package matters.

3. Follow through on every lead and every job you apply for.

Despite my less-than-professional first shot at applying for a job, I was lucky enough to find a job the week after graduation. That job was with the best design firm in New Orleans and, while there, I worked on design projects I could only have dreamed about when I was in school. I enjoyed working there, but after four years, I got the bug to move back to Austin. I knew the city well and had friends there, but I had no idea where to look for a job. I wrote letters to every firm in town (there were only four) and received zero replies. *Who you gonna call?* Faculty, of course!

I called one of my professors, Max Conrad, and asked if he knew of any open positions in Austin. His response: "Do I know anyone in Austin that's hiring? Are you kidding?" Max was our department's liaison with the "Real World." He had just gotten off the phone with an alum in Austin looking to hire a project manager. The lead hadn't even been advertised—I was the *only* person aware of it. I carefully crafted an application letter (recipient's name correctly spelled this time) that opened with a personal referral from Max. I waited a week for my letter to be delivered (email didn't exist yet), then called to confirm that the letter arrived. Bingo! They invited me to an interview that weekend and I had a job offer in my hand as I left the interview. Yes, good timing certainly helped this time, too, but that offer might never have happened without the assistance of faculty.

If your faculty can't help you make a connection, the next best thing is to visit the firm's website. Most company websites identify the firm's Principals, their responsibilities, and their contact info. Because Principals typically make the hiring decisions, identifying them can usually help you find the person in charge of recruiting. If you're feeling adventurous, call the firm and ask who handles recruiting. Once you have a name, locate them on *LinkedIn* (www.linkedin.com) and review their profile for additional intel. For example, if you go to my company's website, you'll find the following description of my role:

> Mark Smith is a Vice President and practicing Landscape Architect at RVi. His responsibilities include concept development, firmwide design oversight, site planning and master planning, hardscape and landscape design, strategic marketing, and firm operations. A lifelong resident of the Gulf Coast region of the US, Mark has worked with design offices in New Orleans, Atlanta, and Austin and has practiced in over 30 states and internationally in Canada and the Caribbean.

Unfortunately, there's nothing mentioned about recruiting in that description. If you visit my *LinkedIn* page, however, you'll find more detail: where I'm licensed, who I'm connected to, and that my professional responsibilities *include recruiting*. A few minutes of research can provide everything you need to do some quality networking.

As you do your research, look for things you might have in common with the recruiter. Did you attend the same university? Do you share a common interest? Perhaps you personally know some of your target's LinkedIn connections? You don't want to come off as being "nosy," but a little intel will certainly help move the conversation along swimmingly. I research most job applicants before I interview them and use what I learn to enhance the conversation; you should do the same. *Establish a personal connection with the recruiter.*

Once you've found the right person, send an email, or call and request an informational interview. While that may seem a bit forward, I don't consider such a request to be an imposition. On the contrary, I see it as a sign of someone who understands networking. Students repeatedly call our office and ask to speak with me. Some are just looking for an email address for a submittal, others come right out and ask if they can visit the office or do a video interview. Assuming you act professionally, and your work is of excellent quality and aligned with what we do, I usually agree to meet; I'm as interested in discovering talented young designers as you are in finding an open position.

Occasionally, through networking, candidates and jobs align in totally unexpected ways. Not long ago, a student called me to request an informational interview. Though we weren't hiring, I agreed to meet with him that Friday. During the interview, I found him to be a promising candidate. I told him that I was impressed with his work and that we'd keep him in mind if a position opened in the future. Well, the "future" arrived sooner than I expected; one of our designers resigned the following Monday. With a heavy workload in the office, we needed a replacement right away. I called the candidate I interviewed on Friday and asked if he was still available. Dumbfounded, he said, "Of course!" He came in for a follow-up interview with my partners that afternoon and we hired him. I hope this tale will help you understand that sharing is much more than just responding to online job ads; it requires networking and putting yourself in the right place. *Network as often as possible and be open to any opportunity that comes your way.*

What if you are responding to an advertisement that provides only a "info@website. com" generic email address for submittals? This type of ad is quite common, particularly among larger firms. Most firms, including ours, use this type of email address to separate large volumes of incoming applications from our everyday business email. If you're determined to follow up with someone but the ad doesn't provide a contact person, I recommend that you call or email the firm, to confirm that your application arrived, and politely ask if you can speak to the person in charge of recruiting. I suspect you'll find that some firms will connect you with the recruiter, while others may just politely say, "Your submittal was received. We will call if we need anything else."

If you do manage to contact the recruiter, you'll need to have done your research on the firm, found some common ground, and be prepared with a few talking points. You might consider something like the following:

I haven't heard back from you since I sent my submittal to you last week. I don't want to bother you, but I just want to make sure it arrived.

My professor told me that he just learned you were looking for an entry-level designer and suggested that I speak directly with you.

I enjoyed visiting your office with my design class this spring and learning about your firm's focus on sustainability. My thesis is focused on sustainable park design—I included an excerpt in the portfolio I just sent you.

Your article in last month's company newsletter, "Designing for an Uncertain Future," was spot-on! My capstone is focused on the impacts of COVID-19 on design and your insight was helpful.

When do you think you might make a hiring decision?

I'll be in town next week for a conference and I am wondering if I could visit your office and introduce myself. I can schedule the visit at your convenience.

There's no guarantee that any of these introductions will get you an interview, but any level of contact you can establish with a recruiter will improve your odds. While reaching out is advised (very few candidates do), I want to caution you against becoming an "annoyance." Calling or writing every day for a week (this happened to me just this week) will be considered a nuisance by any recruiter. Also avoid being perceived as needy or pushy. I received an email from a candidate a few years ago that said, "Dear Mr. Smith: I sent my application to you on Friday. It is now Monday. I've heard nothing. I anxiously await your response. I want to make it clear that I am extremely interested in this position." I'm sure you can see the "pushiness" in this email? At a minimum, I'd give it a week before you try to make contact. *Establish a positive tone and communicate with optimism.*

As you prepare your submittal, also consider its appearance. As it arrives in a recruiter's inbox, the only thing they will see is your email address. Though it happens rarely, when I do see an email with a juvenile-sounding address like MagicManMark@ mywebsite.com, I immediately question its legitimacy. Maybe it's a scam or a virus? Chances are, I'd delete it without even opening it. You don't want your submittal to be confused with a virus, do you? If your email address looks questionable, I recommend that you establish a new one. By far, the best approach for any current student is to use an .edu email account through your university. This type of account looks professional, assures me the address is legitimate, and the association with the university lends instant credibility to your application. *Use a legitimate-looking email address.*

While we're on the subject of naming documents, be sure you create logical names for your email attachments as well. A file attachment with a cryptic name like "R3.0_ msmithV.1.pdf" can also look suspicious. Likewise, a generic name like "cover_letter. pdf" is vague. A better approach is to use a file name that is uniquely yours and incorporates your name, file name, and date. For example, I might name my own attachments, "Mark Smith Cover Letter 2021.pdf," "Mark Smith Resume 2021.pdf," and "Mark Smith Portfolio 2021.pdf," respectively. At a glance, you know who these files are from, what they contain, and that they are current.

Great, I've sent my package. What should I do if a recruiter contacts me? Recruiting is a bit like dating; if you ask someone for a date, you expect a prompt response, right? If all goes well, you'll get a timely reply. If you don't hear anything for a week, you may need to make other plans. Likewise, when we see a candidate that would be a good fit for our office, we contact them immediately and request an interview. If that candidate fails to respond promptly, we usually assume they are no longer interested and move on to the next viable candidate.

Just this week, I interviewed five outstanding candidates (out of 80 applicants) for an entry-level position. Our first choice had already accepted an offer within 24 hours of the interview and our second choice decided he just wanted to go back to school. Given that we are in a *very* fast-paced hiring climate now, I called our third choice that day and left a voicemail asking her to confirm that she was still available. I heard nothing all day. Around 5p.m., I was literally picking up the phone to call our fourth choice when our third choice called back to confirm her interest; a few more minutes and the opportunity would have passed her by. Lesson learned: Be alert for communications and ready for an invitation to interview at any time. Excuses like, "I didn't see your voicemail" or "I was in the shower and didn't hear the phone" won't make a bit of difference if the invitation has already gone to another candidate. *If a recruiter contacts you, respond promptly.*

However you respond to a request, respond thoughtfully. Last year, I received a portfolio from a candidate who seemed to be well-qualified for the position we advertised. Her employment status, however, was unclear and I needed to know when she could potentially start work if given an offer. I emailed, "You have a nice portfolio. I'm interested in learning more about your current employment status. Please call me to discuss further." She responded quickly, but the response was not what I unexpected. No call, just a negative three-word email saying, "I am unemployed." I replied with, "Give me a call, please." I was hoping she would call so we could talk, and I could get to know her better. Assuming the call went well, I would've invited her in for an interview. She never attempted to contact me again. Her communications were so weak that I dropped the conversation there and just moved on to another candidate.

That was an example of a good opportunity to start a dialogue that was squandered. You might challenge me on this and ask, "Why didn't you call her back?" or "You should have emailed with a third request." True, I could have, but it's important for you to understand that recruiters are not looking for candidates that are just "okay" or that need handholding or must be chased down. They are looking for the best candidates, candidates with initiative who will go the extra mile to demonstrate their potential for the position. If you don't have it in you to simply return a call or email with a thorough answer, most recruiters won't bother to follow up. You must prove yourself a worthy candidate at many different levels during this recruiting "dance." Regardless of whether you are sending an email or chatting on the phone, communicating professionally is integral to getting to the next step, the interview. *View every contact with a recruiter as an opportunity to start an on-going dialogue.*

The Cover Letter: Sidebar Checklist

- ☐ Your portfolio must always be ready to share.
- ☐ Communicate professionally throughout the entire recruiting process.
- ☐ Faculty members are your most valuable networking and job lead resource.
- ☐ Every single detail of your job application submittal matters.
- ☐ Follow through on every lead and every job you apply for.
- ☐ Establish a personal connection with the recruiter.
- ☐ Network as often as possible and be open to any opportunity that comes your way.
- ☐ Establish a positive tone and communicate with optimism.
- ☐ Use a legitimate-looking email address.
- ☐ If a recruiter contacts you, respond promptly.
- ☐ View every contact with a recruiter as an opportunity to start an on-going dialogue.

SHARING: YOUR RÉSUMÉ AND PORTFOLIO

OK, your cover letter is done. Let's get on with the rest of your application submittal. As you prepare to share your portfolio, whether in digital or physical form, you should target the firm you want to interview, understand what they do, and prepare a targeted package specifically to get their attention.

We routinely receive "generic" submittals from applicants that appear to have no idea what we do. They *always* fail to impress me. Just imagine you are applying to get into graduate school to obtain a Master of Architecture degree. You wouldn't send your application off to The Juilliard School, would you? Of course not, Juilliard is a performing arts conservatory! Prospective college students research a range of universities to determine which are best suited to help them meet their academic goals. Finding your first job requires a similar level of diligence and research. Talk with your faculty, look for online reviews, visit the firm's website, read their newsletters, and visit their employees' LinkedIn pages. Your goal is to know what the firm does and how they do it. Submitting a well-targeted portfolio that reflects your knowledge of the firm shows that you've done your homework and will increase your chances of getting an interview. *Carefully research the work of every firm you are interested in.*

During interviews, I ask every candidate if they've visited our website just to get a sense of how thorough they are. I'd say 50% have done so and are eager to talk about it. As for the other 50%, I'll just say that it disappoints me to see that they didn't care enough to do any research before an interview. I know from my own experience that the failure to understand what a firm does can make for a bad interview. One of my earliest interviews was with a firm that specialized in large urban design projects. My portfolio contained just four academic projects: a golf course redevelopment, a riverfront park, an equestrian center, and an urban condominium. While I thought it looked good, I was blissfully unaware of the need to align my portfolio with the firm's work and made no effort to organize it for the interview. I really didn't know much about them at all. That morning, I marched confidently into the interview and opened my presentation with my super-deluxe equestrian center project. The interview lasted all of 15 minutes, ending as the recruiter stood up and said, "Thanks, but we don't need an individual with your particular skill set." Bad interview!

In retrospect, it's clear that I failed to thoroughly investigate the work of the firm I was interviewing and, consequently, failed to target my portfolio accordingly. I couldn't blame the interviewer for dumping me; I deserved it. Maybe, just maybe, opening with my fabulous urban condominium project would have been a presentation strategy that would have improved my rapport with that interviewer? Every interview you participate in will be a unique experience because every firm and every recruiter are unique. As you prepare for an interview, understand what the firm does and organize your presentation in response to that; one size (portfolio) does not fit all. This concept of *alignment* with your target is an important one, yet you'd be surprised at how many applicants never give it a moment's thought. *Align your portfolio content with the work of your target firm.*

Format for Sharing

When responding to a job ad that requests a cover letter, a résumé, and a portfolio, most applicants attach their cover letter, résumé, and portfolio as requested. Pretty straightforward, isn't it? Invariably, however, we receive applications from applicants who don't appear to have read our ad at all. Some attach mismatched assortments of DWG, AI, PSD, and WORD files, others attach a separate PDF for every project they have. Still others attach nothing at all and ask if we are hiring. A design portfolio, by definition, is a curated collection of your best work designed to highlight your skill set, style, approach to design, and potential as a professional designer. Even if the ad does not spell this requirement out, you should thoughtfully arrange your work in a portfolio document that provides a singular, organized, and enjoyable viewing experience for the recruiter.

As you can see, a portfolio *is not* a random assortment of individual documents, yet we receive submittals from applicants who do not understand this for every position we advertise. I recently received a submittal from a well-qualified candidate that contained a link to his online "portfolio." I followed the link only to find a single project (of a type our firm doesn't even do). I emailed to request a full portfolio and, in response, received a Dropbox link containing dozens of raw CAD files; no titles, no descriptions, no organization. My final email stated that the only acceptable submittal would be a single PDF containing an organized portfolio; I never heard from that candidate again. Normally, I would have disqualified this candidate without any follow-up dialogue at all, but made an exception because this candidate's résumé gave me the impression he was well-qualified. If it sounds like I was being picky, I was. I would like you to know, however, that recruiters ask you to follow certain submittal protocols because it makes it possible for them to evaluate large numbers of candidates and saves them precious time. Because of this, it is important that you play by their rules. *Before you submit a job application, read the ad carefully; then send precisely what it requests.*

What's the best way to share my portfolio? You can start by using the right digital tools. Every so often, I receive a portfolio in a Word or PowerPoint format. Sounds crazy, right? While these are excellent software programs for writing and making presentations, they are not appropriate for submitting your design portfolio in a job application. Using software ill-suited for this purpose suggests that you don't understand industry standards.

So, what software should I use? First, review the submittal requirements and look for any formatting preferences. Many firms, including my own, require that you provide your materials in a PDF format. There are several ways you can format your portfolio for sharing, as follows:

- **Adobe Acrobat:** Using Photoshop (or other graphic editor program), save each individual graphic or text document as a PDF, then use the Adobe Acrobat "Merge" command to bind them together into a single PDF file. As I pointed out earlier, check the total size of your bound document. Email servers enforce file size limits. AT&T Mail and Google Gmail, for example, both allow up to 25MB of total message size. Remember, however, that this is not universal and that not everyone will be able to receive an email of that size. What's the limit? You can assume an email with up to 10MB of attachments will go through. Some email servers may have smaller limits, but 10MB appears to be the industry standard for the moment. If necessary, use the Acrobat "Optimize PDF" tool to compress your file further. As a final quality control check, open and review your completed PDF to ensure that it will open properly and that each page is in the proper order and that the viewing experience is organized properly, smooth, and enjoyable.

- **Adobe InDesign:** Another outstanding software for portfolio design is Adobe InDesign. InDesign is a desktop publishing and typesetting software application designed specifically for formatting and assembling individual graphics and text files into a single portfolio exhibit. I have been using InDesign (and its predecessor, PageMaker) throughout my career. InDesign provides advanced graphic and typesetting tools that are unavailable in Acrobat. Used together with Photoshop, Illustrator, and Acrobat (collectively, the Adobe Creative Suite), InDesign facilitates the seamless creation, formatting, and sharing of your entire suite of design portfolio documents. I typically create an individual cutsheet for every project in InDesign, which I then save as a JPEG and as a PDF. When I need to assemble them for a submittal, I bind together only those PDFs that are appropriate to my target audience. As with Acrobat, file size is still important. My individual portfolio cutsheets typically range from 1MB to 4MB each and, when combined, create a 31-page portfolio that weighs in at about 35MB—a little large for the average email! When merged and compressed using Acrobat, however, I can create a single PDF of 3.6MB—a file size that can easily be shared through any email system.

- **Online Portfolios:** As file resolution continues to improve and digital files just keep getting bigger, designers need better ways to share their ever-expanding portfolios. With file size limited to 10MB, simply attaching a PDF of your portfolio may not be an option for those of you with larger portfolios; you may need an online portfolio. Fortunately, the market has responded in robust fashion with a wide range of excellent options. Today, I would estimate 10–15% (and growing) of our applicants submit online portfolios. Most of these applicants use portfolio templates provided by developers like issuu.com. A smaller group designs their own portfolio templates and uses file transfer and sharing services such as ShareFile.com or Box.com to submit them. Most online portfolio sites offer an impressive range of professionally designed templates. Setting a template up is easy: you select one of the provided templates, tweak its design to meet your needs and aesthetic tastes, and drop in your content. To share it, you simply send a website link to the recruiter. Aside from being simple to set up and share, most of these sites are also optimized for viewing on any desktop or mobile device. This is a huge advantage since recruiters can also easily view your work on portable devices while working remotely.

If you do choose to go the online route, here are a few additional things you should consider:

- **Cost:** There are both free and paid subscriptions. Though free, most include ads and other distractions. Paid subscriptions offer better template options, more file storage, and ad-free viewing. This last point is important; reviewing a portfolio surrounded by pop-up ads can be distracting for the recruiter. Since most sites offer free demos, sign up for a trial run to determine if it will meet your needs before subscribing.

- **Navigation:** Your portfolio must be easy for a recruiter to navigate. As you review your options, look for a site that is easy to set up and easy for the recruiter to navigate. *Create an enjoyable viewing experience for the recruiter.*

- **Permissions:** Be sure that you understand the site's permissions settings. Because I save submitted portfolios to our server and print portfolios of short-listed students for review with my partners, I will typically need your permission to download and print them. If I can't download, save, or print your portfolio, it may reduce your chances of being shortlisted. I just received a submittal via a popular online portfolio site that I could neither print nor save. After reviewing the portfolio, I tried to save it to my server and got this on-screen message: "The publisher chose not to allow downloads for this publication." You, as publisher, control access to your work. Don't make recruiters have to call you for permission; they may not bother to make the call and just move on to another candidate. *Set online portfolio permissions to allow recruiter downloading, saving, and printing of your portfolio.*

- **External links:** Providing a link to a website can be tricky if not done with care. It's rare, but I occasionally receive links that take me to the wrong website. A few years ago, I received an email containing a link to the candidate's personal website. I clicked on it and was taken to a website that was definitely not his design portfolio—the splash page featured a photo of a middle-aged woman in a swimsuit enjoying herself at the beach. I emailed the candidate to let him know that I found his beach photos but was unable to locate his portfolio. He was understandably very embarrassed by the blunder (it was his mother in a bikini on the splash page) and admitted that he had mistakenly sent me to the wrong section of his family's photo-sharing website. *Test all website links and share the correct URL.*

As you evaluate software, seek software that is developed specifically for portfolio design and sharing, well supported by an established developer, and used universally in your industry. Not only will using the right software help you create a beautiful portfolio and share it effectively, but it will also help you keep it current. Remember; you will be maintaining and updating the content of your portfolio for the rest of your career!

To put this last comment into context, let's consider my portfolio. My portfolio has been through several transitions over the course of my career. Initially, my student portfolio was a multi-ring binder full of hardcopy artwork and photos mounted in plastic sleeves. A few years into my career, however, the introduction of the personal computer and desktop publishing software (DTP) required that I migrate that analog content into a digital format. Thus, I began scanning and importing my work into a PageMaker template; a process that took a couple of years to complete. Everything was going great and then…boom! Adobe acquired Aldus, discontinued PageMaker, and introduced InDesign. Yes, InDesign is great software, but once again, I had to move to a new format. Today, I still use InDesign, but have made yet another concession to on-going digital "progress"—I've imported my content to an online portfolio.

Will this constant evolution in technology ever end? Of course not—it's only going to speed up. Your design portfolio is not a static "one-and-done" project, it is a dynamic on-going commitment to staying current with technology, design trends, and your own professional development and experience. Actively managing and upgrading your portfolio throughout your career communicates to potential employers that you take your profession seriously and that you want your portfolio to represent the best you have to offer. *Create, manage, and share your design portfolio using up-to-date software.*

Presentation Portfolio

Even though creative industries appear to have gone totally digital and the Covid-19 pandemic has limited face-to-face interviews for now, you must still anticipate that a recruiter will need to print your work and that you may need to present a hardcopy at some point in the recruiting process. When I am not working remotely, I typically print every shortlisted candidate's portfolio for review in the office with my partners (no, we don't crowd around my monitor to review them). To facilitate this, your portfolio should be formatted for printing on a standard office copier in an 8½" x 11" or 11" x 17" format. I also recommend that, before sending it to anyone, you should test your portfolio to be sure that it prints as intended. Using standard printer formats may mean conforming to convention more than some of you would like (we *are* artists, after all), but a little conformance is better than a portfolio that won't print properly. *Format your portfolio for printing on a standard office copier.*

If you have your heart set on a custom portfolio format (say, a 5" x 5" square or a 5½" x 8½" brochure) that will not automatically print on an office copier, you should print and bind it yourself and overnight a hardcopy to coincide with the arrival of your digital submittal. Since so few candidates ever send a hardcopy, this approach just might impress the recruiter! A few months ago, I interviewed a student who submitted an exceptional digital portfolio with his application. What *really* impressed me, however, was the presentation portfolio he brought to his interview a few days later. As we began the interview, he opened an anodized aluminum binder and slid it across the table. It was a great first impression! Every detail of the document was beautifully executed, and I could see he was enormously proud of his work by the confident way he presented it. As a leave-behind, he had prepared a wire-bound portfolio printed on glossy stock. We were all impressed with his work and his presentation. Obviously, metal portfolios are not for everybody, but a nicely bound presentation portfolio is. Sadly, a surprisingly substantial number of candidates arrive for their interview with a standard printer copy simply stapled in the corner. From my perspective, it's hard to take that kind of portfolio seriously. Please don't squander a good interview opportunity by presenting a substandard hardcopy portfolio. *Produce the highest quality presentation portfolio you can afford.*

I want to emphasize here that your presentation of your portfolio is just as valuable as your portfolio itself. Done well, your presentation creates a memory point that helps the recruiter remember you and your work; done poorly, the recruiter may not even be able to recall who you are. Some years ago, I received a digital portfolio from a candidate that looked promising, and I invited him in for an interview. When he arrived for the interview, I welcomed him into our conference room and, after introductions, I asked to see his portfolio. He looked at me sheepishly and told me that he didn't bring one. He added, "I assumed you'd print the one I sent with my email." Then...awkward silence. To move this situation forward, I asked our receptionist to print his portfolio so that he would have something to present. That took another ten minutes. It just got worse after that. Even if he had recovered and his presentation had been stellar (it wasn't), I would have had serious reservations about this candidate's lack of planning for such an important presentation. Unfortunately, I will always remember this candidate (though, oddly, I can't remember his name) for all the wrong reasons. *Make your portfolio presentation memorable.*

And, finally, there's no substitute for the real thing. Consider presenting full-size original work if you have materials that are difficult to show in your portfolio. Since my own capstone project was a thick 8½" x 11" report, I used to take the entire document to interviews. While I rarely reviewed it in any detail, the sheer bulk of it always left an impression on the recruiter. I have also been known to present full-size concept sketches and construction drawings for impact during an interview. One word of caution: Bring only the documents you want to show and organize them for seamless presentation; noisily rummaging through a 30-page set of 30" x 42" drawings will only be a distraction during your interview.

Interviews

I think we can all agree that interviews are stressful. They can be, however, even more stressful when you aren't prepared. Most people (myself included) need to rehearse for important presentations. Even if you feel you are a confident presenter, take the time to organize your thoughts and get comfortable with your presentation. Though I've been in the design industry for decades, I practice relentlessly for every interview and presentation I make to be sure it's "perfect." Even the "experts" take extra time to practice their pitch. Steve Jobs rehearsed every presentation for weeks. In his article, "11 Presentation Lessons You Can Still Learn from Steve Jobs,"[2] Carmine Gallo revealed that Jobs was legendary for his preparation, adding that, "Hours and hours of practice made Jobs *look* polished, casual, and effortless." The emphasis on "look" in that quote left me wondering if the author was suggesting that Steve Jobs wasn't naturally polished, casual, and effortless but compensated through practice. I'll never know. What I do know is that most of us get at least a little anxious and thorough preparation will help you overcome anxiety and make a good presentation—nervous or not. A candidate who makes a polished, casual, and effortless presentation gets my attention every time. *Practice your presentation until it's polished.*

Another important aspect of your presentation is knowing your own work. As creative professionals, our clients expect us to know everything about our design solutions and to present them confidently. To do otherwise risks losing their confidence. As a student, you should also know everything about your project and be able to make flawless presentations. A designer who botches project details during a presentation is like a singer who forgets the words to a song during a Super Bowl Halftime performance; we just don't do that. Last month, I interviewed a graduate who arrived for an interview with a beautiful portfolio. As he made his presentation, I began asking questions about his work, as I do in every interview. Which way is north? What's the name of that road? How many acres does the site contain? He was unable to answer *any* of my questions without stopping to read what was on the cutsheet. In many cases, he couldn't answer the question at all; it really felt as if he was presenting somebody else's portfolio. He was unprepared and was understandably embarrassed by his performance. *Know your work; inside and out.*

In addition to knowing your work, you should know how long it will take you to present it during an interview. Most recruiters will limit how long you have for your interview presentation. For example, I schedule most entry-level interviews, both in-person and video calls, to last about 30 minutes. That allows 15 minutes for portfolio review and 15 minutes for discussion. Practice your timing until you can, without a timer, complete the presentation within that window of time. If required, speed up your delivery or reduce your content; you don't want to be cut short in an interview because your presentation goes on too long. If, by chance, you are given more time, you can easily expand your presentation to fill whatever time you might get. *Practice your presentation until you can reliably complete it in 15 minutes.*

Finally, select the right media for your interview presentation. In addition to physical binders, we also have a range of digital options that can be highly effective in the right setting. For an *in-person interview* (most of which have been on hold through the Covid-19 pandemic), I recommend a good old-fashioned presentation binder. It is a tried-and-true media that every recruiter is familiar with and it never "crashes." Organize your materials to focus on work that your target firm is engaged in and follow your

---

[2] Gallo, Carmine. "11 Presentation Lessons You Can Still Learn from Steve Jobs." Forbes.com. 4 October 2012. Web. 5 December 2019. https://www.forbes.com/sites/carminegallo/2012/10/04/11-presentation-lessons-you-can-still-learn-from-steve-jobs/#143ece18dde3

portfolio's lead. Laptops, computers, and portables devices are digital options that we're starting to see used more often for in-person interviews. If you go this route, do so with care. I've seen a handful of presentations on mobile devices, and most were, at best, lackluster. During one memorable interview, the candidate's device crashed; he got so flustered trying to recover his files that he never got back on track. Another student, after his device crashed the night before (without any backup or printed copy), called to reschedule his interview for two weeks. Others find it awkward presenting to an interviewer while trying to swipe the portable screen from behind. And screen glare continues to be a problem for many devices. Though I consider myself an early adopter of technology, I feel that mobile devices are not ideal for making in-person portfolio presentations—yet. I've also seen in-person presentations done on large flat-screen monitors. If you choose this option, make sure the equipment you need is available and set up properly. At a recent student capstone jury, I was invited to join, one student used a flat-screen on a rolling trolley for his presentation. The opening image was wonderful. To move on, however, he had to return to his file directory to locate each project. As he fumbled with the computer, often bringing up the wrong file, he got nervous. In the end, the delays were awkward, and the presentation was weak. Though his design was good, the jurors agreed that his presentation was a disaster. He would have benefited with a little more planning.

For *video interviews*, a digital portfolio is required. Under the current circumstances (the on-going Covid-19 pandemic), most firms are relying on video conferencing for interviews. For a video interview, you'll need to understand the software, take control of the online meeting, and share your screen once introductions have been made. Practice your presentation so that the whole "sharing" experience will go smoothly and within the allotted time. In my experience, most candidates present a PDF of their portfolio, though I've seen a few online portfolios as well. If you make a digital presentation, practice until it's perfect.

Most of the time, interviews go just as you expect them to: introductions, portfolio review, friendly discussion, and a conclusion. And then…sometimes they don't. You should be prepared to set your expectations aside and "go with the flow" if necessary. Some years ago, I was invited to an interview with a well-respected design firm I really wanted to work for. The night before, I studied their website thoroughly, aligned my portfolio with their work, and practiced my presentation. At the interview, as I pulled out my portfolio, the recruiter said, "We can look at that later. Let's go check out a few projects." *What?* Well, that turned into an all-day project tour, lunch, and a lengthy conversation over drinks about the profession, family, design, music…we talked about everything. I had a wonderful afternoon. When we got back to the office, the recruiter hurriedly flipped through my portfolio and ended the meeting by saying, "I'll give you a call." With that closing, you might think the interview went poorly; he didn't seem interested in my portfolio. This, however, was an example of a recruiter who wanted to confirm that I was someone he could work with; he wanted to know my *Story*. Of course, my project history and skill set were important, but he had determined I was qualified long before I arrived. I got a job offer the next day. Job interviews are often as much about you personally as they are about your portfolio. *Be prepared to go "off script" if your interview changes direction.*

I'd like to close this discussion with an observation about interviewers. I wish I could tell you that recruiting is a totally objective process in which personal interaction with a recruiter is not a key factor, but I can't. Your interaction with a recruiter, however short it may be, is a critically important part of the process. Sometimes, these interactions go well and sometimes they don't. While you do have some control over how your side of the interview goes, much of what happens is completely out of your hands. I have already shared a story about an early interview that went poorly because I failed to align my portfolio with the target firm's work (and, if I might add, the interviewer *was* a bit rude). A few years later, I was invited to interview for a position in Austin that I felt I was well-suited for. With four years of experience, I was confident designer and my portfolio now contained solid professional experience. *I should be able to ace this one!* As I arrived for the interview, sitting at the conference table was the very same interviewer who had so brusquely shut me down four years earlier; he had moved to Austin! Even though my portfolio was targeted, I was prepared, and my interview skills had improved, I was told (again), "We don't need anyone with your skill set at this time." He then got up and walked out of the room. Yes, I was flustered (there are more pointed words I could use to describe my feelings, but I won't use them here), but I left knowing, this time, it wasn't all on me; the interviewer had absolutely no interest in relationship building and didn't have the personality to be an interviewer. I should add there is a little irony to this story. Today, I am a Vice-President and Managing Principal with that very company; I interviewed with them 16 years later (this time with the CEO) and found that they did need someone with my skill set after all. If you find yourself in this kind of interview, just give it your best, recognize that sometimes the stars just don't line up, and leave with the determination that the next interview—wherever it might be—will go better. *Be persistent.*

Say "Thank You"

Since most of you have grown up with email and text messaging, I'm guessing that some of you may feel sending a "Thank you" note is old-fashioned. I would counter by saying that, regardless of how we communicate it, we still need to show our appreciation whenever we are given the opportunity to interview. Not only does such a note show that you understand how to network, but it can also extend your dialogue with the recruiter. So, after every interview, be sure to write a short "Thank you" note. It can be a card, a text, or an email (the age of the recruiter should inform us which format is best). Simply thank them for considering you, remind them why you feel that you're a good fit for the position, and close by saying you are interested in the position. I recommend sending an email, rather than a handwritten note, immediately after the interview. An email arrives while you are still fresh in their memory. On top of that, if the recruiter wants to contact you later, your name will AutoComplete in Microsoft Outlook and makes finding you that much easier. While I love hand-written notes, mail is slow. What if your note shows up a week later—*after* the hiring decision is made? If you really want to make a personal touch, send both. Since few candidates take the time to send a "thank you" note, doing so provides you with just one more opportunity to stand out. *Write a short "Thank you" note.*

The Portfolio: Sidebar Checklist

- ☐ Carefully research the work of every firm you are interested in.
- ☐ Align your portfolio content with the work of your target firm.
- ☐ Before you submit a job application, read the ad carefully; then send precisely what it requests.
- ☐ Create, manage, and share your design portfolio using up-to-date software.
- ☐ Create an enjoyable viewing experience for the recruiter.
- ☐ Set online portfolio permissions to allow downloading, saving, and printing of your portfolio.
- ☐ Test all website links and share the correct URL.
- ☐ Format your portfolio for printing on a standard office copier.
- ☐ Produce the highest quality presentation portfolio you can afford.
- ☐ Make your portfolio presentation memorable.
- ☐ Practice your presentation until it's polished.
- ☐ Know your work; inside and out.
- ☐ Practice your presentation until you can reliably complete it in 15 minutes.
- ☐ Be prepared to go "off script" if your interview changes direction.
- ☐ Be persistent.
- ☐ Write a short "Thank you" note.

As a designer, *how* you share your work can be as important as *what* you share. The world expects designers to be creative and, when we share, we typically go to extremes to demonstrate that creativity. We go overboard designing our garage sale signs, we custom wrap every gift we give, we even design our own birthday cards...the aesthetic of *everything* matters.

Consider that birthday card. *Why bother to make one by hand?* You could send an eCard. While an eCard is a caring gesture, it doesn't say much about your creativity. You could buy a hand-crafted card that declares your birthday wishes *and* makes a design statement. It shows you want to make receiving the card a special experience and you care about design. Or you could design and make a card. Now that says much more than just "Happy Birthday." It shows your creativity *and* speaks to the quality of your relationship with the recipient. That you created something *just* for them makes the recipient feel special.

Sharing your portfolio is, in some ways, like sharing that birthday card. The way you package and share your portfolio with a recruiter can be ordinary and unassuming or it can be quite memorable; it's your choice. Just remember that how you package and share a job application submittal is much more than just a bundle of text and illustrations. As a recruiter opens your submittal and reviews it, what he or she sees at that moment is all they must go by as they decide regarding your fitness for a position. The degree to which you help a recruiter see that you understand the importance of tailoring your presentation specifically to your audience will go a long way toward initiating a relationship that may produce an invitation to interview and a job offer. That's what you want, isn't it?

Chapter 6
Bring It
All Together

Just four words: Story, Style, Substance, Sharing

My primary objective for authoring this book has been to help you understand—from the unique perspective of a design industry recruiter who is also a designer—what recruiters actually look for when they review a student design portfolio. I have long felt that there is a need for such a book because, every week, I receive job applications containing portfolios that are little more than random "collections" of student work. They may contain the candidate's academic credentials and past project experience, but beyond that, there's scant indication of what kind of future employee they might be and how they might perform as a professional. Have you ever wondered why recruiters ask interview questions like, "What are your greatest strengths?" or "Are you a team player?" They ask those questions because they want to know about more than just your academic credentials and project experience; they want to know something about *you*.

Honestly, it doesn't surprise me at all that we receive student portfolios like this. I too was once a design student struggling to create my first portfolio, with little awareness of what a recruiter might be looking for. As a student, I naively thought that finding my first professional job would be much like finding every other job I'd ever had: I'd submit my application, a recruiter would review my qualifications, and, assuming I was qualified, "check all the boxes." With that, I'd get the job. In retrospect, I wasn't totally off base on the qualifications part; they *are* important. Your qualifications (those "boxes" recruiters check) support your assertion that you are trained for the job, and they help recruiters decide which candidates to shortlist for an interview. What I *didn't* understand was that recruiters must also evaluate your potential to grow and to work with others and to become a valued designer, a reliable project manager, or—who knows—maybe a future partner, in their firm. An effective portfolio must paint a clear picture of who you are today, *and* it must paint a promising picture of your future potential.

Your portfolio, however, will not get the job for you. Whether you've just begun to assemble your portfolio or you're now adding the final changes, remember that its primary role is to represent you and your qualifications in a way that piques the recruiter's interest and elicits an invitation to interview. If your portfolio successfully endorses your potential and you are invited to an interview, its role then shifts from one of being your representative to one of demonstrating why you are the right candidate for the job during an interview. Think of your portfolio as your "trusted partner" throughout the recruiting process; the two of you must work very closely together if you are to succeed in getting the job.

As the "two of you" initiate your hunt for your first professional design job, it is vital to remember that recruiters are not interviewing your portfolio; they are interviewing *you*. Though your portfolio may appear to be the focus of the interview, it is really you and your ability to present yourself effectively that are on display. It's one thing to have a beautiful portfolio, it's quite another to be able to present it professionally and convincingly; your performance during the interview is *especially important*.

It's been said that the formal job interview was created in 1921, when Thomas Edison developed a written test to evaluate job candidates.[1] In the years since, interview methods have been refined and many innovative technologies that assist the interview process have been introduced. The core reason for doing an interview, however, has not changed; recruiters must get to know a candidate personally before they can confidently make an informed hiring decision. Remember, recruiters don't hire résumés and portfolios—they hire people. For the recruiter, there's a certain *feel* for a candidate that comes only from meeting them personally and engaging in good old-fashioned face-to-face conversation. For you, the candidate, an in-office interview provides the opportunity to have that conversation, but to also see the office environment, tell your story, and (hopefully) initiate a good working relationship with the recruiter.

Despite all the obvious benefits of an in-office interview, recruiters have, in recent years, been moving towards videoconferencing for interviews. Since the early 2000s, the quality and functionality of videoconferencing hardware and software have improved, and many recruiters have found that video technology improves their recruiting efficiency. Used effectively, video interviews save time and money, and they are much easier to schedule than in-office interviews. There is, however, one drawback; recruiters lose that *feel* that comes from shaking your hand, looking you in the eye, and connecting with you personally. Video places distance between you and the recruiter.

Now, if there were any recruiters still on the fence about "going video" as we entered 2020, surely the Covid-19 pandemic sealed the deal for them. As the pandemic spread across the globe, design firms everywhere sent employees home to

---

[1] Smith, Jacquelyn. "Thomas Edison Conducted the First Job Interview in 1921—Here's How They've Evolved Since." *Business Insider.* 21 May 2015. Web. 20 September 2020. http://www.businessinsider.com

work remotely—a scenario (thankfully) facilitated by the availability of reliable video-conferencing products. Hiring came to a standstill at most firms. Any firms still recruiting promptly canceled in-office interviews as a safety precaution and began hosting video interviews. As a result, design school grads entering the workforce in spring 2020 found an unsettlingly quiet job market waiting for them. By fall, with many firms returning to "recruiting" mode, those candidates still looking for work found that the hiring process had changed; virtually all job interviews were being conducted online. In six short months, the video interview went from being "acceptable" to the "new normal." Looking ahead to the day we return to working full-time in the office, I predict that many recruiters will have grown so comfortable with videoconferencing that they will find it difficult to return to doing in-office interviews exclusively. The odds are quite high that your next interview will be a video interview.

Despite the extraordinary physical changes in the workplace precipitated by the Covid-19 virus, the basics of portfolio design, professional communications, and interview etiquette have not changed at all…so you're good there. What *has* changed is the environment in which your interview is hosted; the entire experience now takes place in the shallow two-dimensional universe of a computer monitor. In an in-person interview, you would shake hands with the recruiter, present your portfolio, share a cup of coffee, meet other employees…maybe even get an office tour. Each of these interactions provides you with an opportunity to connect with the recruiter. In an online interview, few of these interactive opportunities exist. Because your portfolio and all your personal interactions will be totally digital, accompanied by the inevitable video freezes, audio distortions, and screen-sharing hiccups, you and your portfolio will just have to work harder to establish that personal connection.

The unprecedented recruiting environment created by the pandemic and the resulting industry-wide acceptance of videoconferencing not only strengthen my pre-pandemic argument for the necessity of incorporating *Story*, *Style*, *Substance*, and *Sharing* into your portfolio, it demands that you and your portfolio perform at a higher level to overcome the absence of in-person interaction. As you set out to inventory your work and storyboard your portfolio layout, evaluate every exhibit and ask yourself the following questions:

- **Does it contribute depth to my STORY?** Beyond its technical merits (e.g., credentials, skill set, project experience), confirm that each exhibit you incorporate into your portfolio contributes in some way to the recruiter's understanding of who you are, both as an individual and as a prospective employee. It must highlight why you are a good fit for the firm and for the position you seek.

- **Does it reveal my unique sense of STYLE?** You're more than a problem solver; you're a designer. Style establishes your unique identity as a designer and sets you apart from other designers. Be certain that your Style is present in every exhibit and contributes to the overall visual continuity of your portfolio.

- **Does it clearly demonstrate my SUBSTANCE?** Your portfolio must prove that you are well-qualified for the position. The best way to illustrate your Substance is by displaying it within the context of your completed projects. Visual evidence of your full range of expertise and skill set is much more persuasive than any résumé infographic will ever be!

- **Does your portfolio's design facilitate SHARING?** If you can't share your portfolio quickly and effectively, it won't serve its core purpose very well. Confirm that every exhibit facilitates a clear understanding of its content and promotes a productive follow-up discussion with the recruiter. Text or graphics that are too small to read, files too large to transmit, or photos with poor resolution compromise that ability and simply don't belong in your portfolio. In the end, your document must be quickly and smoothly transmitted to the recruiter, be easy to open, present a pleasurable viewing experience, and facilitate professional in-person and video interviews.

I'd like to close with this little pearl of wisdom; your portfolio is, and will always be, a work in progress—it will *never* be finished. You will *always* be adding new materials and refining older content. As you make the transition from student to working design professional, your portfolio will begin to evolve from its current role as a job-hunting tool to one of also serving as your professional archive. It will help you organize and preserve the multitude of professional artifacts—projects, art, photos, awards, doodles, newspaper clippings—that are the product of what will hopefully be your long and prosperous career as a designer. Your portfolio is a real-time professional time capsule.

Absolutely...designing a professional quality portfolio is challenging work and requires a substantial commitment on your part to get it right. But it can also be very rewarding. Passionate designers put in the hard work required to create and maintain a professional-quality design portfolio not only because that's what recruiters expect to see; they do it because they are driven to create, they are proud of their work, and they are compelled to share all of it in the best possible light.

Do this for yourself! It's your Story.

Afterword

This book is based upon the importance of effectively telling your story through a design portfolio. Your story is your brand. What is a brand? A brand starts with a reputation based on the first impression you make or how well you communicate and build relationships with others. Your reputation is made up of the opinions and beliefs that others form about you, based on your actions and behaviors. A brand is intentional and can be impacted by your preparation, knowledge, and abilities. In this case, as a job seeker, your brand should be designed purposefully to help a recruiter decide that you are the top candidate for a position. As you work to create your unique brand, your portfolio is one of the most important tools at your disposal.

As a business owner, executive recruiter in the AEC industry, and author of the *How Hard Are You Knocking*? job search book series, I have recruited hundreds of candidates and worked with thousands of job seekers. From my perspective, Mark Smith's book is insightful, pragmatic, and provides an easy-to-follow framework that will differentiate you in a tight job market and get you hired. As a recruiter, I am interested in your story and genuinely want to understand your *Style* to ensure its fit within our team culture. Your life experiences, internships, group, and capstone projects provide the *Substance* a recruiter is looking for when comparing potential candidates.

As a future design professional in the AEC field, your brand is based, in part, on the strength of your portfolio and your ability to align your intentions with experience and substance. Your portfolio must differentiate you from all the other candidates. Your portfolio will influence how others see you and help recruiters better connect with you emotionally and intellectually with your *story*. If that image aligns with the opportunity you seek, you are more likely to secure it.

It is also critical that you show your design *style*. Recruiters are looking for your unique traits that will enhance their team. How you use color, white space, contrast, rhythm, balance, and design to create a design is uniquely you. As you begin your job search, communicate your style, and provide solid visual evidence of your abilities throughout your portfolio.

Mark Smith's book provides a foundation for building your personal brand and differentiating yourself in today's competitive design market through your submittal package. Presenting your story and your unique style, supported by your *substance*, are key factors in getting noticed. Your substance is the material evidence you provide to a recruiter to support your claim that you have the education, skill set, and experience necessary to fill the position you are applying for. This presentation of your credentials should be memorable, show your creativity, and hold a recruiter's attention.

This book should serve as a guide to help you make the transition from student to professional designer. You have worked hard and developed a killer cover letter, résumé and portfolio. Now you need to make sure your package gets noticed. As we wrap this up, here are a few strategies that may help you deploy your brand and launch a winning job search:

1. **Targeting:** Winning the job search game takes preparation and hustle. Don't target just one company, identify multiple target companies where you would like to work, based on location, reputation, and culture, and market segment that the company serves. Create a list of what is most important for you. Is it a team environment? Is it the type of projects the company delivers? Is it the industry or industry subset, such as private real-estate development versus public parks and open space?

2. **Research:** Once you have identified target firms, launch your research for each company. Visit the firm's website and online presence and study any posted job positions. This research will help shape your résumé and uncover key attributes about the company's culture, projects, clients, and services. The research will also help you prepare for your interviews.

3. **Networking:** Share your target list with your personal and professional network including professors, peers, and social media contacts to identify potential connections with your target firms. As you gather information, begin connecting with referrals and applying to open positions. Your goal at this stage is to make that first impression. Submitting an unbelievable cover letter that gets noticed and sharing a portfolio that differentiates you from everyone else are the keys to landing an interview.

4. **Interviewing:** You will face diverse types of interviews, ranging from phone interviews to group interviews. Phone interviews are used to narrow the candidate pool and select the top candidates for face-to-face interviews. Face-to-face or virtual face-to-face interviews provide recruiters with a platform to meet you in person and review your materials. Be prepared. Look professional. Share your story and ask questions that show your interest in the position. Your goal for the interview process is to build a relationship with the recruiter. People hire people they like, have a connection with, and match the company's culture. You have already built your brand and have a fantastic résumé, cover letter and portfolio. Your goal now is to get noticed, win the interview, and land your dream job.

5. **Evaluating offers:** Once you have told your story, won the interview, and received a job offer, you need to consider the culture, the compensation package, and the career opportunity. Confirm this is an environment in which you will thrive. Ensure the compensation package is fair and provides benefits that meet your needs, based on the local market. And, finally, confirm that the opportunity will provide a platform for your personal and professional growth. If the offer and the opportunity are right for you, accept the position and start planning for the first 90 days.

6. **The job:** Your first 90 days on the job will be critical to providing a platform of knowledge, integrating within the team and company, and making your impact. Ensure you understand your role and responsibilities based on your job description and discussions with your leader. Research the markets/industry in which the company operates and understand the depth of services your company provides. Finally, observe the organizational structure within the company and begin to identify potential career paths and opportunities.

In *Design Portfolios: A Recruiter's View*, Mark Smith has provided a clear roadmap to your success in preparing for your job search and for securing your first job as a design professional. This book should be that dog-eared one on your bookshelf for many years to come. Follow his guidance, follow your passion, and you will never really have to work a day in your life. Good luck!

Tim Augustine
Author of the *How Hard Are You Knocking?* job search book series
Vice President, Atwell, LLC

About the Author

A graduate of the Louisiana State University Robert S. Reich School of Landscape Architecture, Mark Smith is a practicing landscape architect with over four decades of professional practice focused on planning and design throughout the US. He is currently a Vice-President and Managing Principal with a national multi-disciplinary planning and design firm with offices located throughout the US.

In addition to everyday planning, design, marketing, and management duties, Mr. Smith has been engaged in design-industry recruiting since 1990 and currently coordinates his firm's recruiting activities. In this capacity, he reviews hundreds of portfolios annually, interviews candidates, negotiates salaries, prepares offer letters, and manages on-boarding activities for new employees. Throughout his career, he has guest-lectured in many university-level design programs on design, professional practice, portfolio design, and student preparation for the profession. Since 2000, he has organized numerous university-level portfolio review sessions for students.

Index

P